**WOMEN WORLD LEADERS PRESENTS**

# Faith Unchained

## CLIMBING TO FREEDOM BY GOD'S GRACE

VISIONARY AUTHORS

MELISSA GISSY WITHERSPOON
CONNIE A. VANHORN

i

Published by World Publishing and Productions
PO Box 8722, Jupiter, FL 33468
Worldpublishingandproductions.com

ISBN: 978-1-957111-46-9
Library of Congress Control Number: 2025911795

# ontents

# Introduction

Welcome to *Faith Unchained: Climbing to Freedom by God's Grace*! The book you hold in your hands and what you are about to read is not just a collection of stories; it's a holy invitation into the sacred journeys of women who have walked through the fire and emerged refined. These chapters and teachings are drenched in truth, raw with emotion, and overflowing with hope. Each testimony is a powerful reminder that no matter what chains have held you hostage—addiction, shame, grief, fear, trauma, unforgiveness, or doubt—God's grace is more than enough to redeem, restore, and set you free! His mercy meets us where we are and lifts us as we climb toward freedom!

The women whose words fill these pages have known the weight of bondage. But they have also discovered something far greater: the unrelenting, chain-breaking love of our faithful God. Their lives are living proof that the same God who delivered Daniel from the lion's den, brought Joseph from the pit to the palace, and gave Esther the courage to stand for her people is the same God who moves today. The Bible is not a dusty book of ancient history—it is alive in us! The same power that raised Jesus from the grave is the power that breaks our chains and calls us into purpose.

Think of Moses: he was a man with a speech impediment and a painful past, yet God chose him to set a nation free. Think of the woman at the well: she was bound by shame and rejection, yet Jesus met her right where she was and turned her into a bold evangelist. Think of Paul: once a persecutor of Christians, he became transformed by grace into one of the most powerful voices in Scripture. Their stories are not so different from ours. We all face Red Seas. We all encounter walls like Jericho. But with faith, obedience, and the grace of God, the seas part, the walls crumble, and yes, chains of bondage are broken!

This book is not about perfection—it's about freedom. It's about surrender. It's about climbing out of the valleys, even with scraped knees and tear-stained faces, and finding strength in the One who never lets go. Through every chapter, you'll find reflections of yourself, echoes of your own battles and victories, and reminders that you are never alone. In every teaching, you will find hope and empowerment to take your next steps. We have the Word of God to guide us. We have the Holy Spirit to empower us. And, through the unity of the Holy Spirit, we have each other to accompany us on our path to freedom.

These testimonies are more than stories—they are weapons of warfare, declarations of victory, and evidence of a God who still sets captives free. The chains that once held these women back are now the very proof that God's grace is at work. Their pain has become their platform. Their brokenness has become the bridge for others to walk across into healing.

It is our prayer that these words will touch your life in a way that transforms you. That, as you turn each page, the power of the Holy Spirit will move in your heart, drawing you closer not only to God but also to us as we share these sacred moments together. May you feel the bond of peace built through shared struggle and shared victory. We pray that in every story, you'll sense the presence of the One who unchains, redeems, and restores.

Whether you are in the middle of your climb or are just beginning, take heart. Let this book ignite your faith. Let freedom stir your soul. God is not done with you. He is writing your story even now as you read this. And through His grace, you, too, can discover what it means to live with an unchained faith.

Welcome to the journey. Welcome to the testimony. Welcome to discovering *Faith Unchained* by God's Grace!

# Melissa Gissy Witherspoon

After more than two decades of substance abuse, Melissa Gissy Witherspoon achieved long-term sobriety and now proclaims that recovery from substance use disorder is possible! *With God all things are possible* (Matthew 19:26 NIV).

Originally from a suburb of Atlanta, Georgia, Melissa lives in Winston-Salem, North Carolina, with the youngest of her four children and her husband, Derek, following her calling to love and support those impacted by addiction. Founder and CEO of the nonprofit Sober-Now, Melissa raises proceeds from her best-selling, award-winning book, *I'm Sober... So Now What? A Journey of Hope and Healing*, bringing hope to prison ministries, recovery centers, sober-living housing, human trafficking safe houses, churches, and high schools.

Melissa is an administrative assistant at her church and advocates for the recovery community, sharing her story of God's love through writing, podcasts, speaking engagements, recovery events, supporting accountability courts, and offering inspiration through her social media pages and Recovery Reflections column in *Voice of Truth* Magazine.

Melissa is a Best-selling and Award-winning Author. She is a Contributing Author in International Best-Selling *Miracle Mindset, 2022,* Contributing Author in Best-Selling *Hope Alive, 2024,* International Book Awards Finalist, 2023 BookFest Award Addiction and Recovery, 2023 BookFest Award Self Help-Inspiration, 2023 Bookfest NY Times Square Billboard Montague.

Stay connected with Melissa at Melissa@Sober-Now.com or www.Linktr.ee/sobernow.com for podcasts and social media.

# Forward in Faith

By Melissa Gissy Witherspoon

*For by grace you have been saved through faith, and this is not your own doing; it is the gift of God—not a result of works, so that no one may boast. For we are what he has made us, created in Christ Jesus for good works, which God prepared beforehand so that we may walk in them* (Ephesians 2:8-10 NRSV).

Faith is not born in comfort. It does not grow in certainty. It is forged in the fire of trials, shaped in the unknown, and strengthened when we step forward—not by sight but by trust and surrender. My journey—one marked by addiction, abuse, brokenness, and ultimately finding redemption in spite of it all—has been a living testament to that truth.

For over eleven years, I have walked the path of recovery from substance use disorder—better known as addiction. With every uncertain step, I have found that trusting God, even in my most fearful moments, has led me to the greatest blessings. The difference between this journey—what one might call long-term recovery—and my many failed attempts that came before it is that this time, God is at the center of it all

My life hasn't always looked like it does today. I wasn't always working in a church or advocating for the lost and broken. In active addiction, I lived a life that many find hard to believe. There were decades leading up to my recovery that might make some clutch their pearls—in fact, I've seen them do it. Some even argue with me, "There's no way you've been where you say you've been—you look so 'normal.'"

But this is my truth—and I'm not ashamed to share it. In fact, God is using it as a living testimony, proof that no one is ever too far gone for His love, grace, and mercy. It's a story of how God broke the chains that once held me captive—how I learned to walk by faith and found the kind of freedom that only comes through full surrender to His will. It's a journey where the gift of His grace met me at every turn, guiding me from darkness into light. And in sharing our darkest moments with others, God's light shines even brighter.

People are often shocked to learn the depths of where my addiction took me. I once frequented strip clubs, walked away from marriages, and was seldom present for my children. I destroyed a promising career in real estate and drove under the influence more times than I like to mention—putting not only myself but also countless others in serious danger. I drained the bank accounts of loved ones who were desperately hoping that inpatient and outpatient treatment centers would finally be the answer. I walked away from friendships without warning and altered my body with plastic surgery and tattoos out of desperation for approval. I auctioned off pieces of my soul and traded my body for money just to get by. I spent countless days and nights in cold, stale jail cells. My criminal and family law cases cluttered up courtrooms and burned through taxpayers' hard-earned dollars.

Somewhere along the way, I began to believe that being in abusive relationships was all I deserved. That kind of chaos became my normal. And when pain becomes familiar, you stop recognizing it as pain—you just survive it. Worse yet, I began to mirror the same abuse I once endured. I reciprocated the very behavior that broke me—because brokenness had become the lens through which I saw the world. And each desperate but failed attempt to break free from addiction left my loved ones heartbroken and terrified, not knowing where I was or if I was even alive.

I spent twenty years living in the exhausting, relentless cycle of addiction—but how did I get there? What would make someone choose all the terrible things I did?

Addiction doesn't start with a needle, a bottle, or a pill. It starts with pain. With unhealed wounds. With unanswered questions and unmet needs. It starts in trauma, in the moments when you first begin to believe that you are unworthy of love, unsafe in the world, and unrepairable. Then, it is fueled by the insane cycle of running away from those horrific feelings and chasing connections that often seem unattainable.

For me, it was a slow fade. A hundred little compromises created choices and circumstances that fueled a desperate need to escape, to numb, to forget. I didn't know how to sit with pain, so I ran from it. I chased anything that made me feel different—better, prettier, braver, more lovable—if only for a moment. Drugs, alcohol, power, control... it was all an illusion—a mask to keep me from facing the girl inside who didn't believe she mattered.

I made choices from a place of survival. But survival turned into self-destruction, and that destruction ruined everything around me and almost cost me my life.

I believed that love was something to be earned. Somewhere along the way, I picked up the message that my worth was tied to performance. Be good. Be quiet. Be perfect. Don't make waves. Smile—even when you're dying inside. In the absence of a secure foundation, I spent years trying to outrun shame and rejection by becoming whatever people needed me to be. The more I hustled for approval, the more hollow I became.

Without a relationship with God to anchor me, I chased counterfeit love and called it connection. That path led me straight into the arms of drug dealers and the throes of manipulative relationships with men who saw my brokenness and used it for their gain, reinforcing the lies that love is transactional, intimacy doesn't exist, and I am only as valuable as what I offer. I wasn't living. I was surviving in a world where affection came with a price tag, and I was always paying the price.

By the time addiction entered the picture, it wasn't some sudden, shocking intrusion. It was a slow fade—an unraveling that at first felt like relief. The bottle didn't judge me. The pills didn't care if I was enough. In fact, they whispered lies—convincing me that with them, I was enough. As long as they were in my system, numbing the pain, fueling me through each painstaking day, I could keep going. For a while, they numbed the ache that screamed, "You're unlovable! You're too far gone. No one could ever want you—not even God." But eventually, the reckless dance with them landed me on the floor of my unfinished basement, where I tried to take my own life.

At my rock bottom—with a toxic mix of alcohol and pills coursing through my veins, I settled on the floor and cut my wrists. This wasn't some desperate plea for help; I fully intended to die, to escape the pain that had consumed me for far too long. I was exhausted. I was tired of hurting everyone around me. Surrounded by the musty stench of despair, I cried out in anguish for God to let me die, convinced that hell was where I belonged.

Every conversation I'd ever had with God up to that point was a cry for rescue—bargaining pleas with no real commitment behind them. "Get me out of this, and I'll do better. Be better." There were many of those moments, but they were always one-sided.

But in that moment of utter darkness, something unexpected happened. A divine intervention—the opposite of what I was begging for. I saw a figure and heard a voice—not audibly, but deep within—that told me if I surrendered completely to God, I would be free. That I had a purpose. And that one day, all of it would make sense.

What followed was a warmth I can't fully describe. A love coursed through me like nothing I'd ever felt before. It was as if heaven touched my soul for a brief moment. That day, what I thought would be my end became the beginning of my spiritual awakening. For so long, I had made substances my god and questioned how a real God could love someone like me or let such pain shape my life. But as I would come to learn, He had been with me all along, even in the darkest shadows. That day in my basement didn't just save my life; it marked the start of my freedom.

I felt I didn't deserve His grace. I didn't understand it. I just knew I was still breathing. And somewhere deep inside, I understood this was not the end. God was not done with me yet. In what seemed like a split second, I had to choose either my old way of life or the one that God revealed was waiting ahead of me—if I would only fully surrender to Him.

I knew this surrender could not be like my previous surrenders—when I had called out for help and made empty promises only to take back the wheel once I was rescued. This time, I had to lay everything at His feet—every part of me. Even if it didn't make sense. Even if I wasn't sure I fully believed the words coming out of my mouth.

My surrender began with, "Okay, God, I don't know what I'm doing, but I trust You… I'm so sorry. Help me."

I actually repeated the words "I'm sorry" like a chant until I was found and then carted off to a rehabilitation center to give recovery another try.

That full surrender in the basement didn't fix everything overnight. It's been a long climb out of the darkness I called home for far too long. There was no instant gratification, no magic cure. Cleaning up the wreckage of my past was a slow, painful process.

But that moment began something. It cracked open the door to a relationship I didn't even know I was worthy of. For the first time, I accepted God's presence instead of trying to bargain with Him. I didn't make promises I couldn't keep. I just showed up each day, asking Him to reveal His will for me.

He met me where I was.

And He loved me through it.

The bondage of self was the most unrelenting stronghold I had ever known. It was the root of my addiction, the source of my despair, and the weight behind my isolation. The belief that I had to do it all, fix it all, be it all—that was the lie. Surrendering to God shattered my faulty belief. This was not a one-and-done event but a repeated occurrence. Each surrender became another broken link in my chain of addiction. Every time I laid down control, fear, shame, or my past at God's feet, I stepped further into freedom.

That was the beginning of my faith journey. It was not a walk of perfection but one of daily progress. A path of continual surrender, again and again, one day at a time. I had to relinquish my pride, my ego, my will, and my plans. I had to learn to say, "God, I can't do this without You." And not once has He turned me away. Not even when I've made mistakes along the way. In fact, He's used those very moments to reveal opportunities for growth, acceptance, and change.

That salvation, that healing, that restoration, that grace—it was never something I could manufacture. I couldn't earn it by saying all the right things or playing the part perfectly. It was, and still is, a gift from God. A gift I receive each time I return to Him in surrender. And when dark thoughts try to creep back in—whispering lies that I'm not worthy—I choose faith again.

As I've moved forward in faith, God has surrounded me with exactly what I've needed. Along the way, I've met the most remarkable people, each one offering a glimmer of hope and shedding light on my never-ending search for His direction.

Faith isn't a one-time decision. It's a daily choice. It shows up in the quiet moments when I ask God to help me stay clean and sober for just one more day. It's in the whisper I hear when I make amends and pray, "God, forgive me my trespasses, as I forgive those who trespass against me." It's in the moments I veer off course—when the enemy tries to confuse me, my ego tries to take the lead, and I forget to put God first as the world presses in with distraction after distraction.

I used to believe I had to come to God clean, fixed, and worthy. But Jesus' life, His choices, His love—they all tell a different story. Jesus didn't wait until his chosen apostles had it all together. He called them as they were.

And they followed Him—not because they were perfect, but because they were loved.

That's what changed me—Love.

It was love that met me on that basement floor, and it is love that still meets me in the quiet when I fall short and ask for forgiveness. Love gave me life when I wanted to end mine. His love gave me strength when I had nothing left, purpose when I thought I had ruined everything, and unity with the God who created me, even when I felt unworthy of His presence.

We all stumble through life feeling unworthy of so many things. The truth is we are human, and, as such, we *are* unworthy. We are flesh. We are *not* perfect. But the One who *is* perfect knows us and our path and, despite our flaws, offers us unity with Him through the Holy Spirit, sharing His perfection and worthiness with us. Only God is purely worthy, and by allowing His Holy Spirit to come alive in us, we become worthy, too. He offers second chances, the strength to make amends, the hope to carry on, and His unending grace. And perhaps the most profound gift I've discovered in recovery—He offers us His written Word, which is alive and breathing, ready to guide us home.

I used to think Scripture was hard to relate to and something reserved for people more "spiritual" than me. But God, in His goodness, placed people in my life who taught me to open the Bible and see it for what it truly is: alive, powerful, and deeply personal. I found my relationship with Jesus in those pages. I discovered a love—unconditional and pure—that I never knew existed.

And what brings me comfort is this: I'm not the only one who needs grace. The Bible is full of people just like you and me—flawed, broken, and unsure... but chosen.

Moses was a murderer with a stutter, yet God used him to lead an entire nation out of slavery. David was an adulterer who orchestrated a man's death, yet God still called him a man after His own heart. Rahab was a prostitute who protected the Israelite spies, and God grafted her into the lineage of Jesus. Jonah ran from his calling, but God still used him to save an entire city.

And Peter—oh my word, how I relate to him. Jesus helped him walk on water, but when his faith wavered, he sank. He denied Jesus three times, yet Jesus still chose him to be the rock on which He would build His church.

Then there's Paul—the very one who wrote the powerful verse I opened this chapter with. He persecuted Christians and was imprisoned, yet God broke his chains—literally and spiritually—and used him to spread the gospel to the ends of the earth.

When Jesus walked the earth, He didn't go into temples to recruit the religious elite—He went along the shoreline and called out to fishermen. He sat at tables with tax collectors and sinners. He stood between a woman caught in adultery and the men who wanted to stone her and said, *"Let him who is without sin among you be the first to throw a stone at her"* (John 8:7 ESV). Jesus handpicked the broken, the outcasts, the flawed, and the people with pasts and pain and reputations. People just like me and you.

If you're reading this and wondering if God's grace is available for you, I want you to know: It is. You are not too far gone. You are not too broken. You are not the exception. Jesus already chose to love you when He gave His life for your salvation. All you have to do is surrender and ask Him into your heart.

Grace doesn't end at salvation—it begins there. Every day, I receive His grace again—not because I've earned it, but because God never runs out of it. He's still calling people like Moses, Rahab, and Peter to follow Him. He's calling me. And He's calling you, too. Not to be perfect, but to be surrendered. Because that's when the best part of our story begins. That's when our chains are broken!

Unchained faith is the kind of faith that allows us to break free from the old labels and walk boldly in our new identity. It's what enables us to forgive others and ask for forgiveness. It's what drives us to stand up and speak when shame tells us to stay silent. It's what calls us to unity—not only with God, but also with each other.

You are not alone on this journey—move forward in faith! The love, grace, and mercy of our Father will guide you every step of the way. Whatever you are walking through, whatever chains need to be broken, may you find the strength to surrender and the courage to embrace the freedom that comes from living out your true purpose. Today, by the grace of God, your chains are breaking away!

> I pray that out of his glorious riches he may strengthen you with power through his Spirit in your inner being, so that Christ may dwell in your hearts through faith. And I pray that you, being rooted and established in love, may have power, together with all the Lord's holy people, to grasp how wide and long and high and deep is the love of Christ, and to know this love that surpasses knowledge—that you may be filled to the measure of all the fullness of God. Now to him who is able to do immeasurably more than all we ask or imagine, according to his power that is at work within us, to him be glory in the church and in Christ Jesus throughout all generations, for ever and ever! Amen. (Ephesians 3:16-21 NIV).

# Breaking Chains of Addiction

### By Melissa Gissy Witherspoon

Addiction is a powerful force that can hold people captive, robbing them of freedom, peace, and purpose. Whether it's substance abuse, pornography, gambling, or any destructive habit, addiction creates strongholds that seem impossible to escape, wrapping chains around the soul and whispering lies of worthlessness, shame, and hopelessness. But Scripture declares the truth that our God is a chain-breaker. He is the One who sets captives free, restores broken lives, and breathes hope into the darkest places.

Jesus said in John 8:34, *"Truly, truly, I say to you, everyone who practices sin is a slave to sin"* (ESV). Addiction is a form of slavery—it keeps us bound in cycles of destruction, often hidden in secrecy and shame. But we cannot heal what we continue to hide. First John 1:9 gives us this promise: *If we confess our sins, He is faithful and just to forgive us our sins and to cleanse us from all unrighteousness* (ESV). Healing begins in the light. Freedom starts with confession and surrender.

Over eleven years ago, I was trapped in the grip of substance abuse—drugs and alcohol ruled my life. I had lost direction, identity, and hope. I didn't have a relationship with God at the time, but He never stopped pursuing me. I cried out in the pit of my brokenness, and God responded—not with condemnation, but with compassion. His grace met me where I was and began to transform me from the inside out.

The journey of breaking free wasn't accomplished by my strength alone—it was by the power of Christ, who declared, *"He has sent me to proclaim freedom for the prisoners and recovery of sight for the blind, to set the oppressed free"* (Luke 4:18 ESV).

Jesus came for people like me—oppressed, blinded, and broken. We are reminded in Romans 6:6 that our old self was crucified with Christ, and we are no longer enslaved to sin. That is the truth I now live by.

Addiction is not just a physical battle—it's also a spiritual and mental one. God began to renew my mind as I immersed myself in His Word. Romans 12:2 taught me that transformation happens when we stop conforming to the patterns of this world and start aligning with God's truth. I replaced lies like, "I'll never change," with promises like, *I can do all things through Christ who strengthens me* (Philippians 4:13 NIV).

When I fully surrendered, restoration began. Second Corinthians 12:9 became real to me—His grace *is* sufficient. In my weakness, He proved strong, surrounding me with people who lifted me up, prayed with me, and reminded me I wasn't alone. James 5:16 encourages us to confess and pray with one another for healing. That's the power of community in recovery.

Today, I live a life of purpose, healing, and hope. John 8:36 says, *So if the Son sets you free, you will be free indeed* (ESV). I am living proof. If He did it for me, He can do it for you.

No matter how strong the chains that bind you are, God is stronger.

Start with these simple yet powerful words: "Jesus, I trust You. Break me free from the chains."

That's the beginning of surrender. That's the moment everything can change. Let Him meet you right where you are, and watch what only He can do—restore, redeem, and set you free with His living grace and mercy.

. . . . . . . . . . . . . . . . . . . . . . . . . . . . . . . . . . . . . . . . . . . .

# Connie A. VanHorn

Connie A. VanHorn has a heart for encouraging others to find their God-given purpose. She serves on the Women World Leaders' Board of Directors and Leadership Team as an ambassador and administrative assistant to staff.

She is an International best-selling author and writes for *Voice of Truth* magazine. Hoping her story will help someone else, Connie passionately shares how her amazing and loving God spared her, an ordinary woman, and gave her a new life.

Connie resides in Winston-Salem, North Carolina, where she has participated in several discipleship classes and taught Sunday school to international students. She has also attended Bible classes at Vintage Bible College.

Being a mother is by far Connie's greatest accomplishment and her first, best ministry. She dreams of changing the world by sharing Jesus and raising world-changers who have a kingdom perspective.

She enjoys being with her children, making bracelets, journaling, fiction writing, and spending most of her time with her family.

Connie wants her readers to know that it's ok to be broken—it's in our broken place that we find God. Come as you are!

See past messy, see past broken, and you might just see a miracle.

# Chasing After God

By Connie A. VanHorn

Just as a caterpillar transforms into a butterfly, believers experience transformation in Christ. We leave behind the old life and embrace a new one, reshaped and set free by God's grace and love.

Before I met Jesus, I struggled to believe in anything beyond daydreams. My faith was tied to what the world had to offer. I was lost, chained to my own doubts and insecurities. I became really good at hiding my true feelings, however. I'd wake up each day and put on a nice dress and a pretty smile.

Eventually, I grew tired of being "just okay." I couldn't keep carrying the weight of the chains that had bound me for so long. The voices in my head were relentless: *You are not special. You are not important. You are not smart. You are not enough.*

I was desperate to break free. My life had been bound by chains of fear, abandonment, shame, and abuse for so long that they had become part of me—like a second skin. I didn't know who I was without them.

From the very beginning, my life was messy. I was raised in a toxic, broken home and bound to the trauma that came with it. Abuse, alcoholism, and addiction were all I knew, and I believed for a long time that would be my story, too.

It started in the 8th grade. I followed a popular girl after school, desperate to belong. That day ended with me waking up in a hospital bed with alcohol poisoning. I had been left alone on a sidewalk—unconscious and choking. Unfortunately, that trauma didn't stop me from chasing the world.

Going out with friends and drinking became the highlight of my week. It was how I coped—how I silenced the pain and convinced myself, if only for a few hours, that life was fine. But underneath it all, I wasn't chasing fun. I was chasing approval, someone to tell me I mattered.

After I turned eighteen, I moved to Hollywood, California, with big dreams and an even bigger void in my heart. I thought I could finally prove my worth by chasing fame and making it as a movie star. But instead of fame, I found myself pregnant and boarding a one-way flight back home.

I grew up in Florida, where the party never stopped. There was always a bar and a new distraction to chase. In my early twenties, I was working at a local bar during Daytona Beach Bike Week—one of the biggest motorcycle events in the world, highlighted by motorcycle races, parties, and street festivals—when a friend handed me an orange, tangerine energy drink mixed with alcohol.

Before long, I was stumbling. The bar owner asked me to leave. I remember wobbling to my car, keys in hand, and collapsing into the driver's seat. That could've been the end of my story.

But then...a whisper broke through the noise, "Throw the keys."

Somehow, I listened. I tossed my keys into the grass and curled up, falling asleep right there in my car. When I woke up, the sun was rising, and shame was sitting heavily on my chest. I thought, *What if I hadn't listened? What if I had driven?*

I had left my baby behind that night. I had almost destroyed my life—and possibly someone else's.

That was a wake-up call. I could either keep walking the path I was on or choose something different. I could break the chain that bound me.

I made the decision that night to never let myself get to that place again—and I meant it. I promised my daughter and myself that I would never drink like that again. I'm proud to say that was over twenty years ago and I've kept my promise.

To this day, drinking is not a part of my life. That night marked the breaking of a generational chain. But I quickly learned that wasn't the only chain that needed breaking in my life. God and I have been on a journey ever since to break every chain that holds me captive and keeps me from becoming who He made me to be.

God can trade our pain for purpose and grow and change us through our brokenness. I didn't realize it then, but He was preparing me to walk through harder things that would reveal His strength in my weakness and His purpose in my pain.

Several years later, I met someone I can only describe as a real-life angel. I would often pass her home on my evening walks. Her windows were always open. There were no televisions, no distractions—just light and peace.

My own house felt like chaos. The constant noises pierced me like a blade. But this woman would sit on her porch, reading a book, her smile as gentle as the breeze. She always wore a long skirt, a tucked-in white blouse, and a white bonnet with her blonde hair in a bun. I had never seen a woman dress that way before. And although it was spring 2013, she looked like someone straight out of an old Amish movie.

One evening, I was sitting at the end of my driveway, watching my children play, when she walked up to me. I opened up and shared that I was pregnant and my doctor said I was experiencing a threatened miscarriage. I told her my heart was breaking and I didn't want to lose my baby.

Without saying much, she handed me a pocket-sized book: *Jesus Calling*. I had never heard of it before. She didn't explain, just smiled and said she'd be praying for me.

This woman, Chere, walked confidently, never blinking at the stares she received from those in our community. It was the first time in my life that I looked at someone in awe of the peace she reflected from within. I wanted what Chere had. I longed for the calm in her home and the joy in her heart.

Peace I leave with you; my peace I give you. I do not give to you as the world gives. Do not let your hearts be troubled and do not be afraid (John 14:27 NIV).

I wasn't part of a church, nor was I saved. Although I had heard about God, I didn't truly know Him. I wanted to believe, but deep down, I didn't think I was good enough to be part of God's family.

I was messy. My life was broken and full of sin. *Why would God want someone like me?* I carried that thought like a weight in my heart for years. But God, in His mercy, was continually chasing after me.

Around the time I lived next door to Chere, I heard a Christian song on the radio. It was the first time I felt a connection to something deeper. Until then, I had felt alone in my circumstances, in my pain, in the heaviness of trying to hold it all together. But the lyrics of that song made me feel like someone had read my soul and put it to music.

I was tired and worn. My heart was heavy, the chains were suffocating, and my spirit felt crushed under the weight of the world. I needed to hear that the struggle ends. That redemption wins. That God could mend a heart so frail and torn. That somehow, a song could rise from the ashes of a broken life. That all the dead things inside of me could be made new again.

God says that faith the size of a mustard seed can move mountains. That's because a tiny mustard seed can blossom into an enormous mustard plant when we let God care for it. Looking back, I believe each of these events was God watering the seed of faith He had already placed in my heart long before I knew Him. I don't know exactly when He planted that seed, but I know it lived in the daydreams that started in my childhood.

One evening, while sitting on my bed, crying for my unborn baby, I reached for that little book Chere had given me. I opened to the devotion for that day, and as I began reading, I couldn't believe what I saw. The words on the page met me right where I was.

I wanted to leap from the bed with joy. I called my older daughter into the room, and we read the devotion together. She felt it, too. Over the next several weeks, my faith began to grow...page by page. And so did my unborn baby.

God was speaking to me through that small book. He was calling to my heart, gently drawing me closer, showing me He had been there all along. He had His hand on my heart before I ever set my eyes on Him.

God knew I'd be messy. He knew I'd stumble and fall. He knew the world would tempt me and that I'd often feel too weak to stand. But He wasn't calling on a perfect person. He had already chosen me to be His just as I was.

And through Chere, He opened my eyes to the peace I had always longed for and offered me a strong foundation.

He knew I would need that for where I was headed...

Not long after meeting Chere, my children and I moved into a hotel. I walked out of the hospital with my newborn baby in my arms, and instead of heading home to a decorated nursery with a rocking chair, we returned to a small room at the Quality Inn. There was no crib, no fresh coat of paint, and no baby shower gifts waiting to be opened.

I sat on the edge of that hotel bed most nights and cried. I had hoped for things to be different. I had hoped my story would turn a new page. But this was our reality—and somehow, even in that low place, I knew God hadn't left us.

He was right there—in the middle of it all. He was there when I cried myself to sleep, praying for a way out. He was there when I felt alone and invisible to the world.

That hotel room became the place where I truly met God. It was where I learned to pray belly down, with empty hands and a surrendered heart. It's where I opened *Jesus Calling* each morning and found words that matched the storm I was facing. It's where I started believing that I didn't need to be perfect to be loved by God—I just needed to be willing to let Him in.

After a total of ten months in the hotel, we moved into a shelter and experienced nine more months of transition, of making do while figuring out how to survive another day and what the next page would hold. Nineteen months total. Nineteen months of being stripped down to nothing but faith.

And still—God didn't let go of me.

He kept showing up. In the kindness of strangers. In the giggles of my children. In worship songs that reminded me I wasn't forgotten. In moments where I should've broken but didn't.

God was teaching me to trust Him in the most difficult moments. To walk by faith and not by sight. To let go of what I thought my life should look like and hold on to what is true: I am loved. I am seen. I am His.

My trials and my pain weren't the end of my story. It was the beginning of a new one built on His faithfulness, not my fear.

I tried to make that little hotel room feel as normal as possible. I hung the kids' artwork on the walls and we celebrated holidays in the lobby sitting area, making it special with what little we had. I kept the beds made and the room tidy. During the day, I opened the windows to let the light in. I wanted my children to feel safe. I wanted them to feel like they were home.

I thought about Chere and her bright, peaceful home and the stillness that lived inside it. I worked hard to create that same kind of peace in our space. I filled our days with parks, libraries, and walks through stores. We spent so much time outside of that room, but I also know now that I found something sacred inside that room. Because it was in that room that God started putting my broken pieces back together. He collected what the world had thrown away.

God knew I still had some fight in me. I didn't have a lot, but I had kids who needed me and a whisper of faith that wouldn't let go.

So, I put on my brave face every morning—the "everything is okay" face—for my children. And every night, after they fell asleep, I'd get down on that cold hotel floor and cry out to the God I was still getting to know. I would cry until there were no tears left. I would beg Him to see me.

And He did! I learned that He wants us to cry out to Him in the night and be ready for battle at dawn. God was with us. He was in that room. He was in the small moments, in the quiet mercies.

> *"Have I not commanded you? Be strong and courageous; do not be afraid or be discouraged; for the Lord your God will be with you wherever you go"* (Joshua 1:9 NIV).

I found a craft frame at a Goodwill store. It was a white frame with a butterfly outline. I brought it back to the hotel and used my kids' little hands to create butterfly wings—their handprints filled the shape. That frame sat next to my bed for all those months.

At the time, it was just a sweet project. But now, I see it for what it really was: a sign of God's presence. His promise that transformation was coming.

Those nineteen months changed me, though I didn't recognize it then. I was still lost and hurting, still buried under the weight of survival. I had very little hope, but I had just enough faith to keep moving.

My mustard seed faith sustained me until God was ready to provide another droplet of hope. Hope is a beautiful thing. It's what fuels us when we're too tired to dream. It keeps our feet moving when everything around us tells us to sit down and give up.

Hope shows up in the most unlikely places—like in a hotel room, a song on the radio, or a stranger in a bonnet. We just have to have willing eyes to see it.

In August 2014, everything changed. I gave my whole heart to Jesus. That day, I became new. Something broke free inside me, and I knew I'd never be the same. From that moment, I stopped running from God and started chasing Him.

> *Therefore, if anyone is in Christ, the new creation has come: The old has gone, the new is here!* (2 Corinthians 5:17 NIV).

I was no longer the same girl who had cried herself to sleep on that hotel floor. I was new. Redeemed. Called. Chosen.

On the outside, I still looked the same. But on the inside? I was a new creation. It was like God had given me brand new eyes—eyes that could see through the darkness and into the light. I began to see people differently. I began to see life differently. He had opened my eyes so that I could live with unchained faith.

I often talk about what I call "chasing butterflies" because that's exactly what my life felt like. God was revealing Himself through the everyday, beautiful things around me as He led me on a path to Him. Actual butterflies started appearing around me often, and I never felt it was just a coincidence. It was God's confirmation to me that He was near—my constant reminder that I wasn't alone; He was leading me to Him.

One day, sitting in my parked car, I was met with something I'll never forget. There, resting on my car window, was the most beautiful blue butterfly I had ever seen. It didn't flutter away. It wasn't startled or scared. It just sat there—in perfect peace, still and steady.

I had never seen a butterfly that close before, not like that. It felt like time slowed down so I could take it all in. And in that moment, something shifted. That was the moment I started seeing butterflies with eternal eyes.

God finds the most beautiful and tender ways to draw us closer to Him.

He knew me—He knew how much I'd need reminders. He knew I was still fragile and easily distracted, how weak I felt, and how tempting and dark this world could be. He knew I would need something sweet, constant, and gentle—a love note from heaven that would anchor me in Him.

That blue butterfly became more than a symbol. It became a quiet and powerful connection between me and God. He was showing me that even when I couldn't always hear Him, I could see Him. And now, every time I see a butterfly, I smile. Because I know God is near.

My journey is still unfolding—like a butterfly's wings fresh out of its cocoon.

The greatest step of faith I've ever taken wasn't just believing in God—it was believing what God says about Jesus. And then believing what God says about me. God says I am loved and redeemed. God says I've been given a new heart and a new life—true life. Not a perfect life, but a better one. A life found only in Christ.

Becoming a Christian is a heart transformation—a rebirth. Much like the butterfly, we emerge from the darkness of our past, transformed and free. The old has passed away, and the new has come.

We don't have to conform to this world. We don't have to live in the same cycles and choices that have defined our families. We can be the ones who break the chains. We can break generational barriers. We can find gratitude even in the transitional places—the waiting rooms of life.

We can dream big, God-sized dreams and walk by faith as we watch those dreams come to life. We can live with unchained faith—fully present, deeply surrendered, and joyfully free.

We can chase after God and, when it's time, spread our wings and let the freedom of His grace carry us—lift us—on His warm, gentle wind... into a life of purpose and peace.

Every day, I am still breaking chains and chasing butterflies. I am climbing to freedom by His grace. Will you climb with me? Will you chase God and embrace the beautiful life He's offering you?

# Breaking Chains of Generational Patterns

By Melissa Gissy Witherspoon

Many of us carry burdens that have been passed down through generations—fear, addiction, brokenness, poverty, shame, or unbelief. Often rooted deep in our family history, these patterns can feel like chains too strong to break. But God. He steps in and calls us higher, reminding us that our past does not define our future.

In Scripture, we meet a man named Gideon, hiding in a winepress, threshing wheat in fear of the enemy. Gideon considered himself the least in his household, which, he proclaimed, was part of the weakest clan in Manasseh (Judges 6:15 ESV). Generational fear, doubt, and spiritual compromise ran deep! Gideon's father had even built an altar to Baal (Judges 6:25). Despite this family's propensity to marginalize themselves, God saw something more in Gideon.

> The angel of the Lord appeared to him and said to him, "The Lord is with you, you mighty man of valor" (Judges 6:12 RSV).

Isn't that just like God? While Gideon saw weakness and failure, God called out identity, purpose, and destiny.

The Lord told Gideon to tear down the altar of Baal that his father had built. This was more than a physical act; it was symbolic of Gideon breaking the chains of generational idolatry and compromise. It took courage to stand against what had always been—to say, "It stops with me."

Like Gideon, many of us are called to tear down the spiritual strongholds that have existed in our families for generations and build new altars to the one true God. Addiction runs deep in my bloodlines, but in my recovery, I have been able to set a new tone for my children—a promise for a future generation built on integrity, truth, service, faith, and a solid understanding that without substances, we can do so much more!

Gideon's story teaches us that God does not require a perfect family background to use us—He just needs our obedience. What matters most is not where we came from but where we're willing to go when He calls. Gideon went on to lead Israel to victory, not because he had the best lineage but because he trusted the Lord who called him. Today, you, too, can break free. You are not defined by your parents' or grandparents' mistakes. You are defined by God, and He says you are chosen, loved, and called.

Jesus Himself came through a bloodline filled with broken people — liars, adulterers, outcasts — yet He redeemed it all. That same redemption is available to you! *For you did not receive the spirit of slavery to fall back into fear, but you have received the spirit of sonship. When we cry, "Abba! Father!"* (Romans 8:15 RSV). We are not bound to repeat the past. In Christ, we are adopted, chosen, and set apart for a new legacy.

Let yours be the generation where it all changes. The chains stop here. Build new altars. Walk in freedom. And trust that God will lead you into a future that will be far greater than your past.

. . . . . . . . . . . . . . . . . . . . . . . . . . . . . . . . . . . . . . . . . . . . . . . . . . .

# Katie Whitehead

Katie Whitehead has a deep love for the Lord and shares that love with those around her. Katie is from Roxie, Mississippi, and is currently a student at the University of Southern Mississippi, majoring in art. With a passion for singing and worshiping, she expresses her creativity as an artist, glorifying God through drawing, painting, and pottery and sharing her art with everyone she meets.

During the summer, Katie dedicates her time to serving as a cabin leader at Camp Garaywa, where she teaches God's Word and shares the love of Christ with girls in grades 4 through 6. She is also a bestselling author, featured in the book *Unseen: You Are Not Alone,* and has been highlighted in *Voice of Truth* magazine.

Katie's favorite Bible verse is 2 Corinthians 5:17 (NLT): *This means that anyone who belongs to Christ has become a new person. The old life is gone; a new life has begun!*

Katie enjoys collecting and painting butterflies, as they remind her of the hope we have in Jesus and the new life found in Christ.

# Who God Says You Are

By Katie Whitehead

Faith is holding onto the Lord and having confidence in Him. Throughout all our storms in life, having faith in God and His promises can keep us together. I have learned many lessons in my faith journey—the most important have been to lean on the Lord in everything and believe the truth of who He says I am instead of the lies from the enemy.

> *Now faith is confidence in what we hope for and assurance about what we do not see* (Hebrews 11:1 NIV).

I used to believe I wasn't good enough— not good enough to serve the Lord, read the Bible, use my talents for Him, or even have my prayers heard. It was a different feeling of unworthiness. I grew up in a wonderful Christian family, surrounded by so many amazing people who were always faithful in serving Jesus. I wanted to be just like them, but I felt so small.

Reading the Bible was difficult. I didn't think I would ever understand where to start, what God wanted me to learn from what I was reading, or how to apply His Word to my life. These feelings of confusion contributed to my I-am-not-good-enough mindset. I loved the Lord so much and always wanted to give my whole heart and life to Him, but I felt blocked.

I was chained to my own *insecurity!*

The enemy was deep in my head, and his voice was loud, constantly convincing me that I couldn't read the Bible well and it wasn't worth the effort—that I wasn't worth the effort!

I believed I would never understand God's Word, so why should I read it anyway? I always thought I would never be as good a Christian as my family or the leaders in my church.

As a result, I became more and more isolated from the truths of God and who He said I was. I began to believe in the lies of the enemy—that I was not good or strong enough. During this time, I never gave up on my faith, although I was greatly discouraged and struggled with anxiety and depression. I sometimes had a lot of hate for myself. I felt defeated by the thoughts in my mind.

As time went on, the weights holding those chains down just got heavier.

One day, I drew a picture of a butterfly and wrote the word "hope" underneath it. At the time, I didn't fully understand the depth of that word. I love sharing my art with friends, so I sent that picture to one of my wonderful friends whom I looked up to. Without hesitation, she shared exactly what I needed to hear. She said that hope is not just a wishful word and instead defined it as "dynamic confidence."

The hope we have in Jesus is our dynamic confidence that, no matter what we go through in life, we can trust He is always there for us and sees our struggles.

I held that word close and continued to search out its meaning. As Jesus carried me through the process, I started to trust in the Lord. God opened my mind to begin to understand the Bible as I read it, which allowed me to find my confidence in Him rather than myself.

*Trust in the Lord with all your heart and lean not on your own understanding; in all your ways submit to him, and he will make your paths straight* (Proverbs 3:5-6 NIV).

Growing up, I struggled to understand my worth. At school, I was often made fun of for different things I wore—like my shoes and belt—and even for how my eyes looked. If it was something about me, someone commented on it.

I felt so small and unsure of myself as I constantly compared myself to others. I thought I needed to be just like others—to use makeup and wear the same style of clothes they did. But a voice whispered deep inside me, reminding me I was already loved and cherished just as I am.

Often, especially when I was upset about what others thought of me, my dad would remind me, saying, "You are a child of God, and that is all that matters. You are beautiful in His eyes and deeply loved by Him."

Those words lingered in my heart. Over time, I began to understand their profound truth.

God created each of us in His image; that alone makes us beautiful. It doesn't matter how many mistakes we make or how far we feel from perfection; God's love for us remains. I learned that leaning into God's deep love creates a path for us to accept ourselves—flaws and all.

I had a moment of clarity when I looked in the mirror and felt God say, "You are beautiful just the way I made you."

In that instant, I understood I didn't need to change who I was to be worthy of love.

> For we are God's masterpiece. He has created us anew in Christ Jesus, so we can do the good things he planned for us long ago (Ephesians 2:10 NLT)

You are God's masterpiece!! He created you beautifully and uniquely!!

I love to create art with my hands. Everything I make is unique. I can never make anything the same; that is the beauty of creating. When I'm working on the pottery wheel, if I don't have a clear idea of what I want to create, I struggle to make anything. However, when I have a plan, I can usually make my vision a reality.

When I know what I want to create, I feel confident I can make it. I can sense the thickness or thinness of the clay in my hands and determine how tall it should be. I know when to shape the inside or outside of the pot and when it's at risk of collapsing. Every aspect of the process has a purpose as a beautiful work of art is fashioned.

God always knows what He is doing. He makes no mistakes. When He created you, He did so with purpose and beauty. You are exactly as He intended you to be.

God continually shapes, leads, and guides us through life as we serve Him. He created us to glorify and serve Him in all that we do. God is always molding us and has great plans for our lives, just like I do with the clay I use to create my own masterpiece!

Oh, how beautiful that is! God is the Potter, and we are the clay! We weren't created simply to exist here on earth. Praise the Lord, we were made for more!

Just as I work with the clay to shape it Into a little vase, the Lord will always shape us and mold us ever so beautifully through His love and grace.

> But you are a chosen generation, a royal priesthood, a holy nation, His own special people, that you may proclaim the praises of Him who called you out of darkness into his marvelous light; who once were not a people but are now the people of God, who had not obtained mercy but now have obtained mercy (1 Peter 2:9-10 NKJV).

As I've continued to grow in my faith, I've realized that stepping out and serving the Lord is another way to discover my worth. I love helping others and serving the Lord. It used to be easy to get caught up in my insecurities, but when I began to focus on helping others and sharing God's love, I felt a sense of purpose that I had never experienced before. I felt the chains begin to release. Serving others allowed me to see myself through God's eyes— someone who is chosen, special, and strong.

The chains that had been holding me hostage to my own insecurities were now breaking away!

When I was asked to write a chapter for this book, I couldn't believe it. It felt like this was a calling bigger than me, far beyond my capabilities. At first, I felt I was not good enough. This work for the Lord seemed impossible, but I soon realized I could accomplish anything God called me to with Him by my side. Not only does He empower me, but He constantly reminds me of my worth.

Writing in this book was God's calling to me, which He reminded me of whenever I felt inadequate. It was as if He was saying, "Katie, I will help you through writing if you just trust Me in the work I have called you to do. I know that if you place your trust in Me, you are more than capable because I will work through you and teach you along the way."

We can always rely on the Holy Spirit and allow Him to work through us. My title, "Who God Says You Are," comes from this. I wanted my chapter to reflect that powerful truth: you can achieve anything if you have faith in God and believe you are who He says you are. With God, your possibilities are endless, and your worth is never in question. He will never make you walk chained to anything! You are free!

*Now to him who is able to do immeasurably more than all we ask or imagine, according to his power that is at work within us* (Ephesians 3:20 NIV).

Knowing and believing are two completely different things. Truly believing in the truth of who God says you are is so important. I grew up *knowing* the truth about Jesus—how much He loves me, how He created me uniquely, and how loving and forgiving He is. However, the lies of the enemy tried to block me from fully *believing* in God's truth and who He says I am. But because I held onto the hope of Jesus, I remembered those truths and planted them deep in my heart. I learned to defeat the lies of the enemy with the truth of God's Word and the light in my life.

We can be chained by the lies of our insecurity and failures or choose to walk closer to Jesus, believing the truth of who He says we are by faith! Faith is believing in the truth of the Lord. We can freely access God's peace when we *know* the truth and *believe* the truth of His love for us.

There was a time in my life when the Lord spoke to me so clearly about His love and grace that was freely given to everyone who believes. I was at an event where there was a demonstration of God's gift to us. I remember very clearly the Lord speaking the words "for you" over and over to me. He died *for me* so that I would be *free.*

Please say this with me—
*For you.*
*For you.*
*For you.*

God was reminding me (and you) of the sacrifice, grace, and forgiveness He freely gave to everyone who believes. At the time, I felt defeated by my failures. I was accepting untrue things about myself and searching for my identity amid the lies. This whisper from God was a reminder of His grace. God has given me so much grace; He gave His life for me—and you. Despite our mistakes and failures, God still offers His grace and forgiveness to us.

*But God is so rich in mercy, and he loved us so much, that even though we were dead because of our sins, he gave us life when he raised Christ from the dead. (It is only by God's Grace that you have been saved!)* (Ephesians 2:4-5 NLT).

If you are like me—struggling to see your true worth—I want to encourage you to embrace and truly believe in who God says you are. You are not defined by your mistakes or how you compare to others. Instead, remember that you are loved and God has a special purpose for your life.

Keep your eyes on Him, surrender your fears, drop the chains, and step out in faith. Holding on tightly to the Lord, trust He will guide you and help you see the beautiful person He created you to be. You are worthy, you are cherished, and you are a child of God.

*For he chose us in him before the creation of the world to be holy and blameless in his sight. In love* (Ephesians 1:4 NIV).

This is our *HOPE!*

When we trade our broken hearts for the truth of God's grace, surrender our fear, anxiety, mistakes, and anything that entangles us, and believe His truth in faith, we begin to find abundant joy and peace in our lives. For Christ is our living hope that we can always lean on. Life takes faith, and we cannot put our faith and trust in just anything or anyone of this world.

Only Jesus.

*Those who look to him for help will be radiant with joy; no shadow of shame will darken their faces* (Psalm 34:5 NLT).

You are who God says you are: chosen, loved, special, and strong in the Lord.

Put all your faith, hope, and trust in Jesus; never let go of Him because He will never let go of you. Turn to Jesus in faith, and He will change your life inside and out. Live a life of freedom today by just taking that first step of faith in believing and trusting in the truth of Jesus!

Hold on tightly to the Lord. He has made you new. He is our hope, and the Potter makes no mistakes!

*Yet you, Lord, are our Father. We are the clay, you are the potter; we are all the work of your hand* (Isaiah 64:8 NIV).

Here are my favorite verses to read when I need reminding of my true identity!

*So God created mankind in his own image, in the image of God he created them; male and female he created them* (Genesis 1:27 NIV).

*Therefore, if anyone is in Christ, the new creation has come: The old has gone, the new is here!* (2 Corinthians 5:17 NIV).

These two verses remind me that we are created in God's image and that, in Christ, we are made new—to reflect our true identity as His beloved children.

As I close my chapter, I want to take a moment to pray for you, dear reader. May you find your way into the loving arms of our God, who created each of us uniquely and with a special purpose!

*Thank you, Lord Jesus, for creating each of us so beautiful and wonderfully different. Help us always remember this truth: You purposefully made us unique and special to fulfill the great plans You have for our lives. We place all our faith and confidence in You; You are our hope.*

*Thank You for the abundant love and grace You freely give us every day. Guide us as we walk with You, embracing Your truth and believing in who You say we are.*

*In Jesus' name, we pray. Amen.*

# Breaking Chains of Insecurity

By Connie A. VanHorn

We live in a world that often amplifies our flaws and shortcomings, making it easy to feel small and insecure. I felt inadequate for much of my life—until I heard a gentle whisper from God reminding me that I am so much more.

At times, it can seem like others only notice our imperfections, our messiness, and the broken places within us, but perhaps that is just our insecurity making us feel that way. We all have struggles, setbacks, and failures, but what if we set those aside and listen for the whisper of hope God speaks to us in our quiet moments?

God can use our pain to usher in growth. In the tears we drop when we are alone, God can build us into something stronger. With our tears that hit the ground, God can move mountains.

Consider Noah, who faced ridicule and doubt while building the ark. People called him a fool as he prepared for rain that others didn't believe would come. Yet, God gave Noah a vision before He gave him validation. Though others might not have believed, Noah trusted the purpose that God put in his heart.

Joseph's story is similar. He was laughed at by his own family when he shared the dream of his future rise to power. They saw him in his circumstances and laughed, not realizing that God was revealing his destination, not his current situation.

David experienced this, too; he was just a small shepherd boy, underestimated by everyone around him. When he stepped up to face Goliath, people looked at his size, sling, and stones as they laughed at the idea of him winning. However, David had trained alone in the fields and now relied on the same God who helped him defeat lions and bears to conquer the giant before him.

When you feel insecure, know that God's plan for your life is perfect. Others can't hear His words or instructions meant just for you. They don't see what you do when you're alone and can't see the nights you cry in silence or the victories you've already won behind closed doors. God sees your heart, is with you, and is preparing you, not just for that moment of victory but for every step throughout your life.

> *Let us not become weary in doing good, for at the proper time we will reap a harvest if we do not give up* (Galatians 6:9 NIV).

This promise tells us to keep pushing forward and be confident in the journey, even when it feels really hard. You might be feeling insecure and tempted to quit, but remember that God will empower you to walk out the plan He has prepared.

We stand before an audience of one—God, who gave you that purpose and dream for a reason.

> *"Have I not commanded you? Be strong and courageous. Do not be afraid; do not be discouraged, for the Lord your God will be with you wherever you go"* (Joshua 1:9 NIV).

That is my favorite verse! It calls us to be strong, CONFIDENT, and have courage. It's a reminder that we are not alone and are secure in God's presence.

God is with you every step of the way.

As you break the chains of insecurity, hold onto these truths. Believe in your purpose, trust in God's plan, and know that you are capable of achieving great things!

. . . . . . . . . . . . . . . . . . . . . . . . . . . . . . . . . . . . . . . . . . . . . . . . . . . . . .

# Olivia Rae Moriarity

Olivia Rae Moriarity grew up in Whittier, California, and lived in Southern California for the majority of her life. Her current home is in the beautiful state of Oregon, where she has happily resided for the past ten years. She loves exploring and discovering more of God's breathtaking creations and wonders in Oregon!

Olivia has a niece and two nephews (all grown), who she couldn't love or be any prouder of if they were her own kids. She loves helping others, spending time with friends, reading, painting, and, most recently, learning more about our Lord and Savior, Jesus Christ!

Olivia is passionate about being a drug and alcohol abuse counselor and helping others on their journey to a sober and healthy life. She also loves to share her testimony of God's grace and His perfect will, knowing the only reason she is here and able to spread His Word is His unfailing love. Olivia hopes her story can reach even one person and bring them to accept the Lord into their life.

*But if from there you seek the Lord you God, you will find Him if you seek Him with all your heart and with all your soul* (Deuteronomy 4:29 NIV).

# Saved by God's Grace

By Olivia Rae Moriarity

My story begins like many who have battled addiction.

As a teenager, I dabbled with alcohol among friends. Then, as a young adult, I embraced the bar and club scene, losing my inhibitions and blowing off steam like so many others around me. Society taught me that drinking was a normal part of life—a rite of passage in the United States when you turn twenty-one. Alcohol is marketed as a way to relax, socialize, celebrate, and enjoy positive experiences. It is frequently associated with fun, attractive people and desirable situations.

But society didn't teach me the danger of overdrinking and the long-term effects it could have on my life and those around me.

Looking back, I can pinpoint the moment my drinking became a problem. In my early twenties, I started frequenting local bars, and even then, I knew something wasn't right. I never knew when to stop. Once I started drinking, I couldn't turn it off. I was always "down to drink," and I quickly earned the reputation of being the "fun drunk." But what people didn't see was that deep down, I was battling something bigger than I could handle.

At the age of twenty-two, I totaled my car and was arrested for driving under the influence, also known as DUI. I spent a humiliating night in jail, went to court, paid my fines, lost my license, and endured years of probation. My blood alcohol level was .24%, almost three times the legal limit. I was blessed that I didn't kill anyone, including myself. Yet, even after all that, I didn't stop drinking.

The years that followed were full of reckless choices. I drank excessively, drove drunk, blacked out, and woke up not knowing where my car was or how I'd gotten home. I am ashamed to admit this went on for longer than it should have. By January 2021, my drinking had spiraled so far out of control that it was no longer about fun—it was about survival.

I was barely functioning—simple tasks like showering felt impossible. My hands shook so badly I couldn't hold a fork. I drank from the moment I woke up until I passed out at night. My body had become completely dependent on alcohol, rejecting even water. I was vomiting what looked like coffee grounds, a warning sign of severe internal damage. I was eventually hospitalized with pancreatitis and told that if I didn't stop drinking, I would die. Even then, I didn't stop.

Over the next few months, I continued drinking, and my body continued to deteriorate. Emergency services were called to my home multiple times because I was so sick from alcohol poisoning. I knew I was killing myself. But as much as I wanted to quit, I just didn't know how. I was terrified— not just of withdrawals but of living sober. I didn't know who I was without alcohol. I was consumed by fear: fear of failure, fear of the unknown, fear of life without the crutch that had controlled me for so long.

One night, I hit rock bottom. Sitting on my bed, shaking and crying uncontrollably, I prayed with everything in me:

"Please, Lord, I need Your help. I can't do this on my own. The only way I can do this is with You. So, I'm giving myself and all of this to You. Please come into my heart, Lord. I want to follow You as my Savior. Amen."

I meant every word of that prayer. It was raw and desperate, and it came from the depths of my soul. The next thing I remember, I was waking up in a hospital bed with tubes and IVs everywhere. I had been in a coma for ten days. The doctors said I shouldn't have survived.

*Lord my God, I called to you for help, and you healed me. You, Lord, brought me up from the realm of the dead; you spared me from going down to the pit* (Psalm 30:2-3 NIV).

As I recovered, I began to understand that my journey was just beginning. I couldn't walk or even stand without assistance. But something inside me had shifted. I had a renewed sense of faith, an unshakable strength I knew came from the Lord. When I struggled to take a step, when I cried from the pain, God reminded me that He had healed me and He would carry me through this, too.

After nearly three months in the hospital, I was released. The doctors recommended I go to a rehabilitation facility because I still couldn't stand or walk on my own. But this was during COVID-19, and the only available facilities were over two hours away, with no visitors allowed. The thought of being isolated again broke my spirit, so I refused. I knew recovery at home would be hard, but I also knew something the doctors didn't: I had the Lord on my side.

With God's help, I pushed myself every day. Each small victory was a miracle. The first time I made it to the bathroom with my walker, I cried tears of joy. I thanked God for giving me the strength to take even those few steps. The doctors had warned me I might need a liver transplant, but in yet another miracle, my last scan showed no signs of cirrhosis. Praise Jesus!

Once I became healthy and gained strength and the ability to walk on my own, I began thinking, *What am I going to do with my life now?* So, I started praying hard and often for God to reveal my purpose to me. In my heart, I knew I wanted to use my experience of recovering from addiction in a meaningful way—to help others and give God the glory all at the same time. And once again, God answered my prayers.

A good friend of mine pointed me in the direction of becoming a certified Drug and Alcohol Abuse Counselor, and I did just that! It is something that I am extremely passionate about and proud of. I'm humbled and in awe that I get to use my experience to help and support those who struggle with the same things I once did; to help guide them to find the eternal love of Christ Jesus is a double blessing!

*Commit to the Lord whatever you do, and He will establish your plans* (Proverbs 16:3 NIV).

During my recovery, my sister Michelle was a source of support. She called almost daily to check on me and tell me she loved me. Michelle and I were never what you would call stereo-typically close sisters. We were six years apart and felt every day of it. Don't get me wrong, we shared a lot of fun times and loved each other fiercely, but we didn't share a close relationship for most of our lives. I'm sure both of our addictions played a role in that. Nevertheless, she was there for me when I needed her.

There was a time when Michelle paid my rent. Another time, she sent me groceries when I didn't have money. We may not have been close, but I was her little sister, and she always felt a need to protect and help me when she was able.

Michelle and I both went to church on and off throughout our lives; however, I don't believe either of us ever truly knew the Lord. You see, it wasn't until that day when I was sitting on my bed crying and shaking uncontrollably that I fully surrendered to Him. When I turned myself and all my troubles over to Him, meaning it wholeheartedly, I then began to know the Lord.

*Submit yourselves, then, to God. Resist the devil, and he will flee from you* (James 4:7 NIV).

Michelle struggled with addiction to alcohol most of her life. Between us, we lost many years to that evil illness. There were times I wouldn't answer my

*Faith Unchained: Climbing to Freedom by God's Grace*

phone, or if I did, I would hang up because I knew she had been drinking. As I found sobriety, I watched from afar as my sister slipped further and further into her substance abuse. Much like me, she found herself in the hospital several times as her body deteriorated from the terrible disease of alcoholism.

My cries from worry and fear turned into frustration and anger. All of my begging and pleading with my sister, warning her that she was going to end up like me, in a coma or maybe even worse, always seemed to fall on deaf ears. She always had a comeback line like, "I'm right as rain," or "I'm fine as frog's hair." But I knew nothing could be farther from the truth.

Eventually my pleas to her turned into prayers for her. I prayed for God to be with my sister so she wouldn't be alone. My heart ached because, due to my own struggles with addiction, I knew the darkness she was walking through. I asked Him to not only heal her but to be with her and ease her pain and loneliness.

*Turn to me and be gracious to me, for I am lonely and afflicted. Relieve the troubles of my heart and free me from my anguish* (Psalm 25:16-17 NIV).

In April 2024, my worst fears came to fruition. Michelle hadn't been heard from for a week, and I knew in my heart that she was gone. A wellness check was done, and she was found in her bathroom unalive. When I was informed her body was found, I felt a wave of grief that I still struggle to put into words. I know she wasn't alone because I had prayed and asked God to be with her, and He is faithful. I envision Him meeting her at the hour of her death and lovingly guiding her home. Believing in this brings me peace and comfort. I pray deeply that she asked Jesus into her heart before she passed, because I yearn to one day be reunited with my big sister in heaven.

*Do not conform to the pattern of this world, but be transformed by the renewing of your mind. Then you will be able to test and approve what God's will is – His good, pleasing and perfect will* (Romans 12:2 NIV).

The pain of losing a sibling, especially to something as cruel as addiction, is truly indescribable. It serves as a heartbreaking reminder that addiction doesn't just affect the individual—it sends ripples through families and loved ones, leaving a void that feels impossible to fill. Finding the words to express this pain is nearly impossible. Terms like gut-wrenching or heartbreaking barely scratch the surface. Honestly, I am still working through grief. Each day, the emotions and the words I use to describe them seem to change. Only through hours of quiet reflection, delving into the depths of my anger, hurt, sadness, and confusion, have I been able to grow in acceptance. And it is through prayer that I've found my calm and serenity. The Lord knows my broken heart and loss for words. He is where I have found my peace, not only for myself but for my sister. Because I truly believe she has finally found hers in Him and with Him.

> The Lord is close to the brokenhearted and saves those who are crushed in spirit (Psalm 34:18 NIV).

Only through my faith in God have I been able to get through my addiction and the aftermath that followed. People are kind and say things like, "I'm so sorry you had to go through all of that—a coma and not being able to walk for so long—how awful!"

I just smile and thank them and say, "Oh, but I'm not sorry! I'm the one who asked the Lord for help! He knew what He was doing. All I had to do was trust His plan!"

Recovery is a marathon, not a sprint, and I am growing one day at a time. I stay in gratitude, knowing that I could have lost my life, but God allowed me a second chance. Now, I continue to do the work to stay on the right path. It is a miracle that after all the physical harm I inflicted on my body due to my alcoholism, today, my brain and liver scans are clear, and I am thriving. Glory be to God. He is amazing!

It is also only through my faith in the Lord that I've been able to carry myself through what is seen as shame and embarrassment with grace and dignity. He broke the chains of addiction and continues to give me the strength to share my recovery story, my faith testimony, through His most pure love, in hopes that it will reach even just one person and change their life.

> But in your hearts revere Christ as Lord. Always be prepared to give an answer to everyone who asks you to give the reason for the hope that you have. But do this with gentleness and respect (1 Peter 3:15 NIV).

I now belong to an amazing Christ-centered church; it is home to me. My pastor's teachings have deepened my understanding of God's Word and how to apply it to daily life. I love sharing my testimony, inviting others to church, and spreading the message of God's incredible grace.

This summer, I plan to be baptized in the Umpqua River, declaring publicly that Jesus Christ is my Lord and Savior. I'll declare it for all the world to hear! Okay, maybe not all the world, but surely whoever is around the river that day. And I'll continue to share the good news, as the Bible teaches us to do, all the days of my life!

> If you declare with your mouth, "Jesus is Lord," and believe in your heart that God raised him from the dead, you will be saved (Romans 10:9 NIV).

Finding sobriety was a grace from God, and it led me to long for a relationship with Him—which is by far the absolute best thing that could have ever happened in my life. The Lord knew I was ready. He knew the way it would happen, and He faithfully took care of me because I asked Him to and trusted in Him. Now, my heart feels freed from the chains and burdens that held me down for so long.

The Lord's timing and ways are always perfect—we simply need to open our hearts to Him. At the right moment, in His perfect timing, He will meet your needs, rescue you, and deliver you. So often, we make life harder for ourselves by trying to take control instead of placing our trust in the Lord and following His will for our lives. Everything is in His almighty hands. Even when we don't understand His timing or His plans, we can rest assured that they are always perfect. All we have to do is trust Him. The most beautiful part is this: all you need to do is ask Him into your heart and follow Him, and He will faithfully show you the way.

It's never too late to turn to God, no matter where you are in life, what you've been through, or what you've done. His love is pure, true, and eternal. His grace and mercy are more than enough to cover anything in your past. If you haven't yet asked the Lord into your heart, let me ask—what are you waiting for? Don't be afraid, my friend. God's power is limitless, and with Jesus in your heart, you are equipped with the strength and armor of God to face any challenge life may bring. With unshakable faith, unchained from whatever is holding you back, you will live a life filled with hope and healing, walking in the peace and purpose He has prepared for you.

> *"Ask and it will be given to you; seek and you will find; knock and the door will be opened to you. For everyone who asks receives; the one who seeks finds; and to the one who knocks, the door will be opened"* (Matthew 7:7-8 NIV).

God wants to save you by His grace, just like He did for me.

The close of this chapter may be the end of our time together, but it's also the perfect opportunity for a new chapter in your life! I invite you to join me in prayer and ask the Lord into our lives and the gift of a pure heart.

*Dear heavenly Father,*

*We humbly ask You to come into our hearts, forgive our transgressions, and wash away our sins. Please cleanse us of all that weighs us down. We open ourselves to You and are ready to accept Your love and embrace a new way of life. We ask that You fill us with Your peace and guide us on a path of righteousness. Thank you for Your grace and mercy and the gift of a fresh start.*

*In Your precious name, Amen.*

Let this prayer be the beginning of a beautiful transformation as you step into a life renewed by His love and grace.

# Breaking Chains of Fear

## By Melissa Gissy Witherspoon

Fear is a chain the enemy uses to keep us bound in shame, addiction, regret, and uncertainty. It's a spiritual weapon Satan relies on to separate us from the truth of God's promises. But Scripture is clear: *For God has not given us a spirit of fear, but of power and of love and of a sound mind* (2 Timothy 1:7 NKJV).

My story begins like many who've battled addiction. What started as casual drinking turned into a dependency that nearly killed me. Years of shame and guilt stacked up, and each day, I was barely surviving, running from broken promises, poor choices, the consequences of those choices, and, most of all, fear. I lived in fear constantly, with no faith in anything but the bottom of a vodka bottle or the next high.

Eventually, I hit both a physical and spiritual bottom. On the cold floor of my unfinished basement, overwhelmed by fear and convinced I couldn't go on, I tried to take my own life. My greatest fear wasn't death—it was being completely alone. In that moment of despair, God met me. He didn't just stop me; He rescued me. I was shown a vision of unity and connection, a life of purpose and healing. But first, I had to fully surrender. I had to trust Him completely, even when nothing made sense. That surrender marked the beginning of everything changing.

> *LORD my God, I called to you for help, and you healed me. You, LORD, brought me up from the realm of the dead; you spared me from going down to the pit* (Psalm 30:2-3 NIV).

Even after 11 years of being sober, fear still tries to creep in. The enemy doesn't give up. He whispers lies about my past and tries to stir up doubt about my future. But my spiritual fitness—my constant contact with God—rescues me. Daily prayer, Scripture, and worship keep me grounded. When fear shows up, I turn to God and remember I am already free.

Faith is the key to breaking the fear of the unknown. When I was afraid of living sober, unsure of who I'd be without addiction, God showed me faith isn't about having answers—it's about trusting Him. *Submit yourselves, then, to God. Resist the devil, and he will flee from you* (James 4:7 NIV).

Several relapses before finally finding long-term recovery reminded me how real fear is—but also how real God's presence is in our struggles. It took me several tries to break the cycle of addiction, and the fear of another relapse followed me throughout the process. Faith doesn't erase fear, but it overrides it. As I continued to trust in God and grow a deep relationship with Jesus, clarity came that helped me discern His voice over the voices of darkness.

Jesus breaks every chain, especially fear. Let Him break yours.

> *"Ask and it will be given to you; seek and you will find"* (Matthew 7:7 NIV).

# Michelle Tascoe

Michelle Tascoe is a financial life coach based in Los Angeles, California.

She has appeared on the Dr. Phil Show as well as the Chelsea Handler Show as a guest financial expert.

Her 15-year coaching track record has earned her the privilege of working with noteworthy coaching clients, executives at Victoria's Secret, Capitol Records, Honest Company, Disney, Warner Brothers, Netflix, New York Times best-selling authors, former Miss New York, and a US Senator.

Michelle has helped her clients pay off tens of thousands of dollars in debt, get 5-figure raises, double and triple the money in their bank account, buy their first house, buy their first investment property, and, ultimately, become debt-free.

Her approach is hands-on and practical. It's not what you make but what you keep that matters most!

At home, she is a loving wife and mom of four children. She loves ministering with her husband, Jeribai, and attends Word of Life Fellowship Church in Northern California, where she is the head of the dance ministry.

# Surrendering in Love and Trusting God

By Michelle Tascoe

God will increase your capacity when you need Him the most because His grace is sufficient and has no limits.

> *Trust in the Lord with all your heart and lean not on your own understanding* (Proverbs 3:5 NIV).

This scripture became my lifeline as I endured a crisis I could not begin to comprehend. There was no rhyme or reason for what was happening. Through this devastating turn of events, I simply could *not* lean on my own understanding, and in my pain, I learned to trust God fully. I began to realize that we live in a fallen world and unexpected things we can't make sense of will happen.

There are some scriptures that you memorize and keep close to your heart to encourage you. Then there are the scriptures that you know inside and out because you lived that scripture. I have experienced this because it was the only truth that gave me solid ground to stand on when my natural world was turned upside down.

My story is this: I lost my baby, Leo Abishai Tascoe, soon after he was born. He was with us for a miraculous 27 hours from the moment he took his first breath until he went to heaven. After giving birth via C-section, my husband Jeribai and I were surrounded by our closest family and friends in our hospital room. I held Leo in my arms and released him into God's arms.

I now understand that God wants me to use our testimony to encourage you and others. It is no coincidence you are reading our story. I hope what I went through—and how God held me—will help you trust Him even more through whatever you face today.

Years ago, I had my third child, Leilani, a beautiful baby girl. At the time, I thought we were good as a family; I was done having kids. As the months continued, however, I could not shake the feeling that we were missing someone. After I agreed in my heart that I would have one more child, the feeling let up, leaving peace within me.

My husband and I were pregnant a few months later, but when my doctor could not find a heartbeat, my world came crashing down. I was shocked because nothing like that had ever happened to me before. My first three kids were quick pregnancies. I was not prepared for the heartache and heartbreak of a miscarriage.

The following year, we were surprised to find out we were pregnant again. And there was a heartbeat! I was so excited because now there was life; I heard it with my own ears.

Six weeks later, the look on my doctor's face let me know that we had lost that baby, too. So many unanswered questions went through my mind. *What is happening, God? Did I not feel the desire of my heart to have one more child? Why did I feel so strongly that someone was missing from our family, but when I agreed to follow through on my heart's desire, I would have two miscarriages?*

That same week, I was at our church conference. The visiting pastor was praying over the whole congregation. I was in the front with my arms raised and my eyes closed. She began to prophesy; as I listened to her speak, I opened my eyes and realized she was prophesying over me.

> "Capacity is determined by receptivity, not by outward things. If you have the will to receive it, says the Lord; if you will make the room for it, says the Lord, I will cause you to walk in capacities you would have never felt prepared for."

The pastor then asked me if I was pregnant, not knowing I had miscarried just days earlier. Then she proceeded to prophesy that there was an anointing for a child:

> "I don't know all the details, but there is an anointing for a child that is about a new capacity... There are some children—every child is gifted—but some children are demarcated. And I declare to you that there is a watershed moment and a child that must come forth that is a demarcation for the future, for what it is you are to step into, because you will not finish in disappointment."

All I knew was to trust God by taking Him at His Word and walking in faith for the capacity that would come.

After two more years of trying, during my last cycle of the year and confirmed by my final pregnancy test in the box, it happened! There were two purple lines indicating that we were pregnant! We practically held our breath, praying we would not miscarry until we passed the 16-week mark. We went to our appointment and received the news that everything was great; our baby was growing in size as expected and had a strong heartbeat.

When I answered the phone the following week, it was my doctor with news we did not expect. Our son had a fatal genetic defect; there was nothing we could do. We were given the option to terminate the pregnancy. What I thought was finally a dream come true immediately turned into one of the most difficult and life-changing chapters of my life.

We made every decision carefully, thoroughly considering our three kids and the testimony of faith we could display. You see, I had an abortion at 19, and now, as a mom of three kids, I could not intentionally terminate a life God had given me, whether we would have a few minutes or hours with him. Even if he was stillborn, I could not get in the way of God's creation being formed inside of me.

The 37 weeks with Leo increased me in so many ways I didn't know were possible.

My capacity for love grew as God showed me to take the time to tell people how much I loved them. My capacity for trust grew as I trusted God for every breath—the amount of amniotic fluid I was carrying was double due to little Leo's growth, making it hard for me to breathe at times. My capacity for being present grew as I focused intently on what was right in front of me instead of the worry and what-ifs of the future. My capacity for courage grew as I stayed the course and ministered to friends and family, encouraging them despite my own struggles. And my capacity for leadership grew as I carried my little lion Leo inside me and saw myself as the lioness leader God chose to be his mom.

On the day of his birth, hundreds of people were praying for us all over the world. Little Leo's life story was shared all over social media. The impact of his 27 hours here on earth glorified God and His faithfulness. So many people said that due to our story, their faith was reignited and their prayer life rose to a new level. Some people shared Leo's story with loved ones and used it to lead family members to Christ!

As I continue healing from losing my son Leo, I continue to learn more and more lessons. I believe that when we experience the loss of a young child, we will be on a continuous healing journey until we pass from this life and are with God in heaven, surrounded by those who have gone before us.

The months after Leo's passing were the most painful part of my healing journey. Every mother who loses a child unexpectedly also loses her hopes and dreams of experiencing all the milestones of her child's life, keeping her on a continuous healing journey. When we go through heartbreak, it's healthy to cry, grieve, and allow ourselves time and space to experience the reality of loss. Grieving is like a tidal wave that sneaks up when you least expect it. I have been hit by the grief wave in this manner multiple times. I have learned that when a wave hits, the way out is through.

What do I mean by "the way out is through?"

When you are in pain, it is tempting to want to resist your feelings, even to evade or ignore them. There is a saying that whatever you resist persists—I can testify to that. I've experienced sad moments—my heart aching as I thought about losing my son—when my internal instinct became fight or flight. I would rationalize it would be simpler to fight the emotions welling up—forcing them out or stuffing them down. Or I would be tempted to take flight and run away in my thoughts—focusing on being busy and ignoring my feelings to build a wall of protection around me.

However, I learned that when I chose to stand still and let the wave of emotions crash on the shore of my heart, God would send His healing.

I discovered this was my way of living out God's Word, which says, *"Be still, and know that I am God; I will be exalted among the nations, I will be exalted in the earth"* (Psalm 46:10 NIV). Being still, as it says in the Bible, has been crucial to my healing journey. Here is what being still looks like for me: acknowledging all my feelings, including hurt and sadness, and asking God to hold my hand and just be with me while I breathe through it all. This experience can feel like it takes an eternity, but in actuality, it usually only takes 5 to 10 minutes. The important thing is recognizing that your feelings are normal; it's okay because you are okay. You will be okay.

Be still and allow God to be with you.

There have been many days when I felt a heaviness in my soul—a spiritual attack often referred to as the sting of death, which sometimes comes when you lose someone you love dearly. It is an experience so traumatic that there is almost a dying inside that takes place; you can't catch your breath, and everything feels overwhelming. It is almost like your body and mind go into shock. There are moments when I ask myself, "Did this really happen?" Then I feel the scar of my C-section, and I know it is all real.

A mentor once told me that a burden shared is a burden lifted. This truth carried me through some of my most challenging days. That encouragement helped me open up and talk with my husband about things that were heavy on my heart.

I wasn't prepared for the difficulty I encountered interacting with friends after losing my son. The toughest part was reconciling my genuine happiness for the joy another was experiencing with their new baby and their child's milestones while being present with the gaping hole in my own heart. Sharing my feelings of loss, emptiness, and pure sadness with a close confidant helped lift the burden from my tender heart. Though it was a struggle to start the conversation, as soon as I did, it was as if my heart had been able to speak up. Using my voice and being heard and acknowledged was part of my healing journey.

I also learned it is okay to take as much time as needed to heal. There is no designated finish line when you are healing from loss. We often want our grieving to be over; *Be done with it already.* This approach only lands you right back at the start again and again. To heal is to continue to endure forward and be okay with the healing process taking as long as it needs to take.

Surrender to the process. It is *for* us and not *against* us. There is a duality of wanting life to return to normal and realizing life will never be the same. I've recognized that though my life will never be the same, I have become a better version of myself by losing my son. Why? How? Because when we lose someone we love, we have the opportunity to grow. We have loved deeply, surrendered so much, and learned how to trust God in a way we didn't know was possible.

Trust yourself.

Trust God.

Trust the process.

This has been my prayer.

The healing journey is paved with trust. I have repeated this cycle again and again, going deeper each time: Trust myself more. Trust God more. Trust the process of my healing journey more. I have found so much comfort in surrendering to this prayer. Trust is another form of intimacy. Oftentimes, we are scared of true intimacy with God—allowing ourselves to come to Him with raw and real emotions and thoughts. God wants us to open ourselves to Him fully, regardless of how hard it may be. That is where new healing begins. I have discovered that it is okay to go through something hard and learn to trust myself in new measures, learn to trust God deeper, and then continue to trust that I am in a process that is meant for good.

Today, I can look back and see how I took steps to trust God with my choice not to terminate the pregnancy in hopes of meeting my son. I learned to trust God that I could carry him to full term. When it was recommended I have a C-section, I learned to trust myself that I could get through the pregnancy, trust God that He would guide me to the best outcome, and trust the process, the doctors, and the nurses through the whole trial.

Healing from loss is something we cannot control—it's a journey that carries its own timetable. As I continue to allow my heart and body to heal from the loss of my son, letting go has been an active exercise of my faith. In fact, I have experienced freedom in not trying so hard to make things happen in other areas of my life when my energy is not there to give.

I have practiced saying no to more things and saying yes to self-care; I've learned to be okay when I'm invited to do something and don't have the energy. There is a release when you choose to let go. It's soothing to our soul to not be "on" all the time. I have enjoyed many days of staying in pajamas all day, letting the laundry sit, and getting creative with leftovers for a meal when I just didn't have it in me to cook and do everyday mom duties. As a result, my world didn't come crashing down. No one got in trouble. Life carried on.

I have identified a push-and-pull energy in my healing journey. Push energy is like pushing a boulder up a hill—everything feels like a chore. Pushing through tough times while not taking time to be still in God's presence prolongs healing because you never give yourself a break, and nothing ever seems good enough.

Pull energy is full of momentum and joy. It is when you feel the Holy Spirit right there with you, helping you get things done quickly and with little effort. You get on a roll and just can't stop because you are accomplishing things left and right.

Discerning one type of energy from the other helps you know how to treat yourself as you heal. When treated appropriately, both are God's grace in action.

Lastly, I have learned to keep having a vision for the future. The Bible says, *Where there is no vision, the people perish: but he that keepeth the law, happy is he* (Proverbs 29:18 KJV). This is so true, especially when you experience the loss of a loved one.

We must never lose hope. God has promised us a hope and a future. He is true to His Word. Hope is like a glimmer of light that carries us to the other side of our healing journey.

I heard a beautiful quote during my pregnancy with Leo:

> "Ten thousand unlit candles can't light one candle, but one candle can light 10,000 unlit candles."

This is what my son did. He was my little glimmer of hope. His little light lit the hearts of 10,000, and the ripple effect continues as we share our story of how we trusted God during a difficult time.

A friend of ours once said, "I was thinking about Leo today, and it brought joy to me that his little life was one that exclusively knew love."

I believe with my whole heart that my son Leo was conceived in love, carried in love, delivered in love, and then surrendered in love.

I have been forever changed by this experience. We may never understand the trials of life, but we can trust God with all our hearts, know that His grace is sufficient, and grow in character as we heed God's call to love more, trust more, be present more, be more courageous, and even be a lioness leader here on earth.

I hope my experience and the wisdom I have gained through my heartache will become tools you can carry. When you are faced with an unfathomable journey, take one step at a time. As you walk through your personal healing journey, our miracle-working God will ensure that you will eventually find your joy again because you can trust Him.

# Breaking Chains of Grief

### By Connie A. VanHorn

*He has sent me to bind up the brokenhearted, to proclaim freedom for the captives and release from darkness for the prisoners* (Isaiah 61:1 NIV).

Grief is a heavy burden we all carry at times, which can feel like chains wrapping around our hearts and minds. For many years, I carried the weight of grief from different parts of my life—my childhood, my mother, and, ultimately, the passing of my little sister Amanda.

Amanda's death in 2022 forced me to examine grief in a new way, as I had never lost anyone that close to me. Initially, my grief masqueraded as anger. I was angry at what my sister's life had become and all the things she missed out on—all the things we both missed out on.

Amanda lost her life to an accidental overdose. In her struggle with addiction, she believed she was invincible, that her pain was something she could control. How often do we stoically claim we can handle everything life throws at us on our own? As a result, we can wander aimlessly—looking for comfort in all the wrong places and filling the empty spaces with substances, material things, and toxic relationships. When those things fail to bring us the satisfaction we desire, we can find ourselves stuck in anger and seeking more.

After Amanda's passing, I realized that my grief was tied to unresolved pain from my past—a past where my sister had been present. Losing her became a turning point for me. Jesus helped me acknowledge what we both had experienced and that my grief was deeply rooted in buried anger—the anger

I learned to keep hidden beneath my hard-earned smile. In processing and healing from the grief of losing my sister, I turned to Jesus, who healed both my grief and the pain my soul was harboring from our childhood.

Through the sadness, I discovered that only Jesus offers true hope.

This can be your story, too!

When we seek Jesus, He offers us comfort along with the freedom to release our pain. We can lay our pain, hurt, and anger at His feet and find peace. Our God can break every chain that binds us!

Understand your worth! You are so valuable to God that He will never let you walk through your grief alone, crippled by chains that keep you bound.

No matter what grief or despair you may be experiencing, God sees you as whole and perfect. When you go to Him, He will use your struggles to refine and grow you into all He has called you to be. As you enter into a relationship with Him, you will stop viewing your life through the lens of loss and begin to view your circumstances—and yourself—through His lens of grace.

God alone can turn your pain into purpose!

Grief can fuel purpose. To this day, my sister's story drives me to raise awareness about addiction and its impact. I now share firsthand that our struggles are not meaningless and can be used to help others.

If you are grieving—a person, a dream, a job, or time you have lost in your life—please know that you do not have to be defined by your loss or imprisoned by your past. God is greater than any force that can come against you, including grief. When you turn to Him, in time, He will break the chains of grief that hold you hostage and will allow you to harness your experiences for a purpose far greater than you can imagine.

· · · · · · · · · · · · · · · · · · · · · · · · · · · · · · · · · · · · · · · · · · ·

# Sonya Johnson

After years of battling addiction, incarceration, and the trauma of having her children removed from her care, Sonya Johnson now lives a life transformed by faith, freedom, and purpose. Her story is a testament that recovery is possible and with God, all things are possible.

Sonya lives in Sarasota, Florida, with her husband and their two teenage boys. She is the Lead Peer Coordinator at a non-profit organization in her community. She draws from her lived experience to walk alongside others facing mental health and substance use challenges and family separation through the child welfare system.

A fierce advocate and trailblazer, Sonya was honored with the 2024 Child Welfare Professional of the Year Award, the 2024 NAMI Champion for Recovery Award, and the Shining Star Award from the Sarasota County Coalition.

When she's not sharing her journey on social media, speaking, teaching, or mentoring, Sonya finds joy in her faith, family, and her God-given mission to be a generational curse-breaker and a light of hope.

You can follow her journey below:
Facebook: https://m.facebook.com/proudbeautifulmom/
Linktree: https://linktr.ee/sonyajohnson
YouTube: https://www.youtube.com/@sonyajohnson0719
TikTok: https://www.tiktok.com/@sonyandsteven
Instagram:
https://www.instagram.com/sonyajohnson0719

# Season of Change

By Sonya Johnson

*For it is by grace you have been saved, through faith—and this is not from yourselves, it is the gift of God— not by works, so that no one can boast* (Ephesians 2:8-9 NIV).

With sweat dripping down my face, I woke in a panic at 3 am. A sense of urgency engulfed me. I thought to myself, *What is happening?* The house was dark; my husband Steven was asleep next to me, and our children were sound asleep in their room. A sudden heavy weight of grief swept over my body. As I tried to collect myself, the reality sunk in that my father-in-law had passed away just the day before.

His room felt so empty, although his clothes and belongings still lay there untouched. I questioned again, *Why am I awake?* I decided to go sit in the living room so I wouldn't wake my husband. I wanted him to rest, so I quietly left our room.

As I sat down on the couch in my living room, alone in the dark, I felt as if a beaming light directed my vision to the coffee table. There in front of me, I saw my father-in-law's Bible, and I felt a heavy nudge from within to pick it up.

I hadn't held a Bible in a long time. I was raised with Christian faith, but at that particular point in my life, I was running from God, lost in active addiction, trying to escape my feelings and numb years of trauma. As I continued to wrestle with the nudge to pick up his Bible, I was consumed by an internal conversation. *What do You want from me, God?* I felt the nudge again, so I pulled out the Bible from beneath the coffee table and wiped away the thin layer of dust that covered it.

I didn't know where to begin. I decided to open it up to a random page and let my finger land on a verse. As the Bible fell open to the middle, I pointed to the bottom of a page. There, I saw a verse that would stay imprinted on my heart forever. It read, *"For I know the plans I have for you," declares the Lord, "plans to prosper you and not to harm you, plans to give you hope and a future"* (Jeremiah 29:11 NIV).

As I read the passage, a wave of peace flowed through my entire body. Overwhelmed and exhausted, I climbed back into bed with my husband and fell asleep.

That verse didn't resonate completely at the time, but throughout my recovery journey, I've come to understand that God gives us peace and strength through His written Word to help us through challenging times. And in that moment on the couch of my dark living room, in the middle of the night—that is exactly what He did for me.

Unfortunately, the days that followed were filled with darkness and constant drug use, with no hope in sight for either me or my husband. Over the next few years, our addictions reached a point where we were no longer capable of taking care of our own children, let alone ourselves. As a result, my mom stepped in to raise our children in her home while we continued living in the destructive cycle of drug addiction.

In 2017, Hurricane Irma headed directly for Florida. While everyone else was scared, I had a hopeful feeling that God was going to bring a season of change with this hurricane. I'm not sure if I was clinically insane from my drug use or if God was speaking life into my desperate heart—possibly both—but I was beyond ready for change.

Hurricane Irma came barreling through as a Category 3 storm, with winds of 120 miles per hour pounding against the house throughout the night. During the storm, Steven lay barely conscious, fading in and out of reality—shivering, sweating, and running a fever as high as 106.1 degrees. Deep down, I knew something was very wrong. This wasn't just withdrawals from opiates; I knew that something far more serious was happening.

Because of the storm's severity, the emergency call center was open, but they refused to dispatch an ambulance to my mom's house. Instead, they advised us to take him to the emergency room after the storm passed.

At the hospital, they ran several tests on Steven. The process was painstaking, and it felt like an eternity as I waited for answers from the doctor. They concluded that my husband's kidneys were failing and that he would die that night if he weren't admitted.

Within 48 hours, doctors diagnosed him with a Staphylococcus Aureus infection that had spread throughout his body, causing sepsis. Over the following months, infectious disease specialists treated complications as the infection spread to his heart, causing endocarditis, then to his lungs, filling them with fluid, and finally to his kidneys, resulting in acute kidney failure. He required a 42-day course of IV antibiotics and had to remain hospitalized to survive. Without the treatment, they said he would surely die.

Every day, I prayed to God to save my husband. I cried out countless times, "God, why is this happening? Please don't take him from me! I need a miracle, Lord!"

What I didn't realize was that God was already working on him while he was there, whispering to his heart, *Be still and know that I am God* (Psalm 46:10 NIV).

God was working on me, too. I found myself in a place of desperation, and the only hope I had was in the Lord. I prayed earnestly and fervently, "Please, Lord, heal my husband. Don't take my boys' daddy from them. We need a miracle!"

God was answering our prayers—in His time, in His way.

Weeks turned into months, and my husband slowly started getting better. Finally, it was time for his discharge. We went to see his cardiologist together the day he was released from the hospital. They listened to his heart, took his vitals, ran blood work, and checked his kidneys before saying, "Based on your hospital records and what we see today, you have about five years to live—if you stop using drugs. If you continue, it will be less."

Those words hit me like a ton of bricks. I remember thinking, *What do you mean, five years? I thought he was better!* We were devastated. We left the doctor's office in denial, and the first thing we did was find drugs and use them. It was the only coping mechanism we knew.

After Steven's hospitalization, everyone, especially me, was terrified he wouldn't make it. He was knocking on death's door every day while still using drugs. It was as if he was possessed, unable to comprehend the severity of his situation, signing his death warrant with every shot and every hit of dope. My mom decided to let us stay with her, hoping it would help him heal or give the kids time with their dad, just in case he didn't get better.

I was just as sick in my addiction, though my health wasn't in immediate danger like his. One evening, I sat in my mom's bathroom using drugs, overwhelmed by a deep sense of condemnation. On the floor of the family home that had been ours for generations, I realized how far I'd fallen.

I thought, *What will I say on the day of judgment when I meet my Maker and have to admit I wasted every gift He gave me?* I wasn't a good mother, wife, daughter, or friend. I felt unworthy and deserving of hell. The enemy had a stronghold on both me and my husband, working to steal, kill, and destroy our souls while damaging everyone around us.

The next evening, while at my mom's house, I had a profound spiritual awakening. Steven sat on my son's bed, drifting in and out of consciousness from drug use. I knelt beside the bed and looked directly into his eyes. Softly, I said, "Steven, I'm so afraid for you. I'm scared to leave your side because I fear you'll die." He gazed back at me, and what I saw pierced my soul with terror—a spiritual darkness seemed to consume him, taunting me through his eyes. Overwhelmed, I fled the room in tears.

As soon as I left the room, it hit me—I had just abandoned my husband, the man God gave me to stand beside "for better or worse, until death do us part." I'd left him alone with that dark force. But I refused to let him go without a fight. I rushed back in and called out to Jesus, the name above all names. I cried out, "Jesus, help me with my husband! Give him back to me and heal his body, in Your mighty Name!" Placing my left hand on his head and raising my other hand to heaven, I wept and prayed with all my heart until I felt something supernatural touch my soul.

In a moment's time, the Lord downloaded three revelations into my spirit.

First, He revealed that my husband and I are one in His eyes, our souls united through marriage. The Lord showed me my husband had been praying in the hospital, and He was answering those prayers through both of us.

Second, I realized I was completely forgiven—past, present, and future. Jesus had carried my sins to the cross long before I was born. All I needed was to believe, and His grace covered everything.

Third, I realized I was called to share the "good news." Later, I found confirmation of this calling in the Bible. It's not just good news—it's the best news! Heaven is real, and this life is temporary. Gaining a heavenly perspective changes how we view everything on earth. What truly matters is knowing and following Jesus.

From that moment on, all I wanted was to follow Jesus. I began reading the Bible, listening to worship music, and spending time with the Lord daily. Yet, I held back one thing—my drug use. I believed I could use "just a little" each day to "stay well." I tried to serve two masters, but it didn't work. My flesh remained addicted, and I kept using. Despite all the grace God had shown me, I chose drugs over Him. But His intervention wasn't over. God never left my side and was preparing to walk with us through the toughest part of our season of change.

> *"Be strong and courageous. Do not be afraid or terrified...for the LORD your God goes with you; he will never leave you nor forsake you"* (Deuteronomy 31:6 NIV).

Steven was arrested for stealing, but instead of jail time, the courts offered him a treatment program through a court-based initiative. This was the beginning of a new path, one that God would guide us through every step of the way. Steven accepted the program, but it came with one major condition: no drug use. Each time he relapsed, he had to serve time in jail, after which they would place him in a rehab facility and, upon completion, transition him to a sober living house. It took him two years to finish because he repeatedly relapsed after leaving treatment. Meanwhile, I was spiraling toward my own rock bottom.

On my birthday, I received both the best and worst gift. I was arrested while leaving a notorious drug house. By the time I was searched and booked into jail, I had racked up four felonies.

For the next year, I went in and out of jail, repeatedly, mostly on probation violations. Every time I got released, I went back to using drugs and continued to live a miserable life of self-destruction, far removed from anything that I valued. My drug use had such a powerful stronghold over me— I was bound by the chains of addiction. Only God Himself could break the power that drugs had over me.

After a long night of using drugs, I heard a loud knock at the door. This knock would change the trajectory of my life. I could barely open my eyes when I heard the words, "Open the door... Police Department!" As the reality sank in, I knew it was time to go to jail—again. But this time, I was done. I was tired of fighting, chasing drugs every day, and doing whatever it took to sustain that life. I was ready to fully surrender.

This time, there was no getting bailed out of jail. I had no bond and no chance of being released. Desperate, I tried calling my mom to speak to my kids, but she refused to take my calls. Everyone was done with my lies and manipulation.

I remember the first time my dad finally accepted my call. He told me, "My prayers have been answered. I can finally sleep tonight because I know you're going to be safe and not overdosing on drugs."

The weight of those words hit me hard. In that moment, I realized this was exactly what my family had been praying for—and no one was coming to rescue me from my consequences.

Now, when I look back on that, I'm so grateful it happened. God had granted me the gift of desperation.

Sometimes, God allows our consequences to catch up with us so we can recognize the errors of our ways. He disciplines His children because He loves us. My gift of desperation didn't feel like a gift at the time, but it was exactly what I needed. It humbled me enough to cry out to the Lord—not to ask for anything, but simply for His presence. I just wanted God to be with me in that dark place because I had felt so alone for so long.

In the weeks that followed, I kept hearing about a place in the jail called the Recovery Pod. People said the living conditions were much better there, and I desperately wanted out of the dark, hopeless cell they had me in. By the grace of God, I was transferred to the Recovery Pod. Little did I know God had perfectly aligned my circumstances to plant the seeds for my long-term recovery.

> *And we know that in all things God works for the good of those who love him, who have been called according to his purpose* (Romans 8:28 NIV).

As I entered the pod, I felt the presence of angels. The space was two stories, with cells stacked along one side. About thirty women sat in the main area, listening to a speaker from the outside world share a message of hope.

While waiting against the wall for the guard to pat me down, I observed the women. Many were familiar faces from my days of addiction. When the meeting ended, they rushed over, hugged me, and said, "Sonya, I'm so glad you're here. Welcome!" For the first time in a long time, people were genuinely happy to see me. I felt welcomed and, for a moment, truly happy. From there, God really started working on my heart.

A group of women brought church to us, letting us worship with music, dance, and raised hands. One song, "Rescue" by Lauren Daigle, moved me deeply. As I listened to the lyrics, tears streamed down my face. In that moment, I realized I hadn't been arrested—I'd been *rescued*. Rescued from the darkness and hell of my addiction. God had heard my cries, and for the first time in my life, I felt peace, contentment, and safety from myself.

With this newfound feeling of peace and a tiny bit of hope, I grew closer to the Lord, one day at a time. I started calling home, and my mom began answering again, letting me speak to my kids. I didn't make excuses or empty promises—I just shared what was happening in my life. I also spoke with my husband. God's perfect will was unfolding as we both entered treatment, separately but at the same time.

Day by day, things began to fall into place. I started visiting my children and rebuilding the relationships I had broken. My parents visited on weekends, and my husband came whenever he could. I'd love to say that it was a magical fairy tale ending, but it wasn't that easy. Once we got out of treatment, the real work began. We had to be patient and continue to work hard every day to maintain recovery and prove to our children that we were going to be the parents they deserve. I'm happy to share that our children have been home with us for almost five years, and life couldn't be better. God has completely restored our family.

In 2021, we became homeowners, a blessing to give our children their "forever home." By 2023, Steven became a business owner, and best of all, God completely restored his health—he is truly a medical miracle!

As for me, I now work as a recovery advocate, sharing hope and proving that recovery is possible. God turned my pain into purpose, and His grace brought freedom to my family.

Our loving God is longing to do the same for you!

Restoration is possible, no matter how far we've fallen. God never leaves us; He patiently waits for our surrender. When we release our faith from bondage and fully submit to Him, He will make a way. I am living proof of His transformative power.

If you let Jesus into your heart, your season of change is possible!

*For I am about to do something new. See, I have already begun! Do you not see it? I will make a pathway through the wilderness. I will create rivers in the dry wasteland* (Isaiah 43:19 NLT).

# Breaking Chains in Difficult Seasons

By Melissa Gissy Witherspoon

Difficult seasons often feel like storms—unpredictable, overwhelming, and dark. In these moments, it can be hard to remain faithful. Challenges may shake our foundation and cause us to wonder where God is or why He has allowed the trial. But in these very seasons, God can refine our faith, break chains of uncertainty and fear, and deepen our relationship with Him.

> Consider it pure joy, my brothers and sisters, whenever you face trials of many kinds, because you know that the testing of your faith produces perseverance. Let perseverance finish its work so that you may be mature and complete, not lacking anything (James 1:2-4 NIV).

God doesn't waste our pain. He uses the fire to shape us, not destroy us.

When we battle strongholds, it can take many tries to overcome them. We may fall back into old habits, return to toxic patterns, or struggle to walk in freedom. But even in our failures, God is faithful. Proverbs 24:16 (NIV) says, *Though the righteous fall seven times, they rise again.* Following God's path in our lives is not about perfection but perseverance. God walks with us every step. Even when we stumble, His grace doesn't run out. His love doesn't give up.

When we face addiction, rejection, abuse, guilt, or shame, the enemy tries to convince us we are victims—trapped and defined by our past. But the Word of God tells a different story. Second Corinthians 5:17 (NIV) says,

*Therefore, if anyone is in Christ, the new creation has come: The old has gone, the new is here!* In Christ, we are no longer victims; we are victorious! We must shift our mindset to match our beliefs to who He says we are.

One of the most dangerous chains holding us captive is the victim mentality, which causes us to claim, "I'll never change. This is just who I am." But Jesus came to set the captives free (Luke 4:18). That includes you! God wants to free you from the mental and emotional prison you've locked yourself in. Guilt and shame are tools the enemy uses to keep us bound, but Romans 8:1 declares, *Therefore, there is now no condemnation for those who are in Christ Jesus.* You are not condemned. You are covered, my friend.

Breaking chains in difficult seasons requires faith, obedience, and surrender. It means praising God when you don't feel like it, choosing His Word over your emotions, and trusting His process even when you can't trace His plan.

If you've tried before and failed, try again with God. Don't give up—your growth is in progress, and so is your freedom. Keep going and keep growing with the Lord!

You're not alone. God is with you. He has never left. And He never will. Your breakthrough is coming!

. . . . . . . . . . . . . . . . . . . . . . . . . . . . . . . . . . . . . . . . . . . . . . . . .

# Jessica Prukner

Jessica Prukner is a spirited mother of three teenagers and a passionate homeschool advocate with over ten years of experience crafting personalized education adventures at home. As a #1 best-selling author in the anthology *Restoration: God Brings Beauty From Ashes,* she inspires readers by sharing her journey of finding beauty in life's challenges. Jessica also pens the beloved column "A Beautiful Mess" in *Voice of Truth,* where she explores homeschooling topics on faith, family, personal growth, and the delightful imperfections that make life interesting.

A devoted follower of Jesus, Jessica beautifully intertwines her faith into every aspect of her life, motivating her to spread love and positivity wherever she goes. Beyond her writing, she shines as a professional speaker and marketplace influencer, empowering others to chase their dreams with purpose and authenticity.

When she's not busy writing or speaking, Jessica cherishes quality time with her husband, Ian, their three kids, and their energetic dogs under the sunny skies of Florida. With a love for the outdoors, she revels in God's creation while encouraging others to discover the hope and peace found in a relationship with Him.

# Be Still

By Jessica Prukner

It was time; turning 40 seemed like such a milestone to me. I was ready to do something radical, something for me, something my mom said was toxic and wrong. I laughed a little as I rolled up my sleeve and gave my left wrist to the tattoo artist. I was ready to be marked with a reminder of my new life motto.

I looked at over 100 fonts until my eyes began to blur, and finally, I decided on one to display the words I would see every day for the rest of my life.

The gentle, muscular tattoo artist carefully placed the stencil on my wrist, unveiling the words he would permanently etch into my skin: Be still.

For the previous four decades, my life was filled with activities and achievements. I had accomplished a great deal and accumulated an impressive list of accolades. God blessed me with a wonderful family, including three amazing children who kept me on my toes, and a successful, loving husband with whom I shared life and business milestones. Friends who deeply cared for me surrounded me.

If you had run into me on the street and asked me how I was doing, my answer would have been, "Great, I am so busy!" No matter what I was doing, I was always fully engaged, involved, and immersed.

My works and actions defined me. My accomplishments fulfilled me. I successfully did so much and then moved on to the next task.

However, before this season, I sat with God for ten minutes daily—enough to check "quiet time" off my list. Now, I was feeling drawn to really be with Him. The more time I spent with Him, the more I realized I had been using activity to fill a void—a need for validation and love I had lacked since I was a child.

My drive to achieve had benefited me in numerous ways, but it also had taken a toll on my health. I just kept hearing in my heart that I needed to *be still*. The Bible verse that kept coming up in little trinkets and pictures on my social media was Psalm 46:10, *"Be still, and know that I am God"* (NIV). I plastered that verse around my house.

Then, I found myself here, embracing the call with a permanent reminder on my wrist. I figured that was a good start in my journey to be still and let God.

If only it were truly that easy.

A few years went by; through the trials of life, I was challenged many times with this idea of being still and letting God. For a firstborn, control-freak personality type, this was clearly not an easy task. Many obstacles kept testing me to trust God. I walked through unchartered territory some days, alone and lost, with only a permanent tattoo reminder on my wrist for direction.

I grew up knowing all the faith verses and singing all the songs, but completely embracing peace and trusting God was easier said than done. I just couldn't let go; I kept hitting a barrier. The struggle seemed unbearable to the point I sought out counseling. One day, in her little office on the couch, my counselor asked me if I trusted God had a plan for my life.

Of course, my answer was an immediate yes. Then, she asked me if I believed that God knew my death date just as He knew my birth date. I responded with another yes, but I noted an asterisk stemming from the story of King Hezekiah in Isaiah 38 when God told him he would die, and Hezekiah asked the Lord for more time. God granted him 15 additional years.

After I told her this story and how I could pray (and possibly control) God's death for me, I realized how ridiculous that sounded. I thought I could control things—that God was not fully in charge. My control-freak tendencies were laughable. I literally started laughing at the idea as I sat in that counseling office.

God is in complete control; even if He did extend King Hezekiah's life, He already knew that would be part of the plan. That day, something changed inside of me. I knew...

I am not God.

I realized I never had the power to control my life; God is truly and ultimately in control of my life, my children, my marriage, and my days.

A few months passed with the routine of everyday life unfolding. Finally, September arrived, marking my birthday month and filling me with excitement. Turning 42 didn't seem as overwhelming or monumental as 40 had been; it would be a simple time of celebration with family. That is, until it wasn't.

Moving to Florida full-time three years prior had significantly affected my birthday month because of something called "hurricane season." We had become accustomed to preparing for and dealing with hurricanes from June 1st through November 30th every year. It was not a fun process, as we lived on the Gulf of Mexico.

Two days before my birthday, September 26th, we spent the day preparing for an impending storm. We had become somewhat pros at this prep; everyone came together and did their known jobs.

We secured the boat and jet skis, placed the outdoor furniture under cover, brought in the volleyball net, and moved everything that could become a projectile. We emptied most of the pool so it could catch any water before it reached the house. The hurricane wasn't forecasted to land anywhere near us or be very bad, so we only moved a few of our higher-end vehicles off the island and decided that since we were staying home, we'd just keep an eye on the water levels rather than moving furniture and valuables from the main level and the garage.

We were ready. So we thought.

The day of the storm arrived. We cuddled and watched movies while monitoring the magnificent weather through our hurricane-proof picture windows. Between the rain bands, the kids and dogs ran around outside.

Around 4 pm, we went out and took funny videos of my mom in the wind, looking like a little wet old lady. Everyone was enjoying the day, watching the storm and laughing. Our water had been shut off as a barrier island precaution, but our electricity was on, and we were confident we were fully prepared. I had just started to cook dinner when the power went out. Then, the wind began to pick up more intensely, and the waves started getting meaner and more aggressive.

Our beach was now gone; water was reaching the middle pond on our property and becoming concerning. The news informed us that the hurricane was approaching offshore; it was about 200 miles directly out from us, passing by to the north. I went outside to check on my husband and found him and my mom soaking wet, trying to fill sandbags, as three massive waves filled up the pool in two minutes.

There was no stopping the rising tide; we were in trouble. I quickly called for the kids, and we began moving my son's entire room up to the main level. We worked together, diligently transporting Lego sets, drums, rock collections, clothes, and furniture to safety.

The water was now collecting outside his doors, filling our patio outdoor kitchen area like a little kiddie pool. We picked up our pace as water started to seep through the door walls. We began grabbing items from the garage and laying down towels in the areas where the water was seeping in aggressively, hoping they might help absorb some of it.

Within minutes, we got all we could from the lower level as the water accumulated by the feet against the doors. We began punching out the breakaway holes in our main level to allow the water to come in so it wouldn't knock the walls out completely. By this time, it was dark. We worked together tirelessly to save our main floor and garage belongings.

We kept a good pace and stayed calm while seeing the concern build in each other's eyes. As we were trying to finish moving the last of the larger items, the loudest crash echoed through the house as the double glass doors to the outdoor kitchen burst open, allowing rushing water and surging waves to pour in.

My husband and a family friend suddenly had wooden outdoor furniture and the patio refrigerator careening toward them. They worked together diligently to use the broken doors as a prop to keep the huge double wooden front doors open to allow the water to flow through our house and prevent it from reaching the second floor. The kids were screaming; it was absolutely terrifying watching the men work as large debris threatened to sweep them out the door. We immediately began to pray and call on the name of Jesus.

Thankfully, they quickly propped the doors open and waded to safety on the second floor. We spent the next several hours in the dark with waves of ocean waters gushing through our house, bringing hurricane winds and sticky humidity.

We told our kids it was safe to go to bed, but there was no sleeping through the storm. Our entire property on the Gulf of Mexico had become the ocean floor. The yard where my kids once played volleyball and the dogs ran after balls now had angry 10-foot waves rolling through it.

Hurricane Helene landed north of us, in Big Bend, Florida, as a Category 4 storm. And it left our lives completely flipped upside down. Around 2 am, while I was trying to sleep, I heard the rushing wind and water cease. I went down and saw the water had receded as fast as it came, leaving a debris line on the interior walls showing the water had risen about 4.5 feet in the house.

Everything was destroyed.

We carefully closed the doors that remained hanging on the house and went back to bed, waiting for daylight to expose what our property had now become. *We are safe. That is all that matters,* I thought as I drifted into an unbearably hot and humid sleep.

The next day, we witnessed what seemed like post-war destruction. I couldn't believe my eyes as I walked down my street. Metal gates were missing, road pieces were gone, and waves engulfed entire parts of my property. Full sections of sea wall were broken through and carried a mile away down the street.

The grass looked like a carpenter had rolled it up. There was total and complete destruction. Water crafts were gone, cars were filled with water, and the property we had tied down safely was now in neighbor's yards blocks away. The damage was unbelievable.

As I looked up the street, a car that had managed to get onto the island pulled up slowly and the window lowered. It was the hands and feet of Jesus. Pastor Willie and someone from our church extended a hand through the window and said, "Whatever you need, we are here."

I immediately started sobbing. We spent the entirety of the next few days throwing away and cleaning up all the debris.

Dozens of people showed up with gloves and shovels to help—people from all walks of life: neighbors, church friends, my kids' school friends' parents, dance and sports families, business friends. I was in absolute awe of the community response.

The demo crew came and sprayed bio-hazardous anti-mold spray.

We still didn't have water or gas or internet, but we had each other, plenty of supplies, and positive attitudes. We knew we would come out on the other side of the storm.

Then came the news reports of another major hurricane headed our way. I almost couldn't believe it was real.

On October 9th, just 12 days after Hurricane Helene, we were hit by

Hurricane Milton.

The forecast for Milton was a Category 5, headed right for us. We had just cleaned up from the first storm, and there we were, faced with what promised to be more devastation. We still didn't have power or even doors on our home, and looting was happening all around us. We had to make the difficult decision to stay or go.

The kids expressed they were too fearful to endure another storm, so, at the last minute, we decided to evacuate to higher ground. A kind friend of my husband offered us a place to stay at his friend's second home. We made the difficult decision to stay close and take shelter in a stranger's home instead of adhering to the mandatory evacuation.

Someone offered to stay at our beach house, and we packed our personal items, animals, and whatever valuables we couldn't imagine living without. I took photo albums and our kids' memory books; each kid took one or two memorable things, and we prepped our house again for a hurricane.

Before we left, I walked around our home, praying for protection. I prayed, cried, and spoke Psalm 91 over my property. I imagined a bubble of God's protection. I worshiped and thanked Him for what He had already done and would do.

I gave God control.

I was just about done praying when I looked up and saw the mightiest centurion warring angels lining my beach, protecting my home from the waters. I immediately smiled and felt a total peace come over me. I knew what I saw; God let me have a glimpse of what was there in the spirit.

We left the island and unpacked into our temporary safe-haven home. We prepared with food, gas, a generator, and water—still in total shock from what had occurred over the last 12 days. There it was as I moved my arms quickly—my tattoo reminding me to *Be still*. I told my husband that weather control wasn't on my payroll; God had it all under control.

The God of the Bible who created the wind and the waves was the same one I was trusting to take care of my family and our home.

Wednesday, October 9th, started like most normal days, except it wasn't. We all sat around trying to go about our normal day, waiting for the slow turtle of a hurricane to show up again. My mom kept herself busy cooking and baking; the kids did some of their school work and built a Lego set we brought with us.

My husband participated in some Zoom meetings, and, at one point, I even took a nap. I usually consider naps only in times of sickness, but after all I had been through, it was important to rest. I spent two hours sleeping as peace continued to flow through me.

As evening came, the winds picked up again. The forecast continued to worsen, projecting a direct hit on Siesta Key. My home was in the direct path of a Category 5 hurricane.

Thankfully, after many prayers, the storm made landfall as a Category 3. It was a total miracle. The person staying at our house described the most unexplainable experience. He watched as the waves and the winds just south of our house destroyed properties but stayed controlled near our home.

Our home was in a bubble of God's protection.

Meanwhile, our family was safely protected and calm as we watched the news and saw the storm wreak havoc. After about an hour of hearing the hurricane shutters banging, the winds died down—we were in the eye of the hurricane. They tell you not to go outside when you are in the eye, but it's hard to resist. We used the break to let the dogs go potty, and while we were outside, the kids danced in the street, laughing and singing.

I got very emotional as I witnessed firsthand the concept of being still. In that hurricane, and even in the storms of life, there is always a calm eye of stillness.

I looked down at my wrist and smiled with tears of joy. Life had thrown some pretty hard storms our way, but there I was, able to rest in Him, to dance and laugh in the street with my kids, to trust and believe in my core that my life is in His hands.

The ability to actually *feel* the bubble of safety, peace, and protection over anxiety and fear was such an overwhelming feeling. I was able to rest in the peace of God, knowing that homes, cars, boats, and personal items are just temporary things that won't last forever. I could see what is most important in life—those I love and my life loving Jesus.

We returned to the house, knowing the second half of the hurricane was still to come. According to meteorologists, the second half is worse than the first. We immediately lost power and the internet. It was 10:30 pm, so we said our prayers and went to bed. We all slept soundly through the night until morning.

We later heard stories from friends and neighbors about how horrible the second half of the storm was. We, however, slept in His perfect peace. We made calls to find out that our house was still standing and only had about a foot of water in it. We had more wind damage, but overall, the house did well.

We were all immediately relieved, but the likelihood of being able to move back in and live in that home anytime soon was bleak. God continued to supply as the homeowner where we were sheltering told us we could stay as long as needed. I sobbed as I held my husband and cried in relief and thankfulness. We lived in a stranger's home for a month; then God opened a door for us to buy a new house and move.

As I write this, our home is still not fully renovated due to supply shortages. And although life isn't as I expected, I can tell you it's significantly better than I could have imagined.

God is in control. And I live each day being still in His peace.

Storms in life come whether we are ready for them or not. I am so thankful I was prepared and had practiced being still and knowing my God. I would have never been able to come out on the other side without God taking complete control of my life.

No matter what storm you face, you can trust His presence and control.

*"Be still, and know that I am God"* (Psalm 46:10 NIV).

# Breaking Chains of Perfection

By Connie A. VanHorn

Do you see yourself through God's eyes? Our world seems to demand perfection, and we often feel chained by our inadequacies. But when you were born, God knew what your future failings and mistakes would be, and He still had a plan for your life. Regardless of your past circumstances, God desires to use you to transform the world.

You are enough, just as you are. And God has the power and is longing to work through you. Our heavenly Father seeks a willing heart, not a perfect person. He stands poised, ready to help you break free from the worldly chain of perfection and use you, flaws and all, for His glory.

Scripture teaches us that the only perfect being who ever walked the face of the earth was Jesus Christ. In Romans 3:23, we are reminded that *all have sinned and fall short of the glory of God* (NIV). Perfection is not a requirement God places upon us; He only desires our willingness to be faithful, available, and teachable.

*Not that we are sufficient in ourselves to claim anything as coming from us, but our sufficiency is from God* (2 Corinthians 3:5 NIV).

Our qualifications for God's work do not stem from our own strength or abilities; they arise from His power operating within us. It's time to break the chains that bind us to the belief that we are not good enough.

God can take our weaknesses and transform them into strengths. He can use our brokenness for His greater purpose, turning limitations into opportunities for His glory to shine through us. Come as you are to the feet of Jesus.

Lay down your fears, doubts, and insecurities. Surrender your weaknesses and struggles to Him. Trust that He can create miracles within you and use you to impact the world in transformative ways.

God doesn't call the qualified; He qualifies the called. He sees your potential clearly and knows the amazing things you are capable of. Trust in His plan for your life and believe that you are more than enough for Him to use in significant ways.

You might be feeling lost right now. Perhaps your life plans aren't unfolding as you had hoped. Or maybe you're in a constant struggle that is stealing your happiness. Trust me, I've been there, too, and I still face those feelings at times. However, we can choose to trust in God's guidance during the hard seasons of life, even when things don't align with our own expectations. Even when things are hard and we feel the furthest from good enough.

The truth is that God's plans are perfect, while ours often fall short. God wants you to live free, leave expectations behind, and take His hand as He leads you into the purpose He has chosen for you.

Our perfect God perfectly chose imperfect you!

Break free from the chains of perfection and become a willing vessel, eager to serve God's kingdom. By allowing Him to work through you in your own corner of the world, you will make a difference. Proudly embrace your imperfections while you trust God to grow you into His perfection. As you do, His light will shine through you, brightening this dark world.

After all, you are God's masterpiece!

. . . . . . . . . . . . . . . . . . . . . . . . . . . . . . . . . . . . . . . . . . .

# Danielle Addario

Danielle Addario is a homeschooling mom of five, a wife, a multitasker, and a professional snack distributor based in Siesta Key, Florida. Her life is wonderfully full, a bit chaotic, and always driven by love and faith.

Homeschooling wasn't originally in Danielle's plans, but now she can't imagine life any other way. Each day is filled with lessons, questions, laughter, and the occasional meltdown—from both the kids and herself! Watching her children grow, learn, and explore the world at their own pace is one of her greatest joys.

Danielle is also blessed to be married to an amazing man. Together, they navigate the beautiful mess of raising a big family, always finding time to share laughter and dance.

When not teaching or tackling the laundry, you can find Danielle spending time with her animals, lending a hand to friends, or soaking up the sun at the beach—her happy place. She has a soft spot for kids, critters, and any excuse to turn up the music and dance.

Life in her home is never dull, and she wouldn't trade it for anything. It's loud, busy, full of love, and exactly where she's meant to be.

# Free to Be Me

By Danielle Addario

Some days, I wake up and the sun is shining. Other days, I wake up and it's a bit gloomy. One thing remains the same: I wake up with the same scars I had the day before. To some, that may sound a bit depressing, but to me, it is empowering.

As I get dressed every morning, I am reminded of my past.

When I put my pants on, my hands run over two small indented scars on my right knee. Then I travel up to a 10-inch scar on the entire right side of my butt and thigh. I have many deep scars, both inside and out. I wear these scars as badges of honor, having learned through my journey with the Lord that my mess is my message. Some of these scars have taken me a long time to accept and even to feel proud of.

I was raised in a very old-school, catholic, loving home. My mom was a homemaker, and my dad was a successful businessman and family man. I have two half-brothers who are so much older than me that I never really lived in the same house with them.

In our home, feelings and shortcomings were not always openly discussed. I remember going to my mom as a young teen, sharing something I had done or that a friend had done, and she would often say, "Don't tell your dad."

That statement right there was a very common phrase in my house. I went along with it because, to me, my dad was perfect! He was the greatest man who ever lived, and I wanted him to see me the same way I saw him. I always felt like I needed to be perfect or try my hardest to do the right thing. Failure and disappointment were not something we easily spoke about.

Fast forward to 18-year-old Danielle. I was an athlete with dreams of becoming a teacher and, most importantly, becoming a mom someday. I had graduated high school and was about to start my freshman year of college. My parents had even surprised me with a new car.

After getting out of an abusive relationship, I tried to numb some of my pain by experimenting with drugs with friends. However, I never got too heavily involved; I just dabbled a little.

I had tried alcohol a couple of times at high school parties and hated it. I am someone who needs to feel in control, and alcohol made me feel like I had none, so I steered clear of it.

Next, I tried marijuana and disliked that as well. It seemed only to make me eat, sleep, and feel paranoid.

Then, a couple of close friends wanted to try OCs, which was the slang term we used for OxyContin, a strong opioid. I liked how it made me feel. It temporarily numbed some of my pain while providing a strong, calm feeling. As someone with a lot of energy, being still and "chilling" was not a sensation I was accustomed to.

One of my brothers also shared OCs with me. He never used the drugs with me, but he gave them to me to share or sell to friends. My brother was my idol growing up; he is 16 years older than me, and I thought he was the coolest person in the world. I looked up to him so much. If they were good enough for him, they must be good enough for me too.

Because I had never lived away from my parents' home, I decided to commute to school, which was only 25 minutes away. I had my first college exam on September 29, 2005. I felt like I aced it and was so proud of myself. I called my mom on my drive home to tell her all about it, but the conversation quickly turned into me crying about an ex-boyfriend who had broken my heart.

As I drove, it started to rain heavily, and in the blink of an eye, I wrapped my car around a telephone pole in a head-on collision. I don't remember much of the accident, as I was immediately knocked unconscious. I flatlined a few times—at the scene and on the way to the hospital.

I remember things I shouldn't have any knowledge of, like the cutting of my clothes and the use of defibrillator paddles to jumpstart me again. It felt as if I were watching a very intense movie from a distance.

Only it wasn't a movie, it was my life.

Then, it all went bright and white. The next thing I remember is waking up in the hospital with both my parents by my side with a breathing tube down my throat. In the first few moments of becoming conscious, I thought I was dead.

I realized I wasn't dead when my dad started to rub my hand and tell me everything was going to be okay. I was so confused, yet oddly unafraid. The doctor came in and told me I had been in a major car accident.

He proceeded to tell me that I broke both my ankles, dislocated my left hip, and shattered my right hip, amongst other injuries. He told me the tube down my throat was there to help me breathe because I was struggling to do so on my own, and the rod through my knee was there to stabilize my hip until I was stable enough for him to perform the surgery needed.

Later, the doctor informed me that, due to my injuries, having and carrying children would be extremely difficult. He said I would most likely never be a mom.

I was crushed. But I was also overwhelmingly determined to prove this man wrong! Who was he to tell me what could or couldn't happen? I love a challenge. If you tell me I can't do something, I promise it will only ignite my passion to do so. So, I focused my energy on proving this doctor wrong.

This helped me get through the excruciating pain of my broken hip, which I was told was as painful as someone experiencing terminal cancer.

I underwent surgery and, after a few weeks, started physical therapy. At that point in my life, I knew who God was, but I did not have a relationship with Him. I was determined to prove the medical industry wrong on my own sheer merit.

The physical therapist came daily; I could not break a 90-degree angle for quite some time. The pain was extreme—taking my breath away and causing me to scream in sudden outbursts at the same time.

My mental strength was fueled by my parents' belief in me and their positive outlook on my prognosis. Thanks to their intervention and insistence, I was eventually able to go home with some in-home medical assistance and equipment.

My parents hired a home nurse and a physical therapist to help with my recovery. They also brought in a hospital bed, commode, wheelchair, circulation machines, and icing equipment. I was heavily medicated with pain meds. After a few months and lots of dedication from myself and the people around me, I learned to walk again. I thought my battle was almost over, but little did I know, it was just getting started.

> *"For I know the plans I have for you," declares the Lord, "plans to prosper you and not to harm you, plans to give you hope and a future"* (Jeremiah 29:11 NIV).

With my injuries healing, I was abruptly taken off pain medication after having been on them for a long time. I quickly learned I had become addicted, which sent me into a downward spiral. I tried to keep my detox struggles to myself and manage without feeling physically ill, but I couldn't handle the sensation of my skin crawling off my body and the restless legs I was experiencing.

I never wanted anyone to know what I was going through, as I lived a life filled with shame, fear, and sadness. It wasn't long before my addiction took over completely. Eventually, the pills I was taking weren't enough, so I turned to heroin. I was just about to turn 19 when I tried it for the first time, and once I did, it became the only thing I used. I started using daily, which quickly escalated to multiple times a day. I felt so guilty every time. I desperately wanted to stop, but I didn't know how.

I tried to maintain my life, but it wasn't easy. Each day, it got harder to hide my addiction and even harder to continue living. I remember praying and asking God to help me, though I didn't feel like He actually heard me. I had been through so much in my short life and could not understand why.

All I wanted was to feel tired and be able to sleep at night without relying on drugs to help me get there. Then, one day, something shifted within me!

Just 13 months after my accident, in November of 2006, my then-new boyfriend took me to his church. Despite being completely high at the time, I recognized that the church was nothing like any I had ever been to before. I felt an overwhelming sense of love and peace. I'm sure there were people in the church who could tell that I was under the influence, but they never cast shame or judgment.

*Do everything in love* (1 Corinthians 16:14 NIV).

I reached out to my cousin and her boyfriend immediately after service. They were two people who had always had my back. They both knew I was on a dangerous path but never shut me out. I confided in them about my fears, expressing that if I didn't get some help, I would eventually lose everything, including my life. They immediately jumped into action, standing by me as I told my parents and my new boyfriend, who had no idea I was even struggling with drugs.

My cousin helped me get into a detox facility and even drove me there. I had chosen what people in our area referred to as "the worst" detox facility—not because it was poorly run, but because it was located in the heart of Boston, in a very dangerous area, right above a homeless shelter.

I had grown up in a "country club community," so no one could understand why I chose to go to that detox facility. To be honest, I didn't fully understand it either. I told everyone that I hadn't hit rock bottom yet, and if I wanted to avoid that fate, I needed to see what rock bottom looked like for others. I was terrified, yet I felt a sense of peace as I hugged my cousin goodbye. I assured her I would be okay and then walked into the locked-down facility. While I was there, I met all kinds of people, including my roommate.

She was a spunky little woman filled with life and jokes—scary, too. Several years older than me, she had been through detox programs multiple times before. She showed me the ropes and kept me laughing when all I wanted to do was cry.

Group sessions and individual therapy filled our days. At night, I would watch movies, use the payphone to call home, and try to rest while tuning out all the chaos that came with being in that place.

It was a time in my life that I will never forget. A few days passed; I thought everything was going well, considering what I was going through. Then it all changed. I walked into my room and screamed!

My roommate was unresponsive, half on the bed and half off, with her mouth open. The nurses stormed in and quickly ushered me out of the room. They tried everything to resuscitate her, but unfortunately, it was too late. She had overdosed.

My heart was broken, and I found myself questioning God. This woman was trying to get clean and put her life back together. Why would He let this happen? I immediately called my boyfriend, hysterical. He let me yell and sob, and then the first thing out of his mouth was, "Can we pray?"

I had never had someone respond to me like that. Out of shock, I quickly replied, "Yes!"

*Faith Unchained: Climbing to Freedom by God's Grace*

He prayed for strength, peace, comfort, and protection as I navigated through the last couple of days I would be at the facility.

I was unsure how he thought that would help as I had just watched someone die, but let me tell you, it did! I felt an unexplainable warmth around me that stayed with me up until the day I left. I also never felt any physical withdrawals. Knowing what I now know, that was all God!

God has had His hand on me throughout the entire process. He shielded me from the things I didn't need to see and exposed me to what I needed to bear witness to, even when I didn't want to.

I remember seeing the scripture Proverbs 31:25 multiple times throughout the first few years I was drug-free.

> *She is clothed with strength and dignity, she can laugh at the days to come* (Proverbs 31:25 NIV).

This is a verse I try to live my life by. Whenever I feel unsure of the present or future, I try to stop and remember where I've been and how God has given me the strength to persevere, grow, and even laugh.

Fast forward to the present day—I have 18 years of sobriety. That boyfriend, who was there for me during my darkest times, is now my husband of 16 years, and together, we have five healthy, happy, thriving children—all of whom I carried on my own! Throughout these years and experiences, I have deepened and grown my relationship with God.

It took me a long time to embrace my past. I did not get where I am overnight! A few months before my 15th anniversary of being clean, I finally mustered up enough strength and guts to tell my three teenagers that I had a drug problem.

I remember it like it was yesterday. We were on a road trip from Michigan to Boston. While driving through the mountains, as my husband kept his eyes on the road, I turned down the radio, looked at my kids, and said I had something big to tell them. I hoped my children would understand and not hate me for my past.

I told them that I was a recovering drug addict and that I had a major addiction just before they were born. While sobbing through it all, I told them part of my road to where I am now. I asked them to forgive me and not to look at me differently moving forward.

To my surprise, they weren't phased at all. They were shocked at all I had gone through and that they never knew. They said they admired the strength it took for me to overcome my addiction, and they even cracked some jokes! The entire conversation ended in lots of laughter. After I shared that with them and saw how they embraced me, I felt as though I could tell the world!

Suddenly, I no longer felt any shame. I no longer had to hide a piece of me from the people I cared most about. I felt safe to share with everyone. My chains were broken, and I was finally set *FREE!*

*I can do all this through him who gives me strength* (Philippians 4:13 NIV).

Four months later, on the actual 15th anniversary of my sobriety, I went with my three teenagers and got the word "Free" tattooed on my inner forearm. It serves as a constant reminder that I am free to be myself and share my story with the world.

Today, I share this story with anyone and everyone. I am no longer defined by my addiction or the things that happened in the past. I love with my whole heart and try to show people that if God can pull me through and set me free, He can do the same for them. He can set us free not just from drug addiction but from any stronghold we must overcome.

Throughout this entire process, God held my hand and guided me. Today, I look in the mirror each day and see a woman who is stronger than the day before. I choose to admire my scars that could have torn me down or even taken me out. I look at them all and remember what I've been through, how far I've come, how blessed I am, and the endless possibilities God has for my life.

I also take notice of that little script tattoo on my forearm and remember that no matter what may come against me or any battles I may be facing, I am never alone and am truly *FREE* to be me!!!

*So if the Son sets you free, you are truly free* (John 8:36 NLT).

# Breaking Chains of the Unease of Solitude

By Connie A. VanHorn

Recognizing that God never meant solitude to be a chain that binds can be transforming. The devil often attacks us when we are alone, confronting us with fear, doubts, and emotional wounds, which can leave us feeling stuck and bound by heavy chains. But being alone with God can help us overcome unresolved trauma and emerge stronger. Isolation can be a sacred place where we can meet with God and submit to Him as He helps us grow into the women He has called us to be.

When I was a little girl, I loved going to a park near my home. I would sit against a concrete wall by the water and daydream about every unrealistic possibility. In that hidden spot, I learned to be alone, which helped me later in life when I was forced into unwanted and unnatural isolation. Even though I didn't understand the purpose as I sat in that park alone with God, my faith and resilience grew. God used that place to protect me from the painful reality around me and prepare me for the future.

Throughout the Bible, we see many people who were changed in their own caves of isolation. David spent years in hiding before becoming king. Jesus trained in quiet solitude for 30 years before beginning His ministry. In their time of isolation, these great men grew in faith and character as God prepared them for His call on their lives.

In my own life, the cave has become a place of peace, joy, and reliance on God. In the cave, I learned to worship and pray, and I began to understand that joy is not absent in our struggles. Even when circumstances are hard, we can find joy in knowing that God is at work within us.

God sees us in our caves. The beauty of isolation is that it is a sacred place where God can mold us. It's not a punishment; it's an assignment. We are only able to grow as deep as we allow God to dig into our hearts. Character takes time to develop, and God is patient with us in the cave.

You, too, can emerge from your cave stronger and more faithful, ready to fulfill the purpose God has for you.

By finding peace in the silence and allowing God's light to shine through our darkness, we can deepen our understanding of ourselves and strengthen our relationship with God. In this process, we learn to release the burdens that hold us back—developing resilience, gaining hope, and deepening our faith. Ultimately, breaking these chains empowers us to connect with ourselves and others so we can live in true freedom.

If you find yourself in a season of solitude, embrace it. Seek God in your secret place, and allow Him to transform you. He is preparing you for something beautiful.

Keep going and count it all as joy, for God is with you every step of the way.

*Consider it pure joy, my brothers and sisters, whenever you face trials of many kinds, because you know that the testing of your faith produces perseverance* (James 1:2-3 NIV).

. . . . . . . . . . . . . . . . . . . . . . . . . . . . . . . . . . . . . . . . . . . . . . .

# Rachael Anderson

Rachael Anderson is a grateful woman in long-term recovery from substance use disorder. Her journey began in the darkness of addiction but was radically transformed by the love and grace of Jesus Christ. Since her recovery began on August 30, 2017, she has devoted her life to helping others find hope, healing, and purpose beyond their pain.

Rachael is the voice behind the recovery movement Addict with Purpose, a social media platform that has reached hundreds of thousands of people searching for light in their darkest moments. Through raw honesty, faith-filled encouragement, and a heart for service, she inspires others to rise from the ashes and walk in freedom.

Born and raised in Utah and New York and now living in Tennessee, Rachael blends street smarts with spiritual strength. She is also a mother, wife, advocate, and speaker who believes that no one is too far gone for God to redeem. Her life is proof that recovery is real, faith still moves mountains, and purpose can be found in the most broken places.

Rachael's story is a testimony of unshakable faith, radical grace, and the beautiful transformation that happens when you surrender to God's plan.

# Restored by Grace

By Rachael Anderson

My name is Rachael Anderson, and I am a forty-five-year-old mother of two incredible teenagers. That sentence seems so simple—perhaps even boring—yet it holds the weight of a life once shattered by addiction, loss, and despair.

For years, I wasn't the mother my children needed or deserved. But after more than twenty years of battling active addiction, today, I live a beautiful life in long-term recovery, free from the chains that once bound me.

I remain in awe of God's mercy, overwhelmed by His grace that brought me back from the depths of destruction and despair. With endless gratitude for this new lease on life, I share my story to reveal the undeniable truth that no one is too far gone for God's redeeming love.

> *But because of His great love for us, God, who is rich in mercy, made us alive with Christ even when we were dead in transgressions—it is by grace you have been saved* (Ephesians 2:4-5 NIV).

## A FOUNDATION I TURNED FROM

I grew up in a dysfunctional Christian household with three sisters. We were all guided by parents who loved the Lord. They were young, it was the '70s—and both were learning how to be parents while coming from two completely different, unhealthy households.

Sundays were meant to be sacred, but they weren't always. My parents did their best to raise us in church, but outside of church, there was a lot of yelling and chaos. This led us kids to feel unloved and desperate to escape a home where we lived in fear. It was hard for them to raise children with love when neither truly knew what healthy love was.

I know my mother believed in God's unwavering love, and that's what she tried to show us, but it was hard, and I couldn't escape the feeling of wanting to get away from the house and the hell I felt like I was living in.

Even though I was raised to know Christ, I never truly *knew* Him, and my heart slowly drifted away. I didn't experience a sudden fall but a slow fade—tiny compromises that grew into bigger rebellions.

We moved from Queens, New York, to Salt Lake, Utah, where I struggled to fit in. My thick accent made me a target for ridicule, and my self-esteem crumbled. We dressed differently and spoke differently, and I felt more like an outsider every day. Even in church, I never sensed acceptance—I was just an outcast with a funny accent. Desperate to belong, I practiced my speech daily, trying to sound like the other kids. But no matter how hard I tried, I never seemed to fit in.

By the age of fourteen, I made a choice that changed everything—I walked away from God. I never stopped believing, but I no longer felt drawn to Him. I mistook rebellion for freedom, convinced that rules meant to protect me were just chains to control me.

At fifteen, I ran away, chasing a world that felt thrilling and full of possibility—but I wasn't prepared for its darkness. I had already started drinking, smoking, and dabbling in substances I barely understood. At first, it felt like power—an escape from the ache inside me. But with every party, every drink, and every high, I drifted further from the girl my parents had raised—and the God who never stopped watching over me. I surrounded myself with people who only fueled my descent, cheering on my recklessness because it mirrored their own. They weren't friends; they were co-conspirators in my slow unraveling.

Looking back, I realize addiction didn't begin with drugs or alcohol. It started the moment I believed the lie that I wasn't enough, that I had to be someone else to be worthy of love. That lie sent me into a spiral that lasted over two decades—a relentless fight for my soul, driven by desperation to fit in and be loved by anyone willing to give it.

> *Do not conform to the pattern of this world, but be transformed by the renewing of your mind. Then you will be able to test and approve what God's will is—his good, pleasing and perfect will* (Romans 12:2 NIV).

## THE LONG DESCENT INTO DARKNESS

Between 1993 and 2017, addiction held me captive. What started as casual experimentation quickly spiraled into a relentless cycle of self-destruction. Alcohol and drugs became chains I couldn't break, pulling me further from who I was meant to be. Yet, under the influence, I felt alive, unstoppable— even safe. It numbed the pain of a little girl who just wanted friends, longed to fit in, and feared being yelled at for everything.

Addiction took me places I never imagined. I faced homelessness, jail, and suffering that stripped me of dignity and left me hollow. I moved constantly after high school, but nothing changed. My parents put me in rehab three times, allowing me to be homeschooled within the program. I even walked across the stage to receive my diploma while still in rehab.

At 22, I was back in New York. Things didn't get better after rehab—they got worse. I wasn't ready. There were nights I wandered the streets of New York City, carrying nothing but a backpack—no destination, no hope, just the constant search for my next high. Clubs and raves became my refuge—

dark places filled with flashing lights and pounding music, drowning out the deafening silence within my own heart. Ecstasy, ketamine, cocaine—these substances became my closest companions, offering fleeting moments of euphoria followed by crushing emptiness.

Eventually, methamphetamines became my drug of choice—my true love and best friend. That's when the darkness swallowed me. I thought I had found something that made me feel whole again—but it was a dark lie. I was falling apart, dying inside, yet my brain couldn't stop thinking about the drugs and alcohol. That little voice in my head craved the euphoria, repeating the same desperate plea for decades: *I need more.*

I was blind to the dangers surrounding me, oblivious to the spiritual warfare I was caught in. The drugs numbed more than just my body—they numbed my soul. I eventually moved back to Utah, believing that if I left New York, I could outrun my addiction. But that didn't last long. I was homeless once again, trapped in the same cycle. I lost count of the nights I had nowhere to sleep and the mornings when I woke up in strange places with no memory of how I had gotten there. I found sanctuary in the devil's playground.

I often wondered why God allowed me to fall so far. *Why didn't He stop me? Why do I have to suffer like this?* But today, I understand. God never left me. I was the one who turned my back on Him. He was there all along—quietly watching over me, weeping for me, waiting for me to look up from the pit I had dug for myself.

I thought marriage would save me. At twenty-five, I married a man who didn't drink or party like I did, hoping his stability would heal my brokenness. For a while, it seemed to work. We had two beautiful daughters, and in those early years of motherhood, I experienced brief sobriety. Their tiny faces were a glimpse of the life I could have had—one filled with love, purpose, and joy.

But sobriety alone wasn't enough. I still thought about drugs daily. Beneath it all, unhealed trauma and pain festered, and without God, my demons returned. I began drinking heavily, telling myself it was just to take the edge off. But addiction doesn't whisper—it roars. Soon, the drugs came back, dragging me deeper than before.

Addiction fed me lies I believed—that I was unworthy of my children's love, doomed to fail as a mother and wife, never enough. I didn't leave my girls and my marriage because I didn't love them; I left because I thought they were better off without me. I believed my presence did more harm than my absence. The devil whispers these types of lies in our weakest moments, attempting to keep us bound to our strongholds and separated from God's love and light.

> *"The thief comes only to steal, kill, and destroy; I have come that they may have life, and have it to the full"* (John 10:10 NIV).

## THE TURNING POINT

In 2017, I hit my lowest point—a darkness so deep I couldn't see a way out. Homeless again, consumed by meth and bath salts, separated from my family, and utterly broken. It wasn't just my body that was fragile—my spirit was shattered. I had nothing left. No hope. No dignity. No reason to believe life could ever be different.

I felt the devil's grip tightening. Some days, I didn't want to live. There were nights I cursed God, tears streaming down my face as I demanded answers. *Why me? Why did You let me fall this far? Where were You when I needed You most?* But deep down, I knew the truth—God had never left me. I was the one who had turned away. He had warned me, but I went anyway.

Incarceration, rape, betrayal, and violence became part of my story. When you walk in darkness, it consumes you. Evil surrounds you. Somehow, what should have destroyed me didn't. But I wasn't living—I was merely existing, lost in the numb haze of addiction. I saw no way out. I was beyond broken. I tried to quit, but I couldn't. No matter how hard I fought, the obsession to use never let go.

But God...

On July 28, 2017, something shifted. Desperate and empty, I walked into my mother's house—not for help, but because I had nowhere else to go. I collapsed on her couch, detoxing for three days as my body shut down from years of abuse. My daughters, only seven and nine, sat on my lap. They didn't care that I was broken; they just wanted their mom.

Then came the knock at the door. My daughter answered, her innocent voice filled with joy. "Yes, yes! My mommy sure is here!" she exclaimed as if announcing a hero's return. But it wasn't a hero at the door. It was three police officers, and soon, I was arrested for outstanding warrants. Rage consumed me—at the police, my parents, my kids' dad, and most of all, at God. I blamed everyone but myself.

I begged to be bailed out, but no one came. Looking back, I see it was God's intervention—an answer to the prayers I didn't even realize I was praying in the depths of my darkest nights.

> Call on me in the day of trouble; I will deliver you, and you will honor me (Psalm 50:15 CSB).

## FINDING GOD IN A JAIL CELL

In that cold jail cell, something inside me finally broke—but not in the way I expected. For the first time, I didn't ask God to get me out of trouble. I didn't bargain or make empty promises. I simply fell to my knees and whispered from the depths of my soul, *God, I can't do this anymore. I need You. Please... just help me. Take away the obsession to get high.*

I wanted to be with my babies more than anything. I wanted to be the mother they deserved. My prayer wasn't eloquent or polished—it was raw, desperate, and real. I cried out with a sincerity I had never known, and in that tiny, cold space surrounded by concrete walls, the presence of the Holy

Spirit filled the room. It wasn't a dramatic bolt of lightning or thunder—it was a quiet, gentle whisper. But I felt it. And for the first time in my life, I knew I was truly heard.

He hadn't abandoned me. He didn't hate me. He had been there all along, waiting for me to surrender. And I did.

A prison ministry volunteer handed me a Bible. On the cover, two shackled hands broke free beneath the words "FREE ON THE INSIDE." It felt like a message meant just for me. As I flipped through its worn pages, I read stories of broken lives redeemed by God—people just like me, maybe even worse—who had found grace and hope behind prison walls.

Tears streamed down my face as a truth I had never fully believed sank in: *If He could save them, He could save me, too.*

Then came an announcement from the guard—the chaplain was inviting inmates to a Bible study. I hesitated. Shame whispered, You don't belong there. You're too far gone. But hope whispered louder. So I went.

That jailhouse Bible study changed my life. I learned again about Jesus turning water into wine, but this time, I didn't see it as just a miracle at a wedding. I saw it as a promise—God could transform something ordinary— something broken—into something beautiful.

> *Therefore, if anyone is in Christ, he is a new creation. The old has passed away; behold, the new has come* (2 Corinthians 5:17 ESV).

## A NEW BEGINNING, A NEW CREATION

I walked out of that jail a different woman. For the first time in my life, the desire to drink and get high was gone. It wasn't willpower. It wasn't because I had finally "figured it out." The chains that had bound me for over two decades had been broken—not by me, but by the power of Jesus Christ. I was delivered.

Instead of craving the next high, I craved Him. There was a hunger deep in my soul, a thirst for something real—something permanent. I didn't just want to survive anymore. I wanted to live. The Holy Spirit whispered to my heart, "You were made for more."

I didn't have all the answers. There were still court dates, broken relationships, and years of wreckage to face. But for the first time, I wasn't afraid—I wasn't walking alone. The road wasn't easy. Many doubted me, and I didn't blame them. My past had shown a different version of me—sick, lost, and selfish. Trust isn't given; it's earned slowly, one day at a time. Though my loved ones doubted, I grew in my faith—and that was enough.

God didn't just save me from addiction; He called me to something greater—my purpose. I felt a pull to help others like me, to be the voice I once needed. My story wasn't just mine; it was a testimony of what God can do with a surrendered life.

He revealed His grace little by little, reminding me He was with me through every challenge. My ever-faithful mother believed this was my restoration. She prayed when I couldn't, and through her prayers, God reassured her—I was on the right path.

With renewed faith and my momma's unwavering support, I rebuilt my life, one day at a time, fully surrendered to Him. When the devil tried to creep back in—and he did—I stood firm, protected by the armor of God. This time, I wasn't defenseless. I had repented. I had been redeemed. I was no longer walking in darkness; I was walking in the light.

*Submit yourselves, then, to God. Resist the devil, and he will flee from you* (James 4:7 NIV).

## THE FRUIT OF FAITH

Today, I stand in awe of what God has restored.

My daughters—those same little girls who once sat on my lap when I was too broken to hold them—are now thriving teenagers. Smart, compassionate, and resilient. Straight-A students preparing for college. Full of dreams and potential. They no longer fear abandonment because I show up—every single day. God didn't just restore my role as their mother—He redeemed it!

He also brought an incredible man into my life. A man who loves the Lord, embraces my past without judgment, and sees me not for who I was but for who I've become. We recently got married—a beautiful reminder that God's plans are always greater than anything we could imagine.

I turned my mess into a message, becoming a voice for those still trapped in the darkness I once knew. Through my online platform, *Addict with Purpose,* I now reach hundreds of thousands, sharing hope, faith, and the truth that recovery is possible—because God makes it possible.

As a certified peer recovery specialist, I use my lived experience to help others break free from addiction and mental illness. I also volunteer in the streets with ministries, bringing the written Word and personal testimonies to those who need hope the most.

Every time I look into the eyes of someone lost in addiction, I see myself. But I also see what's possible. My heart beats for the homeless, for the hopeless—those searching for love in all the wrong places.

These aren't just accomplishments. They're miracles. Graces granted by a God who never gave up on me, even when I had given up on myself.

*He has made everything beautiful in its time* (Ecclesiastes 3:11 NIV).

## LIFE AFTER RECOVERY

Life isn't perfect, and recovery doesn't erase all your problems. I've faced loss, heartache, and disappointment even in sobriety. But now, I don't face those battles alone.

Through it all, God has been faithful. Every day, I show up—clean, sober, and obedient to His will, and He reveals the life He planned for me. A life I never thought I deserved.

His plans for abundance, growth, love, and purpose aren't just for me. They're for you, too—for anyone willing to surrender.

The same God who met me in a jail cell—a woman who abandoned her children—will meet you wherever you are. Whether you're on the streets, in a hospital bed, in the silence of your room, or in the middle of your worst mistake, He is there. Call out to Him with unchained faith. He's waiting, arms wide open, ready to turn your darkness into light—just like He did for me.

> The light shines in the darkness, and the darkness has not overcome it (John 1:5 NIV).

# Breaking Chains of Hopelessness

### By Melissa Gissy Witherspoon

Hopelessness can feel like an invisible prison—one that surrounds us with fear, isolation, and despair. It tells us things will never change, that healing is impossible, and that we're too far gone. But the truth of the gospel tells a different story. Even in the darkest places, Jesus brings light, healing, and hope.

One of the most powerful illustrations of this is found in the story of the Gerasene demoniac in Mark 5:1-20. This man was utterly hopeless. Possessed by a legion of demons, he lived among the tombs—crying out night and day, cutting himself with stones. He was so tormented that people had tried chaining him, but even the chains could not hold him. He had been cast aside by society, isolated and broken.

But then Jesus stepped ashore.

> *And when he saw Jesus from afar, he ran and fell down before him* (Mark 5:6 ESV).

With divine authority, Jesus cast the demons out and restored the man completely. The crowd later saw him *sitting there, clothed and in his right mind* (Mark 5:15 RSV). The transformation was so astonishing that Jesus told him, *"Go home to your friends, and tell them how much the Lord has done for you, and how he has had mercy on you"* (Mark 5:19 RSV).

This story reminds us that no one is too lost for Jesus to find, too broken for Him to heal, or too far gone for Him to restore. He is the hope for the hopeless, the Savior of the outcast, and the lifter of the crushed.

The Apostle Paul writes, *May the God of hope fill you with all joy and peace in believing, so that by the power of the Holy Spirit you may abound in hope* (Romans 15:13 ESV). Our hope is not rooted in our circumstances but in the unchanging character of Jesus Christ. When we trust Him with unchained faith, we understand that no matter what life deals us, there is always hope!

If you're in a place of hopelessness today, know this: Jesus is still stepping ashore. He is still pursuing the brokenhearted. Psalm 34:18 says, *The Lord is near to the brokenhearted, and saves the crushed in spirit* (RSV). You are not forgotten, not abandoned. Jesus sees you—and He is mighty to save.

Let Jesus break those chains. Let Him speak peace into your storm and healing into your soul. Your story isn't over. In Christ, your hopelessness can become a testimony of His redeeming love. There is hope—and His name is Jesus.

. . . . . . . . . . . . . . . . . . . . . . . . . . . . . . . . . . . . . . . . . . . . . . . . . . .

# Natalie Barnhard-Castrogiovanni

Natalie M. Castrogiovanni (formerly Barnhard) is a spinal cord injury survivor, disability advocate, public speaker, changemaker, and Founder and President of Motion Project Foundation, a nonprofit dedicated to helping SCI individuals and those with paralysis reclaim their lives.

After sustaining her own SCI in 2004, Natalie made it her mission to create long-term rehabilitation solutions and advocacy for others facing similar challenges. That mission, fueled by the Holy Spirit, became Motion Project Foundation Inc., and in 2021, she opened the Natalie Barnhard Center for Spinal Cord Injury Rehabilitation and Recovery in Buffalo, NY.

Natalie also established Motion Project CARES, which continues to expand. The upcoming Wheels of Worship program will foster a faith-based community centered around worship and connection.

Natalie's advocacy extends through partnerships with the University at Buffalo and the Christopher & Dana Reeve Foundation, where she serves as a Regional Champion. Her leadership has earned her the Remarkable Women Award, Buffalo Business First's Woman of the Year, United Spinal's Advocate of the Year, Keynote speaker, and a leadership event through M&T Bank.

In 2023, Natalie became a wife, stepmom, and grandmother! She believes through faith, love, and perseverance, life can still be beautiful—no matter the circumstances.

# Perfectly Imperfect

By Natalie Barnhard-Castrogiovanni

I still remember the overwhelming sound of crashing metal, the horrific fear, and the searing, sharp pain. Then—silence.

It was October 22, 2004. I was happy—24 years old, had recently finished my second degree, was looking forward to buying my grandmother's home, and had a boyfriend for almost two years. I was a physical therapist assistant and licensed massage therapist in an orthopedic clinic and was passionate about helping others. My life as a young adult was beginning.

But my life changed forever in that one devastating moment.

I was waiting for my next patient to come in when a 600-pound weight machine came crashing down, crushing my body beneath it. I felt a burning fire in my neck as if numerous sharp knives were stabbing me at once.

There are no words to describe the pain; it was the only part of my body I could feel. The rest of my body did not exist. As I lay on the ground, unable to move or feel any part of my body, complete terror overcame me.

The staff rushed over; five people helped pull the machine off my helpless body. The paramedics arrived, asking me if I could feel my toe. I had no idea anyone was even touching my toe. My tears began to flow. I knew my life would never be the same.

Within minutes, I was rushed to our local trauma hospital for emergency medical care. The impact of the crash shattered my cervical spine at the C5 and C6 levels, damaging my spinal cord and causing paralysis. I could not move my arms or legs but only turn my head. I lay on a table with a neck collar, tears streaming down the side of my face.

My mom had arrived. I gazed at her and said, "My life is over. It will never be the same." She tried to reassure me that things would be okay, but I knew how devastating my injury was. I barely remember being wheeled into surgery because I was so desperate for the horrific pain to stop.

The days that followed my life-saving surgery are blurry. I woke up on a ventilator, completely paralyzed and unable to speak. I was so scared and confused—not understanding why I couldn't talk or breathe on my own. My mind was going in so many directions as I grappled with the reality that I might never walk again.

I was in shock for the first couple of weeks and couldn't even cry. As I became more aware, I felt lost—like I was in a nightmare I could not wake up from. Three weeks later, my mom and best friend were in my hospital room when the gravity of my situation hit me all at once, and the floodgates crashed open.

As I started to cry uncontrollably, so many thoughts and questions ran through my mind: *Why did this happen? Why me? What am I supposed to do now? How can I live my life in a wheelchair, paralyzed?*

The vibrant, energetic, and caring woman I had been vanished. All that remained was uncertainty and fear. In those darkest moments, I clung to my faith, knowing others were praying for me when I could not speak or pray for myself.

I had lost everything—my career, the hope of purchasing my grandma's house, and even the boyfriend I envisioned a life with. My goals, dreams, and independence were all gone! Every part of my life was shattered. I was mentally and emotionally crushed, confused, scared, and angry. I prayed this was a nightmare I would wake up from. This was not the plan I had for my life!

I often think of us as clay. When something traumatic happens, our clay breaks. We sometimes try to put it back together ourselves, but it does not always stick. That day, my clay shattered into millions of pieces, and I had no idea how to put them back together. Every single aspect of my life was now different. I was broken.

> *Yet you, Lord, are our Father. We are the clay, you are the potter; we are all the work of your hand* (Isaiah 64:8 NIV).

A pastor visited my hospital room—the timing was nothing short of a miracle. I was having a meltdown as he sat down and prayed with me. He shared a verse that would become my anchor: *"For I know the plans I have for you," declares the Lord, "plans to prosper you and not to harm you, plans to give you hope and a future"* (Jeremiah 29:11 NIV).

I clung to those words, though I could not see how God's plan would unfold. All I could think was that this was my new reality. I was now a quadriplegic and needed so much help and care. How could God use me?

I tried to trust God but felt like I had lost so much of myself. I had so many questions. I had used my physical body and hands as gifts to help others heal; why would God allow that gift to be taken from me? I could not understand.

My mom often prayed with me, sharing that God had a bigger purpose for me. She encouraged me to trust, pray, and believe that He was going to use me in ways bigger than I could ever imagine. As moms often are, I would eventually see that she was right. However, at that time, I could not see beyond grief and mourning the loss of who I used to be. I had to grieve for how I used to be and begin rediscovering who I had become. All I could do was hope, pray, and trust that God would have a new purpose for me.

*Now to him who is able to do immeasurably more than all we ask or imagine, according to his power that is at work within us* (Ephesians 3:20 NIV).

I left my hometown, friends, family, and entire support system to go out of state for specialized spinal cord injury care and rehabilitation. My daily rehabilitation was grueling. Sometimes, I was so depressed I didn't want to get out of bed. It was not just about rebuilding physical strength but also about learning how to live with my disability.

Every task and every movement was a struggle. I had to learn how to eat, brush my teeth, and do the simplest, most basic daily tasks we often take for granted. There were so many moments of frustration and tears. But in those moments, I prayed.

*"So do not fear, for I am with you; do not be dismayed, for I am your God. I will strengthen you and help you; I will uphold you with my righteous right hand"* (Isaiah 41:10 NIV).

After months in rehab out of state, I returned home, where my family and I had to learn to navigate life with my injury. My parents became my caregivers, taking on every aspect of my care; they were terrified. They had to make big adjustments, including moving my bedroom for accessibility.

As we packed up my old room, filled with pictures and memories of my past life, I broke down, facing my new reality. Home, once my safe place, now forced me to confront the shattering truth of my situation: my old life was gone.

The next two years were filled with anger, anxiety, and frustration as I adjusted to my injury, needing help with everything. The breakup with my boyfriend left me feeling unlovable and questioning my worth. If someone who claimed to love me couldn't handle this, how could anyone else?

My self-worth was shattered. I didn't think I would ever find true peace.

Eventually, I realized I needed specialized therapy unavailable in my hometown. I spent another eight years out of state, including four years living in a hotel and attending therapy five days a week to rebuild strength and regain physical function. Being surrounded by others who understood my struggle gave me a sense of community and hope.

Slowly, I began to see that my injury didn't define me—it was just part of my story. I found purpose and meaning again, realizing God's plan for me wasn't over; it was only beginning. My education as a therapist and my experiences in recovery were preparing me for something greater. I just needed to trust His plan and fully accept my injury.

> *Do not be anxious about anything, but in every situation, by prayer and petition, with thanksgiving, present your requests to God* (Philippians 4:6 NIV).

Grateful for the care, resources, and knowledge I was receiving, I could not help but wonder about others who could not afford to leave their communities or access long-term recovery programs. I felt a stirring in my heart to create something to change that. God put a passion in my heart to help others with similar catastrophic injuries.

He was showing me my purpose!

*The Lord is my strength and my shield; my heart trusts in him, and he helps me. My heart leaps for joy, and with my song I praise him* (Psalm 28:7 NIV).

I began a nonprofit, initially called Wheels With Wings, to help the immediate financial needs of people with injuries. I also started doing advocacy work and started a Buffalo chapter of the United Spinal Association—a national advocacy organization. Being part of this organization empowered me. I was part of something bigger than myself and longed to do more for my community.

Throughout the following years, I traveled back and forth from Buffalo to Atlanta to visit family and create events for our nonprofit organization. We were supporting individuals with spinal cord injuries by providing quality-of-life grants. Our mission was clear: to provide resources, advocacy, and hope. We were making a difference, but there still was so much more in my heart that God was calling me to do.

The dream and passion God put in my heart was to build a place where people with paralysis could find physical healing as well as emotional, mental, and spiritual renewal—a place of connection and support. God was calling me to use my experience as a therapist and patient to do something bigger than myself.

I left Atlanta and returned to Buffalo to build the recovery center I envisioned, but coming home was more difficult than expected. Without daily therapy and the friendships I'd made, I felt isolated and disconnected. Depression crept in, threatening the progress I had fought for.

Then, my health spiraled—a bowel obstruction led to surgery, and I battled pneumonia twice. One episode was so severe my heart stopped, and doctors gave me a 50-50 chance of living. Miraculously, I survived, convinced God still had a purpose for me.

Yet, I couldn't stop wondering: *When will I move from trials and survival to happiness and joy?*

> There is a time for everything, and a season for every activity under the heavens (Ecclesiastes 3:1 NIV).

Eventually, I surrendered everything to God—my pain, plans, and even my search for love. I stopped trying to control everything myself. I prayed for guidance and support. The idea of starting a recovery center terrified me. How could someone like me, with no business background, do something so big?

*Trust in the Lord with all your heart and lean not on your own understanding; in all your ways submit to Him, and He will make your paths straight* (Proverbs 3:5-6 NIV).

After years of struggle, prayer, and perseverance, my dream became a reality. I renamed my nonprofit Motion Project Foundation, Inc., a name that reflects the journey of recovery, the movement of the body, and the drive to keep moving forward. We were putting "Recovery in Motion."

In 2021, that vision came to life with the opening of The Natalie Barnhard Center for Spinal Cord Injury Rehabilitation and Recovery in Buffalo, NY. Our center offers a welcoming space for long-term recovery, combining cutting-edge therapy, advanced robotics, and personalized programs with support groups and social events. More than just treatment, we are a family dedicated to supporting the whole person.

Recovery is about more than physical progress—it's about rediscovering purpose, building confidence, and fostering connection. True recovery isn't about being defined by your disability or your wheelchair; it's about freedom and living your best life.

The journey to creating the center was anything but easy, filled with obstacles that tested my faith. Fear was constant, but failure was never an option. Each time I felt overwhelmed, I turned to God, trusting His plan.

*"Be strong and courageous. Do not be afraid; do not be discouraged, for the Lord your God will be with you wherever you go"* (Joshua 1:9 NIV).

God's presence was evident in the people who supported me, and together we overcame every challenge. Seeing the center's impact today is a miracle. But my work isn't done—I feel called to expand, creating programs that empower and support people in their recovery. I've been the therapist and the patient, and now I use both perspectives to help others heal.

Recovery takes a community. Through advocacy, social groups, and spiritual wellness, we help people adapt, overcome, and draw closer to God.

> *And we know that for those who love God all things work together for good, for those who are called according to His purpose* (Romans 8:28 NIV).

My ultimate vision is a comprehensive facility with advanced rehab, accessible housing, aquatics, and holistic wellness—open to all, regardless of finances. I trust God will provide the resources to make this dream a reality.

Through it all, my faith has been my foundation. I have been at the bottom of the highest mountain. Yet through faith, God carried me one step at a time until some of the darkness started to move, and I finally started to see a little bit of light—a little break in the clouds—and then finally some sunlight. In the beginning, I thought I would never be happy or see the sunlight again.

Surrendering to God has not been easy. We often want to control our own outcomes. But this was something I could not do on my own. Fully letting go to my Lord and Savior has freed the chains binding me, allowing me to accept my injury fully.

With my acceptance, I felt freedom unlike I had ever experienced. I was no longer a prisoner of my paralysis or disability. My wheelchair no longer confined me. God taught me that I don't need full physical function to be used for his glory! I am in awe of God's work in my life. I began to value myself and stopped dating below my standards, surrendering and praying to God for the right partner—someone who would see and value me for who I truly am.

God answered that prayer and blessed me with an incredibly loving, caring, and supportive man I now call my husband. Steve sees beyond the wheelchair—he sees me. He loves the woman I am and completely adores me. Because of his own journey with an injury and a father who had muscular dystrophy, he understands the challenges that come with being with someone who has a disability.

God had the right man for me. Steve did not run the other way; he embraced me as if he was made for me and had trained throughout his life for a relationship with me. God is first in our marriage, and we are building a life filled with faith, love, adventure, and purpose.

Wow!! *God is so good!*

I am finally in a season of joy and happiness. It is all a testament to God's faithfulness and promises.

Looking back, I see all that God has done in my life. The prayers He has answered, the ways He has restored what I once lost. My clay—once shattered into millions of pieces—has been put back together and reshaped into a stronger and more resilient shape than ever before. Praise God!

God had a plan and purpose the entire time. He has shown me I am made in His image to do His incredible work. All that happens in our lives can be a testament of faith. Our trials and suffering might even propel us to do something for God's glory we never imagined.

> Consider it pure joy, my brothers and sisters, whenever you face trials of many kinds, because you know that the testing of your faith produces perseverance (James 1:2-3 NIV).

If you are facing a challenge, know that God has a plan for you. Each of our stories is a bit different, but we can trust that the challenges and questions can all be answered by turning our faith to Him and letting Him break our chains. Your pain and struggles do not have to be the end of your story. They could be the beginning of something you might have never even imagined.

Lean into your faith, seek support, and remember—you were made in God's image. He made you ON purpose and WITH purpose. He will never let you go.

*But those who hope in the Lord will renew their strength. They will soar on wings like eagles; they will run and not grow weary; they will walk and not be faint* (Isaiah 40:31 NIV).

God has shown me that no obstacle is too great for His grace. His peace is rooted in his unchanging character, which is not dependent on our circumstances. When we struggle, we simply need to pray to Him to receive His beautiful and perfect peace that will guard our hearts.

He can and will break the chains binding you and keeping you from living the purpose He has designed for you. I pray my story inspires you to face your own challenges, no matter what they are, with courage and hope, building your faith so you may also become unchained.

I am perfectly imperfect—a testament to faith and the human spirit. My story is one of loss and pain, struggle and perseverance, healing and restoration. Through God's grace, I have gone from despair to living a life full of purpose. And so can you!

*I can do all things through Christ who gives me strength* (Philippians 4:13 NIV).

# Breaking Chains of Loneliness

By Connie A. VanHorn

What happens when we cry out to God in loneliness and desperation? He sends an army!

God wants us to cry out to Him for help, and in response, He sends help.

> The righteous cry out, and the Lord hears them; he delivers them from all their troubles (Psalm 34:17 NIV).

Loneliness can make us feel isolated and disconnected from the world, putting us in a dark place from which it is incredibly tough to exit. Staying in a place of loneliness can prevent us from receiving help and enjoying the community God longs to provide us. It can make us miss out on the blessings of connection and support that can come from others.

Even more striking, when we allow ourselves to stay isolated, we can inadvertently walk away from the purpose God has prepared for us!

So many different things can hold us captive in loneliness—shame, guilt, or feelings of unworthiness that surface as we engage with others. I've personally felt the weight of all of these in my life. I've stayed in loneliness for longer than I needed to because I was afraid to open up to others, fearing rejection.

Sometimes, the weight of our problems can be so heavy that it seems easier just to stay quiet. But let me share what I've learned: there is power in the telling!

*Faith Unchained: Climbing to Freedom by God's Grace*

Breaking the chains of loneliness requires us to take the first step—telling a trusted friend, joining a group or ministry (like Women World Leaders!), or finding a church community. God uses other believers to lift us up and encourage us, and by stepping out of our comfort zones, we create space for those connections to grow into something beautiful!

I love the example in the story of Elijah in 1 Kings 19. After a huge victory over the prophets of Baal, Elijah found himself isolated, feeling alone, and fearing for his life. He fled into the wilderness, where he expressed his feelings of loneliness, even asking God to take his life.

God responded to Elijah's loneliness in a powerful way. He provided an angel to bring Elijah food and water, strengthening him for the journey ahead. God then spoke to Elijah, revealing to him that he was not alone. This encounter not only addressed Elijah's physical needs, but it also reminded him of the greater community and purpose he was a part of, ultimately helping him overcome his feelings of isolation.

God has the power to transform our loneliness and pain into a greater purpose. Even in our most challenging moments, He is aware of our struggles and can offer the support and encouragement we need to overcome feelings of isolation.

When we open our hearts and allow others into our space, we are not just inviting help into our lives, but we are allowing God to work through us to be a source of hope and light to others who may also be struggling with loneliness.

Let's break the chains of loneliness together and enjoy the community God has created for us.

. . . . . . . . . . . . . . . . . . . . . . . . . . . . . . . . . . . . . . . . . . . . . . . . . . .

# Tiffani McPadden

Tiffani McPadden is a compassionate dental assistant at Premier Community Healthcare, a certified recovery coach, a board member of The Hope Shot, and a prevention facilitator with Alliance for Healthy Communities. Through her personal and professional experience, she advocates for healing, hope, and prevention in her community.

Tiffani shares her powerful journey of resilience, overcoming addiction, grief, and loss. Her story honors the memory of her mother, Kathleen McMaster, whose love and belief in her continue to inspire Tiffani's life of service.

Tiffani's work reflects her unwavering commitment to helping others find light after darkness. She is a proud wife, mother of five, and grandmother, drawing daily strength and purpose from her faith and family.

Tiffani McPadden proves that healing is possible—and that love, especially a mother's love, endures forever.

# Through the Lens of Grace

By Tiffani McPadden

> *Even though our outer nature is wasting away, our inner nature*
> *is being renewed day by day. For this slight momentary affliction*
> *is preparing us for an eternal weight of glory beyond all measure,*
> *because we look not at what can be seen but at what cannot be seen;*
> *for what can be seen is temporary, but what cannot be seen is eternal*
> (2 Corinthians 4:16–18 NRSV).

I was raised in the heart of the church, surrounded by its teachings, immersed in its fellowship, and deeply anchored in a sense of belonging to God. Faith wasn't just a part of our lives—it was the foundation upon which our family stood. Every Sunday morning and evening, as well as Wednesday nights, my family and I faithfully gathered at our local church. Together, we joined services, participated in programs, and embraced events designed to radiate God's love into our community.

The melodies of my childhood still linger in my soul—"Jesus Loves Me" sung with innocence and joy, and the hum of "Amazing Grace" resonating with unshakable truth. Weekly Bible memory verses guided my spiritual journey, beginning with the cornerstone of Scripture, John 3:16: *For God so loved the world, that He gave His only begotten Son, that whosoever believeth in Him should not perish, but have everlasting life* (KJV).

These words weren't just recited—they were planted deep in my heart, shaping my understanding of God's immeasurable love and His desire for a relationship with me. His love wasn't just a story; it was a living promise.

Faith ran deep in our family, anchoring us through generations. My dad's family is Christ-fearing, and my bonus dad's family reveres the Lord. My maternal grandparents, Jim and Dena McMaster—known to me as Grandpa and Grandma Mac—lived their faith boldly as missionaries in Senegal, West Africa, serving with New Tribes Mission. After returning to Florida, my grandfather continued his ministry, becoming a deacon and then a pastor, while my grandmother wrote inspiring articles for the mission's magazine. My Aunt Krystal's family were also missionaries in Senegal. My Aunt Kim's family is God-loving, and my Uncle Kevin, who lived on the edge, often shared how God showed up for him as well.

My parents stayed busy in church small groups. My mother, in particular, was a beacon of faith. She lived with an unshakable trust in God, leaning into Him during difficult seasons and sharing His love with everyone she encountered. This connection fostered a love for people she didn't fully understand but chose to embrace.

In elementary school, I was a diligent student—hardworking, attentive, and always giving my best. A social butterfly, I befriended everyone while remaining a quiet observer, seeing life from every angle.

The school counselor was my favorite person to visit. Our conversations fueled my curiosity, expanding my mind and unlocking new levels of awareness. During this time, my reality became a split view. Through one lens, I viewed life as shaped by my family and my understanding of God. Through the other, I saw life shaped by the worldly events unfolding around me. And as a new level of maturity emerged, events began to affect my inner psyche and belief system. Quietly, I started questioning God.

You see, my sister and mother were experiencing life on life's terms while I watched from the sidelines, questioning: *If God loves us and we serve Him faithfully, why does He allow these frightening things to happen? Why do we live by certain principles that set us apart from the world yet still remain part of it? If He has the power to change our circumstances, why does He allow His people to endure such hardships?*

My view of God was beginning to shift into a negative light. I began to wonder, *What is the point of living for Him if His people face the same struggles as those who don't?* I felt trapped in a tug-of-war between faith and doubt.

My heart wrestled with the paradox of faith—trusting a God whose ways I couldn't fully grasp and whose plans I couldn't always see. I continued attending church with my family but filtered every sermon through my worldly lens. I questioned, doubted, and poked holes in what I heard until I ultimately denied both faith and God.

As I grew older, the questions only grew louder. By middle school, I had set aside my lens of faith, no longer leaning on the teachings and truths that once guided me.

These years were defining—weird, fragmented, and choppy. I began to construct my own framework—a patchwork of ideas shaped by what I thought was right, good, and, above all, fun. I ventured into the ways of the world, blurring the moral boundaries my parents had set. The places I went, the things I did, the conversations I entertained, the mockery I laughed with, and the company I kept—I thought I was finally living the "real life."

The ways of the world felt thrilling and exciting. Yet, alongside the highs came moments that were low, frightening, and dangerous. There were firsts—alcohol, drugs, and sexual experiences. But there were also firsts in pain—abuse, abandonment, and slander. The world wasn't just thrilling; it was miserable, too.

In my lowest moments, my soul cried out to God, but then my willful mind remembered I had set aside my spiritual lens. I manipulated others to meet my needs, all while convincing myself I was a good person who didn't need God.

When my mother fell into depression, I discarded my lens of God altogether. I wanted nothing to do with Him or His ways. Abandoning my faith completely, I dove into rebellion without hesitation.

This marked the start of a dark chapter—years of pain, poor choices, and the heavy weight of separation from God. Yet, through it all, a gentle whisper remained—the Holy Spirit was persistently nudging me back to Him. And I now recognize that the prayers of my parents, grandparents, and family carried me through.

For the next fifteen years, my life was a blur of sin and brokenness. Alcohol and marijuana became constants in my life, offering only a false sense of escape. I dropped out of high school my freshman year due to pregnancy. Moving in with my boyfriend, I convinced myself that I could build a life apart from my family and faith.

When my parents issued an ultimatum—to marry or move back home—I chose marriage, rushing into a union that quickly unraveled. More of life on life's terms—wrong friends, harmful environments, and substance use—led to divorce just a year later. By the age of 17, I found myself a single mother, broken and overwhelmed, fighting desperately for custody of my daughter. The weight of my choices pressed heavily on my heart, and the fragments of the life I had tried to build lay shattered around me.

And yet, God never left me. Even through the chaos, I was blessed to witness God's presence in my mom's spirit. She was so different—in the best ways— and I wanted what she had. She shared God with me, and I made an effort to reconnect with Him.

His presence was a gentle whisper in my soul, a quiet yet unwavering reminder that He was still there, patiently waiting for my return. In rare moments of stillness amid the chaos, I felt Him near—glimpses of His unfailing love, assuring me that even in my brokenness, He had not given up on me. *The Lord is near to the brokenhearted and saves the crushed in spirit* (Psalm 34:18 RSV).

While I struggled to piece life together, navigating shared custody of our daughter between two homes, a motorcycle accident introduced me to prescription painkillers. The numbing of physical pain quickly gave way to clouded judgment and set me on a deeper spiral into darkness.

During this time, I signed away my parental rights for my daughter—a decision made in a medicated haze but one that pierced my soul with unbearable regret when the fog lifted. Consumed by anger and resentment, I blamed God.

The devil whispered, "How could God allow such pain if He claims to love you?" The whispers grew into shouts: "Look at the mess He put you in!"

My drinking escalated, and I sought solace in toxic relationships, partying, and fleeting pleasures that left me feeling emptier than before.

I worked various jobs, made new friends, partied, and bar-hopped, only to find myself in dangerous situations once again. I kept manipulating others to meet my needs, all while convincing myself I was a good person who didn't need God. This lifestyle eventually led me to meet Justin. We shared mutual friends and spent every night partying, only to wake up, go to work, and then do it all over again. Before long, I moved in with him and soon discovered I was pregnant.

We moved into a new home and prepared for life together as a blended family—besides the baby we were having together, Justin had two children, and I had one. I kept in touch with my family but maintained distance, knowing I wasn't living within the boundaries they had set. Shame became the wall that separated us.

The Holy Spirit continued tugging at my heart, reminding me of the faith and family foundation instilled in me. My uncle and aunt stepped in, helping me fight for my parental rights to regain time with my daughter.

Through the pregnancy and court hearings, my longing for God grew. My worldly perspective crumbled in the light of redemption. I clung to my family's faith and listened to their prayers.

Shortly after I gave birth, the courts restored my parental rights for my first child, and with it came a prescribed parenting plan. Days turned into years. Justin and I built a life around our blended family while my desire for faith in God remained.

> And do not be conformed to this world, but be transformed by the renewing of your mind, so that you may prove what the will of God is, that which is good and acceptable and perfect (Romans 12:2 NASB).

I wish that were the moment I turned my life around and ran to God, but I was not yet ready to surrender. I was navigating life as a girlfriend, mother, and best friend. Amid the uncertainty of things around me, my deep soul connection with Justin was a constant.

Justin worked hard in drywall while I stayed home. Our older children visited, and one eventually moved in. We were figuring out parenthood while still partying at home. Many of our friends had young kids, too, creating the illusion of normalcy as we indulged in "righteous carousing" once the kids were in bed. And it didn't take long for drinking and other substances to become frequent again.

Then Justin's worst nightmare happened—his mother passed away. This devastating loss escalated our nightly partying, which became a way of coping. The partying led to countless fights and sour nights. We kept our families in the dark; no one truly knew how bad things had gotten.

Eventually, life reached a breaking point   it was no longer working for us.

Searching for change, I decided to enroll in college. Shortly after, we received a devastating call that my Grandma Mac had passed away. In my grief, I made a promise to start living in a way that would honor her memory. This promise sparked a shift in my heart—God became important, and I began to see life through the lens of His grace.

As Justin and I navigated life, my mom and I grew closer. I also discovered

I was pregnant with our second child. My mom urged me to surrender my lifestyle, embrace my relationship with God, and share that gift with Justin and our children. She believed in our family and was confident we could thrive if we refocused on God. Her words of faith were gentle reminders to stay steadfast.

*Let us not become weary in doing good, for at the proper time we will reap a harvest if we do not give up* (Galatians 6:9 NIV).

We welcomed our second child, moved into a new home, and focused on growing Justin's drywall business. I enrolled in dental assisting school, reading my Bible and devotionals with my mom to honor Grandma Mac's legacy. We worked to connect with both sides of our families, and life seemed to be moving forward.

Our children were healthy and cared for, Justin's business was thriving, and I completed dental school, landing a job. We worked hard, shared the same circle of friends, and raised our children alongside theirs. On the surface, we looked like a thriving, functional family.

Then came the night that shattered the illusion.

What we expected to be a fun, typical evening turned into a nightmare. I became a victim of drug-facilitated sexual assault—a moment that shattered me to my core. I felt dead inside—like black, decrepit decay had overtaken my soul. But instead of turning from God like I had in the past when things bottomed out, God became my best friend. In my darkest hour, I clung to Him, desperate for light amidst it.

My mother helped me sift through the overwhelming emotions, providing support and guidance while Justin took care of things on the home front. This made space for me to allow God's restoration to begin. When I finally fully surrendered and desperately begged God for His will, He breathed new life into me. *Restore to me the joy of your salvation, and grant me a willing spirit, to sustain me* (Psalm 51:12 NIV). God answered my plea instantly. I felt unworthy—yet deeply grateful.

Justin had been doing unlicensed drywall work, and someone reported him to the state. What seemed like a setback became a blessing—it pushed Justin to study, pass the exam, and earn his state license. We were striving to live with integrity.

We moved into a new home, embracing a healthier lifestyle—seldom drinking and avoiding substance misuse. But time and again, we failed. A promise of "just one drink" on the weekend often ended with an empty bottle three nights later.

Finally, Justin joined a recovery program, attending meetings every night for 90 days. This became the turning point—where everything began to rise with God's presence. Following His lead, we transformed our lives by changing our people, places, and things.

We joined a community that lived substance-free and practiced spiritual principles. Through them, we met God in a new way, seeing Him with fresh clarity. As we centered our lives on spiritual truths, I began working from home for our drywall business, and our approach to family, parenting, friendships, and work was completely transformed.

We found joy in a substance-free life—vacations, zoo trips, beach days, nature walks, skating, movies, birthday parties, and simple nightly routines. We became grandparents and welcomed a new niece into our lives. The greatest blessing was my Grandpa Mac officiating our magical wedding, surrounded by family and friends.

As we committed to our recovery, COVID-19 hit the nation. Rooted in spiritual principles, we practiced love, kindness, and goodness in both our personal lives and business community.

God led us to our forever home, and our drywall company flourished, enriching our lives. During this challenging time, God also blessed us with Hub Pro—a business growth support group that carried us through the coronavirus times.

Sadly, my father passed away from cancer, but in God's perfect timing, when my mom visited, she helped us find a church to call home. Then life dealt another blow—I was diagnosed with ovarian cancer, requiring surgery and chemotherapy. In this season of suffering, I found my deepest connection with God. He carried me through every treatment, wrapping my family in His love.

Blessings followed. One of our children reintegrated into our lives, and God strengthened our drywall business for His glory after we endured an attempt to slander it. Justin founded The Hope Shot, a movement to support those struggling with substance misuse. As we battled cancer and embraced this calling, our family and friends rallied around us. Through it all, we saw God's hand in every moment.

Our faith deepened during a Breaking New Grounds sermon when we realized how the spiritual principles we were living by align with Scripture. The living, breathing Word of God became active in our hearts, breaking chains and unlocking a new freedom. Daily meditation with Him became routine, granting wisdom, perspective, and an unexplainable love for people.

We focused on growing The Hope Shot and, through a partnership with Alliance for Healthy Communities, opened All Ways Center, the first prevention and recovery resource center in our area. God blessed it abundantly, changing lives and enabling recovery to become a lived-out testimony.

Just as things were improving, the greatest blow of my life hit—my mother passed away, shattering something inside me. It took time, prayer, maybe a few screaming tantrums, and the love of my community to gather my broken pieces. God sent a counselor who helped me place those broken pieces in new positions, confirming His goodness.

Looking back, I see how God wove a golden thread through my life, turning every painful moment into a testimony of His grace, one day at a time. My childhood struggles shaped my parenting. My child who was born out of wedlock became a blessing to our mothers. My divorce, motorcycle accident, custody battle, and reckless choices became the very experiences that now allow me to connect with those I serve.

What began in sin, God redeemed—our blended family and our community have become a testament to His greatness. He held my spiritual lens even as I made a mess of my life, and when I finally chose to see through it again, I saw Him in everything.

God is so good. He was, is, and always will be—the great *I Am*.

# Breaking Chains of Doubt

By Melissa Gissy Witherspoon

Doubt is a chain the enemy loves to use. It often starts as a quiet whisper: "You're not enough. You're not worthy. Who do you think you are?" Over time, that whisper grows heavier, becoming a weight that prevents us from fully stepping into the purpose God has designed for us. One of the most deceptive forms of doubt is imposter syndrome—that sinking feeling that we don't belong in the very places God has already prepared for us.

When we learn to see God through a lens of faith, trusting His will for our lives, even the devil's deceptive whispers of doubt can become opportunities for growth. Each time doubt tries to creep in and we choose to listen for God's voice instead, our trust in Him deepens. What the enemy meant to harm us, God uses to strengthen, refine, and prepare us for a greater purpose.

In my own journey of recovery, there were many moments when I believed I wasn't good enough. Years of unhealed trauma had buried my confidence and clouded my understanding of my worth. Even after getting sober, I questioned whether I had anything of value to offer. I certainly didn't believe I was worthy of becoming an author or sharing my story. I remember thinking, *Who would want to hear from someone like me?* But when I started trusting God's plan more than my own fear, everything changed.

*For we are God's masterpiece. He has created us anew in Christ Jesus, so we can do the good things He planned for us long ago* (Ephesians 2:10 NLT).

You are not an accident. You are not broken beyond repair. You are not an imposter. You are God's masterpiece, handcrafted for a purpose that only you can fulfill.

Faith reminded me of who I was when doubt tried to define me. I started to believe that maybe, just maybe, God could use my story—even the messy parts. And He did! What began as a simple act of obedience—writing down my truth—turned into thousands of copies of hope shared for free through a nonprofit. I didn't do that. God did that.

The enemy tried to silence me with doubt, but God turned my mess into a message. He took every scar and transformed it into a testimony of His grace. That's what He does. He breaks chains—not just of addiction, but of doubt, fear, and insecurity. Isaiah 61:1 says, *He has sent me to bind up the brokenhearted, to proclaim freedom for the captives and release from darkness for the prisoners* (NIV). That's the promise. We're not just saved; we are set free!

If you're in a season of doubt, take heart. Every time you choose to trust God instead of fear, you grow stronger. Your voice matters. Your story matters. You matter. Let faith be the lens through which you see your future—because when God breaks chains, they stay broken!

Starting today, live in freedom from doubt by speaking God's truth. Your authentic self is beautifully and wonderfully made. The story God is writing through you has only just begun.

. . . . . . . . . . . . . . . . . . . . . . . . . . . . . . . . . . . . . . . . . . . .

# Cindy Rosenthal

 Cindy Rosenthal grew up in the southern part of New Jersey and lived in Albany, New York, for almost eighteen years before moving to Florida four years ago. She has two associate degrees, one in Applied Science and one in Health Services Administration. Cindy went on to complete her bachelor's degree in Health Services Administration and currently works as an Office and Compliance Manager in healthcare. Before going into healthcare, Cindy spent twenty-six years in banking finance as a mid-level manager.

Cindy's greatest joy is music and worshiping the Lord. She spent thirteen years singing with a ministry group called Kol Simcha, which means Sound of Joy in Hebrew. Cindy had opportunities to minister with Kol Simcha all over the world and saw hundreds of people come to know Yeshua (Jesus) as their Lord and Savior.

Cindy has written for *Voice of Truth* magazine and is a contributing author for the Amazon #1 Best Selling Book *Hope Alive: Debilitated to Exhilarated with God*. Her heart is to help people; she hopes her story will inspire and give encouragement to whoever reads it.

To contact Cindy, email: cindalarose@yahoo.com

# Faith—Not for a Minute but for Always

By Cindy Rosenthal

Growing up, I was unaware of what faith truly meant. Now, I understand it well—especially what God says about faith.

> *Now faith is the substance of things hoped for, the evidence of things not seen* (Hebrews 11:1 NKJV).

When I came to know Yeshua (Jesus), I believed life would be easy and all my problems and sadness would be over. However, I quickly learned that this would not be the case. I discovered God does not promise a life free of challenges, but He does promise to be with us as we face those challenges.

> *Let your conduct be without covetousness; be content with such things as you have. For He Himself has said, "I will never leave you nor forsake you"* (Hebrews 13:5 NKJV).

This was a very difficult lesson for me to learn.

At times, I've had to depend on faith and nothing else—longing to understand what God was doing in my life and why He was doing it. As I've grown in the Lord, I've looked for something to learn every day. Early in my walk with Yeshua, I recognized He alone is constant and never changing. I am reminded of that in Hebrews 13:8, *Jesus Christ is the same yesterday, today, and forever* (NKJV).

God has shown me through many experiences just how essential my bold faith and trust in Him is. He has proven His promises to me—He is always the same and always with me.

I'm about to share with you one of those BIG experiences!

I had been looking for my first apartment for many months and finally found it. I moved into it in May 1997. I used all the money I had to furnish it—even cashing in a 401K retirement account. My new apartment was so beautiful. I loved it and felt blessed by it. I would come home from work at night and look around, so thankful to be in that lovely place that God provided. It was just such a sweet little apartment.

One night, three months after settling in, I attended a weekly prayer meeting. The weather was nasty—a thunderstorm with heavy rain. The prayer meeting was at my congregation, a little over half an hour from home. I told the rabbi that if the weather did not improve, I would be leaving at about 8:30 PM. Later, when I looked outside, I saw the conditions were significantly better, so I stayed at the prayer meeting.

It was a wonderful time. We sang songs of praise to God and prayed for many things. I really felt the presence of God in that meeting. I ended up not leaving until almost 11 PM—little did I know what I was going home to. As I drove up the street toward my apartment, I saw many police cars and fire engines. I thought to myself, *There must have been a terrible car accident.*

I was very wrong.

I pulled into the parking lot and was stopped by the property manager, who asked where I lived. When I told her, she said, "We must talk."

I parked my car. I remember screaming and crying when she told me the worst news. While I was at the prayer meeting, my apartment was struck by lightning and burned down.

I listened as I was given details of what had happened. I was in such shock that I only heard about ten percent of what was said. I called my mother; she came right over.

They let me into the apartment to see the damage. When I saw it, I was so shocked I almost passed out. The fire department had to help me. I just couldn't believe what had become of the beautiful new apartment I had only lived in for three months. I was beyond devastated.

The next day, my mother and I were allowed in for exactly one hour to get out odds and ends and some clothes, but that was it. When I asked what happened, the fire investigators explained it to me.

The apartment complex consisted of connected buildings, each with four identical units—two upstairs and two downstairs. The kitchen in each unit was very large; mine had a stackable washer and dryer in the corner.

The lightning had struck the building at the wall of my apartment, right at the corner of my kitchen where my washer and dryer were. The electricity entered the building between the outside wall and the wall of my apartment and struck the power line of my dryer. The dryer had exploded and obliterated the whole kitchen.

The fire then spread upwards, taking out the whole top of the building. As a result, there was no longer a wall adjacent to where the washer and dryer had been; you could see right into what little remained of the apartment across from mine.

Everything in my apartment was completely destroyed—by fire, smoke, or water. The apartment directly below me was leveled when the whole ceiling collapsed due to the weight of everything from my apartment. The common area was destroyed as well.

The only section that was not wiped out was the first floor of the apartment on the other side of the building. It was very interesting—there was a small wall covered with mirrored tiles; not one was even chipped. However, even that couldn't be saved because of the possibility of trapped water and mold behind it.

I could only ask myself, *What now?*

The next days were devastating; it was so hard to wrap my head around what had occurred. I just couldn't understand why God would allow something like that to happen. I didn't know why He would take everything away from me.

I cleaned up the few clothes I was able to salvage. It took several wash cycles to get the smell of smoke out of them. I lost things that could never be replaced, including things that had belonged to my grandmother. When she passed, I received a three-piece outfit she made. It was now destroyed. My heart was broken.

That Friday night, I went to a Sabbath (Shabbat) service. The rabbi told the congregation what had happened and said he was very happy I wasn't there when the tragedy occurred. He prayed for me and asked everyone to please keep me in their prayers.

After service, people hugged me and gave me financial offerings to help. It was comforting. A few weeks later, there was a shower-type party for me to help replace things I lost. People in my congregation were very generous.

It took over five months for the building and apartment to be rebuilt. Over that time, I picked up odds and ends, replacing what I could and working hard to save money as people gave me additional offerings. Eventually, I moved back into the apartment, amazed at the help I'd received to refurnish it and replace much of what I had lost. God provided for me. I lived in that apartment for seven years.

Not only did God provide, but He had also protected me.

During the investigation of the fire and the lightning strike, I learned more about it. It had occurred at approximately 9 PM. If I had left that prayer meeting at the time I told the rabbi I was going to leave, I would have arrived home just about the time the incident occurred. I was told that if I had been anywhere in the apartment, the way the fire had spread, it is not certain I would have been able to get out. Furthermore, if I had been in the kitchen when it happened, I would have been killed instantly when the dryer blew up.

Over the years, as I've thought about the fact that I could have been killed, I've considered what the Lord did that night. He kept me at that prayer meeting to protect me. He knew what was going to happen.

The Lord is always our protection; He alone is where our faith should be.

> *The Lord is my strength and my shield; My heart trusted in Him, and I am helped; Therefore, my heart greatly rejoices, And with song I will praise Him. The Lord is their strength, And He is the saving refuge of His anointed* (Psalm 28:7-8 NKJV).

After seven years, the Lord showed me it was time for change. I moved to Albany, New York, where I spent the next almost eighteen years. During that time, my faith was tested many times. I changed careers and went back to school. Then, in 2013, I had a mutual separation from a job that blocked me from any unemployment support, leaving me with no income. My whole documented income for that year was $7,000. I survived on credit cards and am still working to dig myself out financially. However, I've continued praying and keeping my faith strong.

After those eighteen years in Albany, NY, I moved to North Florida in January 2021, and a year and a half later, I moved to South Florida. While I was packing and getting ready to move to South Florida, something else truly amazing occurred.

Three days before moving to South Florida, I was driving a beautiful rental car while my car was being serviced. I was on my way home from picking up boxes and bubble wrap. It was storming out, and as I was sitting at a red light waiting to turn into the development where I lived, my car was struck by lightning. I heard the strike; I saw it, and I felt it.

Then, it happened again.

I said out loud, "Oh! The car was just struck by lightning." I was scared and sat there for a couple of minutes, not really knowing what to do first.

I called the rental agency. They said they would send a tow truck, but it would take at least an hour and a half. I told them I was in the middle of the street; they instructed me to wait. I then called my rabbi from Albany, NY; he was shocked and immediately prayed for me.

While I was waiting, an off-duty police officer came and looked to see if maybe he could see if a fuse would help to start the car, as there was no sound when trying. This was unsuccessful. He told me to be patient and that he would call other on-duty police; they came to help me. One stayed with the rental until the tow truck came, and one took me home.

The lightning had struck the street and the undercarriage of the car. The undercarriage of the car was fried. The rubber tires had protected me from being hurt or killed.

Several weeks later, I received an email from the rental company. The email indicated that unless I filed a claim with my insurance company, I would be responsible for payment for the damage to the car. The damage totaled $9,600. I wasn't paying a cent of that cost for a lightning strike. I wasn't even sure they believed I had been struck by lightning.

I contacted my insurance company and told them what happened. The claims representative could not believe the rental agency was making me file a claim for damages from a lightning strike. She heard the emotion in my voice and said they would take care of it from there—that I had no further responsibility.

Over the next couple of months, I received a couple of calls for information. Thankfully, I didn't hear anything further.

A year later, I was in my car in my eye doctor's parking lot when I thought I'd been struck again. But that time, the lightning hit a tree less than five feet in front of me. I couldn't move from the car for fifteen minutes. I was pale when I finally walked into the doctor's office. The staff told the doctor, who asked me if I wanted something to calm me down. I was appreciative but told him I had to drive home. As I later returned to the parking lot, I saw the pieces of the tree lying near my car.

It's no surprise that I now struggle with being outside during thunderstorms, especially when driving. People often tell me that South Florida is the wrong place to live if I'm afraid of storms.

A year after my car was struck by lightning, I faced some severe storms that left me terrified. I found myself calling friends and counselors to pray for me because I felt overwhelmed. Counselors and professionals diagnosed me with post-traumatic stress disorder (PTSD), a label I was reluctant to accept. However, I had to reflect on my reactions during those storms and consider that perhaps they were correct.

The key question was what to do next. Should I continue living in fear, or should I take steps to heal and overcome the trauma and anxiety I experienced? I ultimately decided I didn't want to live in fear; I wanted to embrace God's faith, so I knew I had to take action.

> For God has not given us a spirit of fear, but of power and love and of a sound mind (2 Timothy 1:7 NKJV).

I've had to learn to focus on the Lord whenever I am in or approaching a storm. I pray when I look at a weather report and see that lightning is possible, especially if I have to go out or drive. I use the scripture above along with Psalm 91:11-12 to stay focused on God.

*For He shall give His angels charge over you, To keep you in all your ways. In their hands they shall bear you up, Lest you dash your foot against a stone (Psalm 91:11-12 NKJV).*

I read and pray these scriptures every morning. They are powerful.

Circumstances and events have tested my faith, but God has strengthened it by staying with me continuously.

We are strengthened in our faith as we stay close to God. And we can be assured that He will always stay close to us. As Christ-followers, we can share Abraham's commitment to God's promise and reap the benefits of faith as he did. *He did not waver at the promise of God through unbelief, but was strengthened in faith, giving glory to God, and being fully convinced that what He had promised He was also able to perform* (Romans 4:20-21 NKJV).

Although I have been saved and have been promised eternal salvation in the arms of our Father, on this earth, I still experience trauma and face challenges that are difficult to navigate. Perhaps you can relate. In many ways, faith is a choice. God can use every experience we go through as an opportunity to test our faith and deepen our relationship with Him.

As stated in James 1:2-3, *My brethren, count it all joy when you fall into various trials, knowing that the testing of your faith produces patience* (NKJV). While I may not know what the Lord has in store for my future— and neither does anyone else—I am certain that God has seen me through all I have faced, and He will continue to do so. With that in mind, I can— and always will—place my trust in Him.

God will keep me safe and direct my path. And He will do the same for you.

*You will show me the path of life; In Your presence is fullness of joy; At Your right hand are pleasures forevermore (Psalm 16:11 NKJV).*

I attend service on the Sabbath (Shabbat), where many prayers are shared that are comforting and uplifting. There is a prayer of blessing said at the end of every service that sometimes brings me to tears. It comes from Numbers 6:24-26: *The Lord bless you and keep you; The Lord make His face shine upon you, And be gracious to you; The Lord lift up His countenance upon you, And give you peace* (NKJV).

All I have gone through has changed my understanding of faith from something vague and distant to a powerful force that is present in my life. I now recognize faith is not just for a season; faith is a lifelong journey with God—one that calls for boldness.

With my faith unchained, I am free from the grip of fear and ready to walk into the future with confidence, trusting His plan. My solid faith gives me the courage to face anything head-on, including the storms.

I pray if you don't yet have that kind of faith, you will allow God to develop it in you, too. I can promise He will. He is a patient and ever-present God who is always working in our lives. I mean, how many people can say they have been hit by lightning twice?

# Breaking Chains of Envy

By Connie A. VanHorn

*A heart at peace gives life to the body, but envy rots the bones* (Proverbs 14:30 NIV).

Have you ever experienced feelings of jealousy or been caught in a rut of comparing yourself to others? Certainly, we are all tethered by and battle chains of envy at different times in our lives.

Envy can weigh us down, stealing our joy, peace, and, at its extreme, our purpose. Envy can lead us to compare ourselves to others and give rise to feelings of inadequacy, resentment, unnecessary competition, and stress.

Here's the good news! God calls each of us to a different path, and He has perfectly designed *your* path specifically for *you*.

By focusing on all God has blessed us with rather than what we think we lack, we will begin to break free from the chains of envy. After a time, we will start to recognize that God has perfectly positioned us to fulfill His plan.

When I first gave my heart to Jesus, I was stuck in the comparison trap. I would constantly compare myself to the Christian women around me, hearing whispers from the enemy that said, "You will never be as good as them." I would tell myself, "They are prettier, smarter, more put together, and know the Bible better than I do."

I struggled to silence those negative voices and see myself through God's eyes. This created unhealthy feelings of envy and held me back from my calling.

But God's Word tells us who we are!

The more I learned about God through His Word, the more my self-view shifted. I started to see myself and the beautiful women around me for who God made us to be, and my perspective changed.

I now know that we all grow at different speeds and have special and unique gifts and opportunities from God. So, I stopped comparing myself to others and, instead, celebrated the growth and successes that God continually gives each of us!

If you feel stuck in envy, remember that God has a special plan for your life. By recognizing His goodness in your own life, you can have a heart filled with gratitude rather than envy. Pray and ask God to help you release any feelings of envy you have towards others. Pray for a heart that finds joy in the blessings and strength to break free from comparison.

God has a unique journey for you. His plans are always good—embrace them and break the chains of envy in your life.

*For you created my inmost being; you knit me together in my mother's womb. I praise you because I am fearfully and wonderfully made; your works are wonderful, I know that full well* (Psalm 139:13-14 NIV).

*Dear God, Thank You for the gift of community with other believers. Teach us to celebrate the successes of others and praise You for our own blessings. Fill our hearts with gratitude and contentment, knowing that Your plans for us are perfect. Thank You for the beautiful path You have perfectly prepared for us. Amen.*

# Lynn Strickland

With 30 years of experience as a nurse, primarily in home care, Lynn currently serves as the Vice President of Education for Concierge Home Care. She is dedicated to making an impact on the lives of seniors in their communities.

Lynn achieved the title of bestselling author with *Hope Alive,* in which chronicles her journey through COVID-19. This experience also inspired her to open a nutrition club, where she and her family serve their North Carolina community.

Lynn enjoys making memories with her family through board games, cookouts, and travels. She serves in her local church, on the praise team, and works with youth as their camp nurse.

Lynn's faith has been a cornerstone of her life, nurtured by her wonderful grandmothers. She believes that her faith and relationship with God are what keep her here to share her story.

Lynn hopes to inspire readers to cultivate unchained faith!

.

# Just Say Yes

By Lynn Strickland

*And without faith it is impossible to please him, for whoever would draw near to God must believe that he exists and that he rewards those who seek him* (Hebrews 11:6 ESV).

Unchained faith! What does that even mean? Does it mean we do not have to be tied down to unbelief? Does it mean having so much faith that nothing is impossible? Does it mean we don't have doubts and struggles? Those two words, "faith unchained," bring up so much emotion and thought.

*Now faith is the assurance of things hoped for, the conviction of things not seen* (Hebrews 11:1 ESV).

Three and a half years ago, my world as I knew it came to a halt. COVID-19 struck me like a freight train! The night I was diagnosed and found myself in the emergency room marked my first moment of unshackled faith. I had to make some crucial internal choices. *Do I wallow and just let this happen to me, or do I start praying, believing, and claiming that God is going to take care of things?*

The latter felt like the better option. During my conversations with God, which were quite frequent, I experienced a peace that was beyond explanation. His presence washed over me, reassuring me that I would make it through this—that I would live. He urged me to hold on to Him, reminding me that the journey wouldn't be easy.

I decided right then that I believed what He was telling me, and I had to hold on to that promise with every seed of faith I could muster because, for the next several months and years, I would need that foundation of faith to survive.

> He said to them, "Because of your little faith. For truly, I say to you, if you have faith like a grain of mustard seed, you will say to this mountain, 'Move from here to there,' and it will move, and nothing will be impossible for you" (Matthew 17:20 ESV).

After spending 92 days in the hospital—56 of which were in the intensive care unit, one year on oxygen, six months in a wheelchair, and two years of recovery, I'm here to share the rest of my story filled with countless miracles.

His purpose for all of it was more than I could ask for or imagine. He saved me for a purpose, and it would take *FAITH UNCHAINED* to get through all of it!

> Now to him who is able to do far more abundantly than all that we ask or think, according to the power at work within us (Ephesians 3.20 ESV).

Throughout my journey with COVID-19 and my near-death experience, I used social media as a journal to keep friends and family updated and document my testimony in real time. God continually affirmed that this entire ordeal was for a purpose and for His glory. I couldn't shake the feeling that I was meant to write my story to share with the world, but I struggled with how to begin.

Self-doubt began to find its way in, and the enemy tried to hold me hostage in every way possible. I fought so hard against that adversary.

*In all circumstances take up the shield of faith, with which you can extinguish all the flaming darts of the evil one* (Ephesians 6:16 ESV).

*But let him ask in faith, with no doubting, for the one who doubts is like a wave of the sea that is driven and tossed by the wind* (James 1:6 ESV).

Through a friend, I was introduced to an author's class. After praying about it, I decided to take a big leap of faith and purchase the class. The next six months became a whirlwind of God's confirmation and guidance. Each lesson and encounter confirmed that I was on the right path. That step of faith not only empowered me to fulfill God's plan for my life, but it also opened unexpected doors. Shortly after starting the class, I was invited to share my testimony at a women's conference.

Sharing my story with others inspired them, but it also helped sharpen my understanding of my healing and the purpose God had planned through my experiences. It was a powerful reminder that our trials can lead us to these really great moments for ourselves and those around us.

Then, through that same friend, I was introduced to Women World Leaders, and they asked me to speak on their podcast. God was moving and working through many avenues. I finished the author's class and started to work on my book. God had more plans. Through all of this, I was still recovering from my near-death experience with COVID-19.

The following year, Women World Leaders asked me if I wanted to write in their next book, *Hope Alive.* Giving my yes was so scary, but it was also the easiest decision I ever made.

*What if I'm not good enough?*
*What if no one wants to hear about my journey?*

*What if?*

These questions played continuously in my mind, creating a wave of feelings and the fear of rejection. I questioned if my story would resonate with anyone. But deep down, I knew that sharing my story could bring hope and encouragement to others.

I had to push through the doubts, fear, and vulnerability to trust that God had a purpose for my life and the story He had given me.

*BUT GOD...*

I knew by giving God my yes, He would not only show up for it but also become the new voice in my head.

This is what I would hear...

*What if God plans to use you and your story to bring others joy, peace, and hope, all while demonstrating just how awesome He is?*

*What if your experiences—no matter how hard and painful—could be hope for someone who feels lost in the darkness? What if, by sharing your story, you inspire others to trust in God's plan for their own lives?*

So, I simply kept saying yes, not knowing where it would lead. But I was certain that God had saved me more than once—physically, mentally, and spiritually—and that His plans are always better than my own.

> For I know the plans I have for you, declares the Lord, plans for welfare and not for evil, to give you a future and a hope (Jeremiah 29:11 ESV).

*Hope Alive* was released in the spring of 2024, and through that book launch, I was invited to do some book signings at local nutrition clubs near my former home in Florida. This was a dream come true!

During this time, I was not only recovering from my illness, but I was also learning new things, working my full-time job, and writing. I was selling my home of 30 years and moving in with my husband's parents to help care for them for a year.

Then... God completely surprised me!

After this whirlwind of change and new experiences, God did something only He could do—He guided us to buy a house and relocate to North Carolina.

God was orchestrating every single piece of this journey. While visiting nutrition clubs, God stirred my heart, and I felt Him urging me to open one of these clubs in North Carolina.

What next?

"OK, God, I have said yes to everything you have asked, but opening a business in a state we just moved to, in a community where I know almost no one? I'm not sure I can do this."

Old feelings of doubt and fear began to creep in once again with that same old, nagging, negative voice. However, I was more prepared this time and battled through with God's faithful words and reminders.

*This is CRAZY!*

*If God is leading me to do this, why does it feel impossible?*

I felt like I was losing my mind to believe this was a possibility. All I could do was cling to the miracles God had already done in my life. I needed to trust Him again. If I could trust Him to save my life, I could certainly trust Him in this new thing.

I took a deep breath and said, "OK, God, let's go."

*Here we go...*

I talked it over with my husband, my daughter, and her husband, as they would be assisting me with this new journey. Given that I was still traveling back and forth to Florida for work, tackling this alone was not an option or even possible!

They said *yes* almost immediately, and we started looking for a location—still not knowing why God decided this was a good idea. I felt like this was crazy! We did not have a ton of money, and we knew He would have to work some miracles for this to happen. None of the locations we found in the town where we lived worked out; too much money and too much work to get it together.

I started to doubt God's plan again. *Was I actually crazy? Did I hear God wrong?*

*But God's plans are good, and He will fulfill His promises.*

At that moment, I heard a voice, loud and clear: "Not so fast!"

I was sitting in my hairdresser's chair, and she told me that someone was selling their club in the next town over, near where we attended church. So, I spoke with the owner. She let me know that the people who were supposed to take over had canceled the night before.

*What?! OK, God, I hear You.*

She didn't ask for any money for the business; she only wanted someone to take over the rent. They even left us supplies and an ice machine. And the setup was already aligned with our needs, requiring minimal renovation.

Four weeks later, we were open. I won't dive into the details of those four weeks, but I can say that God was present and working through all the renovations, decorations, permits, and inspections to ensure we opened on time, even while I was in Florida the entire time managing my real job. In Matthew 18:20, Jesus says, *"For where two or three gather in my name, there am I with them"* (NIV). I felt His words guiding us throughout the process.

We were working together here and in heaven!

*Now what, God?*

> Jesus said to her, "Did I not tell you that if you believed you would see
> the glory of God?" (John 11:40 ESV).

The word I chose for the year, six months before I knew anything about
opening a club, was "Renew." I selected this word because I felt I had healed,
and it was time to renew my body, mind, and spirit.

> But they who wait for the Lord shall renew their strength; they shall
> mount up with wings like eagles; they shall run and not be weary; they
> shall walk and not faint (Isaiah 40:31 ESV).

When it came time to name the store, God reminded me of my word for
the year, so I chose "Renew Nutrition." The name "Renew"—with a
butterfly— symbolizes my coming out of the cocoon of sickness, disease,
and the chaos of my old life into a new world filled with strength in Christ
and endless possibilities for the future.

Almost dying certainly gives you a new perspective. God brought us
customers—not always as quickly as I wanted, but exactly the ones we
needed at the right time. He blessed us with new friends, a supportive
community, and a place to serve Him. He knew that this location would
be close to our church and that we would benefit from that connection to
carry out His work. When our customers walk into our club, they tell us
they're not just buying a drink; they feel safe, sense something different, and
know that God is present in this place.

We play Christian music over the speakers, and customers have the
opportunity to stop by our prayer wall to submit their requests. They can
also highlight their favorite Bible verses in the store Bible, knowing we will

pray over that wall every day. When they receive their drink, it comes with a handwritten Bible verse, and many times, they tell us it was exactly what they needed to hear that day. All of these encounters are orchestrated by God; we never know who will receive which verse on any given day. Customers often share these moments on their social media, allowing others to be inspired and witness the experience.

Many conversations about life and God happen in our store every day, and He continues to work through this entire journey for His glory to bring others to Christ. Have I experienced doubts, worries, and days when I have cried out to God, reminding Him that He told me to do this? Absolutely, I have—and I still do. But each time, He shows up and reminds me that He has me.

I remember one such morning after a very slow week, wondering, *God, I have to pay the rent. How?* I sat there early in the morning and cried out to Him. *You said to do this, God. I am scared; we have used all our savings, and Christmas is coming. God, why would You put us in this position?*

Tears were streaming down my face when a customer walked in. I will never forget her words. She said, "I'm so grateful for you, your smile, and this place. I feel peace and know that Jesus is here. Know that you are making a difference."

I thought, *God, you certainly know how to remind me with a powerful "I told you so" at just the right moment!*

Not an hour later, another sweet customer came in and said, "This place is more than just selling drinks; it's a safe space."

I understood then that God was saying, "Keep going; I have planned this out perfectly, and it will bring you what you need and Me glory! You just follow Me, and I'll take care of the rest."

*Yes, Lord, yes! I'm Yours; this business is Yours!*

Business has continued to grow every week, and we are now paying the bills, and, more importantly, we are touching lives daily for Christ!

What does *Faith Unchained* mean to me?

It means I'm no longer chained to self-doubt. I can trust God in all things! It means saying *yes,* even when it makes absolutely no sense. Holding on to every promise with all my strength. Believing that God will fulfill His word, even when there seems to be no way. Going to Him immediately when doubts creep in. When others thought I wouldn't survive COVID-19, He knew that three years later I would be writing my second book, living in a different state, owning a nutrition store, and using all of this to bring Him glory and honor!

He is so amazing, and I am incredibly grateful that He uses big storms and messy situations to grow us and His kingdom. I encourage you to find your own definition of faith unchained and to live it out boldly and loudly every day, continuing to just say *YES!*

> *Though you have not seen him, you love him. Though you do not now see him, you believe in him and rejoice with joy that is inexpressible and filled with glory, obtaining the outcome of your faith, the salvation of your souls* (1 Peter 1:8-9 ESV).

Removing self-doubt and learning to trust God can be a crazy hard ride. Here are some things I learned; I pray this helps you along the way.

1. *Acknowledge Your Feelings:* Recognize self-doubt and believe you can change your thought patterns and allow a different voice to fill you with truth.

2. *Ignore Negative Thoughts:* Identify negative thoughts and who they are from. The enemy wants us to stay chained to doubt! God wants to set us free.

3. *Focus on Strengths:* Make a list of your strengths, accomplishments, and positive qualities. Remind yourself of past successes to build confidence. Remind yourself what God has already done!

4. *Set God-Size Goals:* Believe God is bigger; hold to Ephesians 3:20.

5. *Limit Comparisons:* Avoid comparing yourself to others. Everyone has their own journey; comparison can fuel self-doubt and keep you stuck in a comparison trap.

6. *Find Support:* Surround yourself with like-minded friends and mentors who encourage you. Sometimes, an outside perspective can help you see your worth.

7. *Practice Self-Compassion:* Treat yourself with kindness and understanding. Show yourself GRACE!

8. *Go to God in Prayer:* Pray about everything before giving your yes! Seek God's guidance and wisdom through open communication.

Most importantly, *KEEP GOING!* Allow your faith to be unchained as you climb to freedom by God's grace!

# Breaking Chains of Negative Thinking

By Connie A. VanHorn

Recently, I had the opportunity to share about dreaming big for God with my daughter's class. I focused on the concept that we will become what we think about ourselves.

Negative thinking prevents us from the life and purpose God has intended for us.

As I spoke, I used the example of magnets, explaining to the children how negative thoughts can act like a cluster of magnets: each detrimental thought drawing in more negativity as they clump together and weigh us down. This process changes how we see ourselves as we begin to believe the lies our negative thoughts inflict on us!

The devil is so enamored with using negative thinking against us that he even challenged Jesus with temptation and doubt!

In the wilderness, the devil approached Jesus, attempting to lead Him astray with doubts about His identity and purpose. He challenged Jesus, saying, *"If you are the Son of God, turn these stones into bread"* (Matthew 4:3 NIV), pushing Him to question His faith and the hunger He felt.

Instead of giving in to the temptation, Jesus countered the devil's negative thinking by relying on God's Word, declaring, *"It is written, 'Man shall not live by bread alone, but by every word that comes from the mouth of God'"* (Matthew 4:4 NIV).

Jesus' strong belief in the Scriptures helped Him ward off the temptation to think negatively and showed us how dedicated He was to God's truth. Jesus proved that having faith and relying on God's Word is stronger than any temptation or detrimental thought.

God wants us to seek the truth! What we think about ourselves is who we will become. The truth is in His Word! This was a difficult lesson for me to learn because I grew up believing the lies the enemy was whispering in my ears. However, God persistently reminded me of His truth; I just had to choose to listen to and believe His sweet and beautiful words.

We are daughters of God, daughters of the true King. When we embrace our identity in Christ, we begin to see ourselves in a new light. Instead of focusing on our imperfections, let's focus on the truth of who we are—loved, valued, and worthy.

When we do, we can trust that the magnets of negativity will begin to detach, leaving us unburdened and hopeful, feeling as light as feathers as our thoughts shift to the truth about who God says we are.

We hold the power to break free from negative thoughts and replace them with God's truths, allowing us to step into the purpose He has created us for, wearing our crowns with courage and confidence.

You are meant to shine brightly and dream big because you are loved and empowered by the One who created you. God loves you and has a beautiful purpose waiting just for you!

Don't let your own words determine your worth. God has already defined you!

*Now to him who is able to do immeasurably more than all we ask or imagine, according to his power that is at work within us* (Ephesians 3:20 NIV).

. . . . . . . . . . . . . . . . . . . . . . . . . . . . . . . . . . . . . . . . . . . . . . .

# Amanda Spearin

Amanda Spearin is a former U.S. Army Captain who served in Germany and Washington D.C. With a deep passion for criminal justice, Amanda earned a bachelor's degree in psychology from California State University, Fullerton, and a master's degree in criminal justice - forensic psychology from Liberty University. Dedicated to making a difference, Amanda volunteers with a faith-based anti-human trafficking organization and works in criminal defense.

Beyond Amanda's professional and military background, she is an endurance athlete who thrives on pushing physical and mental limits. Amanda has completed multiple 100+ mile endurance events, embracing challenges that test perseverance and faith. However, her greatest joy is her marriage—sharing a love for the outdoors and spending time on the trails with her husband.

Above all, Amanda is passionate about faith and redemption, and she hopes her testimony will inspire others to trust in God's transformative power, no matter where they are in their journey.

# Unchained from Regret

By Amanda Spearin

Time travel would be incredible, wouldn't it? Imagine having the ability to go back and undo a bad decision before regret could even take root.

Regret serves as a stark reminder that we must live with the mistakes we've made. But what if I told you there's a way to have fewer regrets in life? The way to accomplish this is simple: Do God's Word. Notice I said *do,* not *know.* Doing God's Word is vastly different than merely knowing it.

Judas Iscariot knew God's Word. After all, he was one of the twelve apostles. Judas heard Jesus' teachings every day for years, yet he still betrayed his teacher and Lord by leading His captors to Him in the garden (John 18). If Judas had done God's Word from the outset, he likely would have forgone the decision he eventually regretted (Mark 27:3).

The most important thing to realize about regret is that if we give it to God, we can trust He will use it for His glory, empowering us to climb to freedom by guiding us into repentance, transformation, and renewal through His grace.

I became a Christian in 2016. For much of my life, I believed I had no regrets. But the truth is, it wasn't that I didn't have regrets; I had simply convinced myself otherwise. I clung to Romans 8:28 so strongly that my understanding of it became unbiblical.

*And we know that God causes all things to work together for good to those who love God, to those who are called according to His purpose* (Romans 8:28 NASB).

This verse means that God, in His infinite power, uses all things for His glory and orchestrates them for the good of those who love Him. It does not mean God needs our wrong decisions to fulfill His plans.

As a result of misunderstanding this scripture, I never lingered in regret, telling myself, *This is how God meant things to unfold.* Looking back, I realize that may have been a coping mechanism—a way to shield myself from the pain of regret. After all, feeling pain also meant admitting I was wrong. Despite the comfort I found in Romans 8:28, I failed to grasp an important truth: as Christians, we must have remorse for the times we have sinned against our Creator—something I lacked.

God gives us commands and boundaries. The closer we follow Him, the fewer regrets we will have. We must learn to recognize when God is saying *no*, even when circumstances seem favorable.

This is where I lay my case. Despite faithfully praying over a situation, I made a foolish choice when I was newly married. I prioritized my career over my marriage. At the time, choosing what looked like a great opportunity seemed right, but it led to immense regret. Thankfully, through God's grace, I have since overcome it. *Praise the Lord!* My hope for you, my friend, is that sharing this chapter in my life will help you heal from your own regrets and find peace in God's redemptive grace and love.

My story begins in 2023, a year of major transitions for my family. We celebrated college graduations, my brother embarked on his journey in the Air Force, I transitioned out of the Army, and most significantly, I got married!

My husband and I tied the knot at a beautiful hilltop church in sunny Southern California. After the wedding, I moved to North Carolina, where my husband was stationed at Fort Bragg. I had just completed my master's degree and was working remotely as a tutor for Liberty University. Tutoring part-time from home was a drastic change after years of 12–18 hour workdays in the military!

Yet, I wanted more. My passion has always been rooted in the criminal justice field, which my bachelor's and master's degrees reflect. Having served five years as a military police officer, I began missing the law enforcement community. After a year away from public service, I felt the pull to return.

Meanwhile, my husband faced a decision. He could either sign another contract with the military or exit service within the next 18 months. Selfishly, letting the military dictate our next move didn't sit well with me. After all, that was one of the main reasons I left the service.

On top of that, both of our families are from Washington, and we longed to be closer to them. Ultimately, we decided he would leave the military in the fall of 2024 and hoped to move to the Pacific Northwest—Washington, at last!

My husband planned to return to school while I worked full-time, so the job hunt began. I sent hundreds of applications across the Pacific Northwest, enduring interview after interview but receiving no job offers. Then, finally, the breakthrough came. I received two offers, both in Washington. I wholeheartedly believed this was God's way of confirming that Washington was meant to be our home.

Both positions were with the federal government, offering a shift from law enforcement to a more relaxed public service role. One was in Seattle, the other in Spokane. With family in both cities, we weighed our options, but Seattle stood out as the best choice due to its career growth opportunities and thriving tech industry, which aligned perfectly with our professional goals.

Federal hiring usually takes six to twelve months, which is why I started applying a year before my husband and I planned to move. However, I received my final offer in just two months. The agency wanted me to start immediately. Having just married in July, I wanted to spend as much time with my husband and knew he was committed to the military until fall 2024, so I requested a delay. We settled on a start date of November 2023.

My husband and I sought counsel from our family, but truthfully, I had already made up my mind. Still, I couldn't shake the internal struggle. *Is this really God's plan?*

We prayed about it. We asked God to close the door if He wanted me to stay. But the job offer had come, so I reasoned He must have wanted this for our lives. There didn't seem to be any clear obstacle preventing us from making the move aside from the fact that I would be going to Seattle nine months before my husband could join me.

I am an avid planner, and we—perhaps more so I—were focused on the long-term goal: my husband would leave the military and go to school while I worked full-time to pay the bills. Then, we'd buy a house, have kids, and live happily ever after in Washington. I even joked that we could treat it like a year-long deployment, except this time, I was the one voluntarily leaving.

I fixated on the security of having a stable job before my husband left the military because I didn't want to face the uncertainty of that transition.

Though people we loved and trusted understood our long-term vision, my move to Seattle didn't make sense to them. Looking back, this was red flag #1, something we should have considered more carefully.

Red flag #2 was that moving across the country without my husband arguably didn't align with God's Word: *"So they are no longer two, but one flesh. Therefore, what God has joined together, no person is to separate"* (Matthew 19:6 NASB). Granted, we weren't separating in terms of divorce, but we were choosing to live over 2,000 miles apart.

Since our relationship had been long-distance from the start, I convinced myself that we could handle being married long-distance for a little while. I didn't realize that God was about to show me the profound difference between a marriage and a committed relationship.

Red flag #3 was that I am not a city person, yet I accepted a job in a major city. I let my pride take over, knowing deep down that this might not be the best situation.

If I had to pinpoint my biggest regret, it would be October 2023, the moment I signed my offer letter. That single decision cast me into deep sadness and regret.

When the time came for me to leave, packing my things felt surreal. We had just settled into our first apartment together, and now I was *re*-packing my things to go. Getting on that plane was one of the hardest things I've ever done. It was a five-hour flight, and I cried the entire way.

Thankfully, once I arrived in Washington, I stayed with family, which helped ease my heartache for a little while.

The next few months flew by with the holiday season. My husband visited for three weeks in December; it was wonderful. For the first time in months, we were under the same roof!

Being apart made us realize the value of simple moments: morning coffee, reading our Bibles together, and movie nights.

Meanwhile, God was working on my heart. Deep down, I had no peace. Guilt crept in over choosing a "great opportunity" 2,000 miles away from my husband. The supposed stability of my government job was losing its appeal, but I was too embarrassed to admit it even to myself.

I felt lost, desperate for a sign—a burning bush moment from God—to tell me to quit my job and move back to be with my husband. But instead of surrendering, I kept pushing forward toward our long-term plan.

Every day, I walked to work, passing homeless encampments and watching people openly using drugs on the streets. I tried not to let it affect me. I'd arrive at work in the safety of a federal building to my monotonous job— churning out work just to meet numbers. I knew I was capable of so much more.

By March, I started questioning just how sustainable our long-term plan really was. My job required me to be in the office five days a week, with no remote work option. On top of that, there was no employee parking, so I was forced to take public transit every day. These small inconveniences started to pile up, each one making it harder to ignore the growing weight of my regret.

As I was taking the bus home one night after jiu-jitsu, two men started arguing. One threatened to pull out a gun. I was right in the middle of their verbal fight.

I wanted to run, to remove myself from the situation. But I was trapped on a moving bus with nowhere to go. By God's grace, the bus driver pulled over. The moment those doors opened, I darted out. That was the last time I ever took that bus.

My office window overlooked the harsh reality of the fentanyl and homelessness crisis. People were slumped over, casually making drug deals in plain sight, cooking food over open barrels in their encampments, and counting stacks of cash, presumably from drug money. I even saw a man casually walking around an encampment wielding a large machete.

As the weather warmed, the chaos ramped up. Each day, I passed yet another homeless encampment, some just a hundred meters from my home. The news was filled with stories of escalating violence, drugs, and disease. It wasn't just headlines; it was my daily life.

I lost count of how many times I stepped over discarded needles, watched people inject themselves, or saw them collapse in a drug induced stupor. And then there were the gunshots echoing through the night as I lay in bed. Just another normal day.

I was constantly on edge. Five months had passed. Five months of missing my husband, walking past every flag except the American flag, watching the homeless population grow, and witnessing open drug use on nearly every street. It all built up until I finally hit a breaking point.

My burning bush moment came the day after Easter. As unfortunate as it was, the situation completely changed my outlook on life.

I was standing in the kitchen, chatting with my mom over the phone, when she told me that she and my dad were separating. Tears instantly welled up in my eyes. I had known this day might come, but that didn't make hearing it any easier. I held myself together through silent tears and shock.

Without hesitation, I called my husband. The moment he picked up, I was already sobbing. I hadn't sent a text, no warning, just raw emotion. All I could say was, "My parents," and he knew exactly what that meant.

That night was unbearably lonely.

My world came crashing down. I wept, sobbed, and cried out to God. I cried so hard that I was left with a pounding headache. I don't even remember eating dinner.

As my head hit the pillow, my childhood flashed before my eyes. Grief overwhelmed me, the pain unlike anything I had felt since losing a family member. I was facing this tragedy alone, without my husband, because I had chosen to leave.

Regret set in. I blamed myself. Negative self-talk and thoughts crept in: *You took this job. You decided to move across the country.*

About a week later, I flew to North Carolina. I needed to be with my husband to feel his comfort, love, and support. The emotions were overwhelming, and my entire being ached. The news of my parents' separation stirred a mix of emotions: grief, anger, confusion, and even a sense of relief. But above all, it reinforced the importance of having a firm foundation. While it felt like my family had fallen apart overnight, my faith in Christ remained unshaken.

As I sat in the airport, waiting to fly back to Seattle, I called my mom. For the first time, I admitted that moving there without my husband had been a mistake. My mom has a remarkable gift for being a steady source of support. She already knew how I felt, perhaps even before I fully admitted it to myself. With her gentle wisdom, she helped me silence my self-sabotaging thoughts and encouraged me to reconsider our long-term plan.

My feelings of regret continued to stir within me. I knew I needed to share how I felt with my husband, but I was afraid of disappointing him. Moving to Seattle had been a huge decision, and now I was questioning whether it had been a mistake.

I began to see Seattle as a dead end, maybe God's way of closing a chapter before it even started, using the experience to grow me spiritually. God allows us to go through trials; if we go to Him in prayer and submit to Him with obedience and perseverance, He often reveals His purpose.

After nine months in Seattle, I quit my job and moved back to North Carolina. Nothing else mattered except being with my husband. Admitting that I regretted accepting the job and moving to Seattle took vulnerability and humility. For a long time, I struggled with the word regret, seeing it as a sign of failure. But I've come to realize that regret, when acknowledged, can lead to spiritual growth, transformation, and even repentance.

The Bible speaks of two types of regret: regret from a sinful choice and regret from a foolish choice.

Regret from a sinful choice is exemplified by Judas Iscariot. After betraying Jesus, he realized the gravity of his actions and attempted to undo them by returning the money he was awarded for his deed. However, we can surmise that his regret did not lead to true repentance, as he ultimately took his own life by hanging himself.

Peter is an example of someone deeply reckoning with foolish regret. Although he was the leader of the twelve apostles, he ran away when the soldiers came to arrest Jesus. To make matters worse, he later denied his Lord. Peter did not intend to sin, but his actions revealed his spiritual immaturity and fear in the moment. Luke 22:62 tells us that he wept bitterly.

After His resurrection, Jesus, knowing Peter's remorse over his foolish choice, asked to see Peter specifically (Mark 16:7).

I can relate to Peter.

Regret occurs because, unlike God, we are not all-knowing, and we make mistakes. God knew my decision before I made it, just like He knew me before He formed me in my mother's womb (Jeremiah 1:5).

The biblical answer to overcoming regret is confessing it to the Lord. In His love, mercy, and grace, the Lord is faithful to forgive.

> *If we confess our sins, He is faithful and righteous, so that He will forgive us our sins and cleanse us from all unrighteousness* (1 John 1:9 NASB).

I can't pinpoint the exact day I truly repented for my foolish choice; it was a prayer I repeated over and over in the months after returning home from Seattle. But through those prayers, God softened my heart and helped me move past my regret. And friends, the Lord provided even in the midst of this trial.

Today, my husband and I are happily living in Washington, working jobs we would have never discovered had I not moved to Seattle. More importantly, our relationship with God has deepened, both individually and as a couple. What once felt like a mistake, God has used for good. He took my regret and turned it into redemption, reminding me that nothing is wasted in His hands.

If you're carrying the weight of past choices, let this be your reminder: God is still writing your story. When we turn to Him with a repentant heart, He is faithful to forgive, restore, and lead us into the fullness of His grace. Trust Him because even in our brokenness, He is making all things new.

> *Therefore if anyone is in Christ, this person is a new creation; the old things passed away; behold, new things have come* (2 Corinthians 5:17 NASB).

# Breaking Chains of Regret

By Melissa Gissy Witherspoon

Regret is a powerful emotion. When left unhealed, it can become a prison—used by the enemy to whisper lies like "You're disqualified," "You've messed up too much," or "God can't use someone like you." The enemy, also called "the accuser," wants us to dwell on our mistakes rather than God's mercy.

> *"The thief comes only to steal and kill and destroy. I came that they may have life and have it abundantly"* (John 10:10 ESV)

One of the most powerful examples of regret in Scripture is experienced by Peter. Peter was bold, passionate, and determined to follow Jesus. But when pressure came and fear set in, he denied Jesus three times.

> *The Lord turned and looked straight at Peter. Then Peter remembered the word the Lord had spoken to him: "Before the rooster crows today, you will disown me three times." And he went outside and wept bitterly* (Luke 22:61-62 NIV).

At that moment, Peter was crushed by the weight of his failure. His denials of Jesus were based on fear, ego, and self-preservation—worldly desires that separated him from God's will. That's where the enemy loves to keep us: ashamed, broken, and convinced we are beyond forgiveness.

But Jesus didn't allow Peter to stay in a state of regret. After the resurrection, Jesus personally sought Peter out and restored him. As recorded in John 21:15-17 (ESV), Jesus asked Peter three times, *"Do you love me?"*—once for every denial. Each time, Peter affirmed his love, and Jesus responded, *"Feed my sheep."* In doing so, Jesus replaced Peter's regret with purpose.

This is the heart of the gospel: Jesus doesn't ignore our failures; He transforms them. Regret doesn't have to be a chain—it can be the birthplace of repentance and restoration. Romans 8:1 (NIV) reminds us, *Therefore, there is now no condemnation for those who are in Christ Jesus.*

The devil wants to use regret to hold us captive, especially when our decisions are driven by pride, ego, or worldly pressure. But Jesus offers freedom.

> *For godly grief produces a repentance that leads to salvation without regret, whereas worldly grief produces death* (2 Corinthians 7:10 ESV).

We can break free from regret by surrendering our past mistakes. When we confess, repent, and receive His grace, the chains fall off! If you're stuck in regret, remember: God isn't finished with you. Like Peter, your failure doesn't disqualify you; it prepares you for a greater calling. The enemy speaks shame. Jesus speaks purpose.

You are not what you've done; you are who God says you are. And in Him, you are free, chains of regret broken!

• • • • • • • • • • • • • • • • • • • • • • • • • • • • • • • • • • • • • • • • • • • •

# Kelly Williams Hale

Kelly Williams Hale is a speaker, author, and life coach. She is passionate about Jesus and encourages others to deepen their personal relationship with Him. Her teaching and online courses help Christian women walk in their unique calling to bring God glory.

Partnering with the Holy Spirit, Kelly teaches women how to be courageous and confident in Christ. Her speaking topics include spiritual growth, emotional resilience, and leadership.

Kelly is happily married (third time's a charm!), a mom of three—each born a decade apart—delivering her youngest at 44 years old. Kelly is living proof that our mess truly becomes our message and past mistakes don't define future success.

To connect with Kelly, you're invited to join her Facebook group, *Sisters Who Shine,* or visit thebebravelife.com.

# Seeking His Kingdom– Not Their Approval

By Kelly Williams Hale

*Am I now trying to win the approval of human beings, or of God? Or am I trying to please people? If I were still trying to please people, I would not be a servant of Christ* (Galatians 1:10 NIV).

I've always loved being around people, listening to their stories, and learning about their lives. But for a long time, I didn't realize I was also living out a story of my own—a story I was writing with every choice I made, even when I wasn't fully aware of it. In my twenties, I made decisions before I was mature enough to understand their long-term consequences. I married my high school sweetheart when neither of us truly understood what marriage required. Just six months after our wedding and a week before my twentieth birthday, I gave birth to my daughter. By the time I was twenty-two, I was a single mom, holding the pieces of a broken marriage and facing an uncertain future.

With my young daughter in tow, I decided to return to school and pursue a career in graphic design. It wasn't easy, but I found a way for it to work—

including relying on food stamps and government assistance. I did what I had to do to get by, but emotionally, I was struggling. I didn't know who I was or what I truly needed. I was simply surviving. Deep down, I felt lost. It seemed like I had no real choices—just reactions to whatever life threw my way.

Trapped in the cycle of people-pleasing, I couldn't see that I had real choices. Every decision I made was tied to meeting others' expectations rather than honoring my own needs or desires.

We face decisions every day—some small, like which type of bread to buy, and others life-changing, like where to live or whom to marry. But for years, I didn't realize I had the power to choose for myself.

I was the oldest of four children. By the time my mom was twenty-five, she was trying to manage all of us and a busy household. My dad had been drafted into the Vietnam War at nineteen and returned home with painful memories he couldn't escape. He turned to alcohol to cope, and that struggle deeply impacted our family.

I'm not sure my parents knew they could make life choices, either. They were simply trying to survive. They moved through life on autopilot—taking the easiest route, making quick decisions, or avoiding hard choices altogether. I know I've been guilty of the same.

Entering my late twenties, I found myself in a new relationship. This time, I married a man who seemed to have it all together—he was charming and had a good job. On the surface, our life was good. But the red flags were there, and I chose to ignore them. Insecurity kept me from seeing the truth. I had no boundaries and fell into the familiar cycle of hoping things would somehow get better.

I told myself that if I just tried harder or prayed harder, my husband would eventually change. He constantly belittled me and tore me down, and, in my desperate attempt to keep the peace, I convinced myself it wasn't worth speaking up or making a fuss. Once again, I was simply surviving.

One day, while riding in the car with my husband and our eighteen-month-old son, I tried to share how I felt, but he continually cut me off. I felt suffocated. The next day, I scheduled a counseling appointment—I couldn't keep it bottled up any longer.

During one of my first sessions, after listening quietly, my counselor said, "I'd like to recommend a book. *Codependent No More* by Melody Beattie. I think you'll find it helpful."

I couldn't help but roll my eyes. Codependent? My mom had said that for years, but I always brushed it off. Sure, my childhood was rough with an alcoholic dad, but I thought I was fine. Hearing it from a counselor hit me differently. I decided to read the book, which changed my life. It was like a switch flipped. I finally saw why I made—or avoided making—the decisions I did. I understood why I kept ending up in toxic relationships.

I learned that our environment, circumstances, and family dynamics all play a part in shaping us. We don't realize how deeply the experiences we have as kids affect our future decisions. Once I became aware, everything started to make sense.

I had learned to be passive, letting people treat me poorly to avoid conflict. Growing up, I walked on eggshells, always reading the room before I spoke. As the oldest child, I played the peacekeeper—helping my mom, doing my homework, and volunteering. Doing things for others made people happy, and their approval made me feel worthy.

People called me "a good girl" and "so well-adjusted." I wore that like a badge of honor. On the outside, I was the perfect child. But inside, I was searching for validation.

Thankfully, with the help of my counselor, I had an epiphany: I had been controlling people by *not* letting them take responsibility for their actions. *Wait, what?! I was only doing what needed to be done. It wasn't going to do itself, right?*

This "doing" part of my personality followed me well into adulthood. I lived for the approval of others. But here's the truth: I could spend my whole life chasing that approval, and God would still love me the same—whether I did everything perfectly or did nothing. His love is not something I have to earn.

Learning about codependency and the patterns I'd developed in my relationships was eye-opening. The more I read and reflected, the more I realized my marriage was verbally abusive. That realization hit me hard. I had chosen a man who felt familiar—someone who, on a deeper level, made dysfunction feel like home.

During this time, God became my anchor. As I learned more about myself, His presence guided me. I was beginning to feel free—free to be the person God created me to be. Not everyone was thrilled about this "new me," especially my husband, as I no longer allowed him to bully me into doing things his way. I started speaking up, standing up for myself, and asserting myself in ways I hadn't before. I made mistakes along the way, and our communication wasn't great to begin with, so things definitely became rocky.

I learned that I have control over my own situation. I didn't have to let my husband dictate everything. I gave him opportunities to take responsibility for his actions, but let's just say it didn't go over well. The process was tough but necessary.

Ultimately, my second marriage ended. And even though I was learning about my identity in Christ, I felt a lot of shame. How could God use me, a twice-divorced, single mom of two kids from two different men, for His kingdom?

Here's the thing: we will make bad decisions. We will take the wrong turn at times. It's part of being human, and it's how we grow. The key is recognizing that we must take full responsibility when we make mistakes. We can't blame others for our decisions. If we want to step into the future that God has for us, we must own our mistakes, admit them, and seek forgiveness.

Take King David, for example—a man after God's own heart, yet he made some huge mistakes. He slept with Bathsheba and had her husband killed to cover it up. Yikes, right? How do you move past something like that? But the beautiful thing is that God still loved David and didn't abandon him. God knows we are human. He created us with all our flaws, and He's not surprised when we mess up. The truth is, God doesn't abandon us when we fall short—He's right there, ready to help us get back on track.

We may stumble. Our mistakes may delay God's plans, but He will not forsake us. His love remains constant, no matter what. And the beauty of God's grace is that He allows us to take the test again. And again. And again. His love and patience are limitless.

David's story is a powerful reminder of God's faithfulness, even after failure. As a young shepherd, David saw God protect him from a bear and a lion. So when he faced Goliath, he didn't rely on armor or strength—he relied on faith, trusting God for victory. And isn't it so easy to forget how often God has carried us through hard things? Like David, we must remember our past victories.

For a long time, I thought I wasn't "good enough" for God to love me—especially knowing how many mistakes I'd made. I used to beat myself up over my shortcomings. But God's love isn't based on our perfection. It's not about being flawless; it's about His grace and mercy. And His grace is available to all of us—no matter where we've been or what we've done. His love doesn't change based on our performance.

It's easy to step away from God when we know we've messed up, but that's exactly when we need to move toward Him. He's not disappointed in us; He's waiting for us to come closer.

During my thirties, God truly showed up—or, more accurately, I fervently pursued Him. My faith was growing. I began reading the Bible and praying more, trying to understand who God wanted me to be. No longer just going through the motions, I started to hear His voice.

When I came across Jeremiah 29:11, it hit me like a ton of bricks. *"For I know the plans I have for you," declares the Lord, "plans to prosper you and not to harm you, plans to give you a hope and a future"* (Jeremiah 29:11 NIV).

Understanding and accepting God's grace is crucial to finding freedom from our past. When we realize grace isn't something we earn but a gift freely given, we can finally stop striving for perfection and embrace our humanity. For me, embracing this was a slow process that required time and patience.

> *But he said to me, "My grace is sufficient for you, for my power is made perfect in weakness." Therefore, I will boast all the more gladly about my weaknesses, so that Christ's power may rest on me* (2 Corinthians 12:9 NIV).

When you were young, were you asked, "What do you want to be when you grow up?" As a little girl, I don't remember wanting to be anything specific, but I do remember wanting to be like certain people.

Growing up in the '70s and '80s, we didn't have the distractions of cable TV or the internet. Life was simpler, yet I still compared my world to the lives I saw on screen. My heart longed for what looked like a perfect life.

One of my biggest influences was *Little House on the Prairie*. Laura had Pa, the perfect dad, and Ma, the perfect mom. In each episode, she learned lessons about love and family; by the end of the hour, everything always worked out. I longed for a sense of belonging and the perfect family dynamic I saw portrayed. More than anything, I wanted to be Laura Ingalls.

We all compare ourselves to others, especially when it comes to how we look. There's constant pressure on women to fit a certain image—including our figures, hair color, height, and fashion choices. We compare everything—from our spouse to our house, job, and finances. This robs us of joy and causes us to reject the unique and beautiful person God created us to be.

When my son Dallas was three, he memorized Psalm 139:14: *I am fearfully and wonderfully made* (NIV). It was a perfectly timed reminder for me.

God knew us even before we were formed in our mother's womb. Before we had a name, we were already a bright, shining star in God's eyes.

Our uniqueness is evident in our fingerprints, eye color, and even the shape of our noses. These differences make us who we are. Have you ever recognized that no two blades of grass are the same and every snowflake is unique? It's the same with us—God's design for each of us is intentional and beautiful.

Our differences are proof that God created each of us with individuality and purpose. We have different personalities, skin tones, hair colors, and even quirks—like that cowlick that keeps you from ever having a perfectly smooth hairstyle! So why is it so easy to forget how special we are?

Because we have an enemy who also has plans for us.

The devil loves to tell us that our differences are flaws, saying, "God can't use you. Just look at your imperfections."

I believed those lies for a long time. But the truth is that God creates each of us uniquely for a specific purpose. Our perfect God took the time to create you, and He has big plans for your life.

God didn't just create us with unique features; He also gifted us with special talents and abilities. Some of you may already know what your gifts are. Maybe you love to cook and make others feel at home—that's the gift of hospitality. Perhaps you have a compassionate heart and naturally empathize with others—that's the gift of mercy. You might have the gift of leadership and or encouragement. The key is to recognize and celebrate all God has equipped you with.

> *For we are God's masterpiece. He has created us anew in Christ Jesus, so we can do the good things he planned for us long ago* (Ephesians 2:10 NLT).

When my daughter Christie was four years old, she was telling my dad *all* about her day. At one point, he turned to my mom and said, "Does she remind you of anyone?" Apparently, I was the same way as a child—a big talker. My school report cards always included "talks too much!" I'm so thankful for the gift of communicating, even if I—or others—didn't always see it as a gift.

For years, I tried to fit in. I thought I had to act and look like everyone around me. But God didn't want me to copy anyone else. He wanted me to be who He said I was—a speaker, an author, a woman who encourages and inspires others. These are my callings from our Creator, given to me to use to bless others. Following His call brings far greater fulfillment than chasing validation through people-pleasing. When we serve the Lord, the empty spaces left by past insecurities are filled with His promise and hope.

> *Do not conform to the pattern of this world, but be transformed by the renewing of your mind* (Romans 12:2 NIV).

Turning forty was a huge milestone for me. I had moved into my own house, gotten a great job, and was surrounded by a circle of supportive friends. I was living a life that, although not perfect, was fulfilling. It was the first time in my life that I felt like I was creating the life I wanted rather than just reacting to what life threw at me. My relationship with Jesus was thriving, and I finally fully accepted myself—my mistakes, past, and the messy middle.

In March of that year, I met a woman at a jewelry party. She and I instantly connected. During our conversation, she casually mentioned her son, an artist who painted the mural at the church down the street. Something in my spirit fluttered.

Just a few weeks later, I found myself talking to Buddy, her son. We began exchanging emails about art and life. We had a lot in common, and by

June, we decided to meet in person. When we did, I was captivated by how different Buddy was from what I had expected. He was outgoing, positive, and full of life—a complete contrast to the brooding artist I'd imagined! What struck me most was how he treated me and, more importantly, how he treated my son, Dallas. He didn't just accept Dallas into his life—he became a true father figure, something Dallas had longed for.

A year later, Buddy and I got married. Looking back, I can clearly see how God orchestrated our meeting. I had prayed for a man who would love and care for my children, and that's exactly who Buddy was.

I also became a mother again—at forty-four! I had prayed for another child. Austin has brought so much joy to our lives, and I am so grateful.

Reflecting on the twists and turns of my life, I see how far I've come. The struggle truly became my strength. From the uncertain, insecure woman I once was to the confident, empowered woman I am now, the journey has been anything but easy. But through faith, perseverance, and a deep belief in God's plan for me, I've been able to create the life I always dreamed of.

As I continue to grow, I know God has more in store. One thing we can always count on is change and, with it, the opportunity to evolve. I'm excited to see what God will do as I keep seeking Him first.

Through every high and low, God's hand remains steady. We don't have to spend our lives trying to please people to fill empty spaces or quiet the fear of abandonment. God's grace assures us that we are never alone. When He is at the center of our hearts, we no longer live chained to yesterday's pain. Instead, we walk in freedom—whole, complete, and filled with the joy of serving for His glory. And that is where true wholeness is found.

> *But seek first the kingdom of God and his righteousness, and all these things will be added to you* (Matthew 6:33 ESV).

# Breaking Chains of People-Pleasing

By Connie A. VanHorn

For many of us, including myself, childhood experiences can shape our self-worth and how we view ourselves. Growing up, I faced trauma that made me feel like I needed approval from others to be valued. I learned that if I kept everyone happy, I would feel accepted.

This caused my true self to shrink and created a chain of people-pleasing in my own life. I felt that I had to say yes, be available, and put others' needs before my own, even at the expense of my well-being.

In Luke 10:38-42 (NIV), we learn about two women, Mary and Martha, who experienced the struggle of people pleasing. When Jesus and His disciples visit their home, Martha is busy preparing and serving, while Mary sits at Jesus' feet, listening to His words. Martha feels overwhelmed and frustrated, believing she must be the perfect hostess.

She eventually asks Jesus to tell Mary to help her, but Jesus gently reminds Martha, *"Martha, Martha," the Lord answered, "you are worried and upset about many things, but few things are needed—or indeed only one. Mary has chosen what is better, and it will not be taken away from her"* (Luke 10:41-42 NIV).

How many of us have felt this way as we strive to serve others—whether in the kitchen or even in ministry? It can be hard to tell the difference between assisting others with joy and getting caught up in the people-pleasing trap.

Like Martha, I can easily find myself overwhelmed as I try to juggle too much in an effort to make others happy. This happens even when, or maybe especially when, I'm not appreciated by those I minister to. However, I am learning that while serving others is wonderful, allowing the fear of disapproval to guide my actions is a trap that limits me.

God wants us to BREAK FREE from the focus of pleasing others and seek wisdom to offer care and assistance as He instructs!

When I feel the urge to please others, I ask myself, "Am I serving out of love, or am I doing this because I fear rejection?"

God calls us to serve joyfully, not out of obligation or fear. Helping others should come from a place of love and a desire to help, not from a compulsion to please others, thereby securing our place as "popular" or "necessary to have around."

God loves you because of who you are, not what you do. You can break free from the chains of people-pleasing that hold you captive by asking God to show you your true identity in Him and give you the strength to set healthy boundaries in relationships. Service should reflect your love for God and others, not be a way to seek validation. Rest in the truth that you are enough because of *who You are.*

God invites you to a life of freedom, where you can love and serve without being held captive by the need for approval. Though we are all called to serve in some way, like Mary, there will be times when God calls you to sit at the feet of Jesus and receive His love. This will ultimately empower you to serve from a place of joy and freedom.

Break the chains of people-pleasing by seeking to please God. His will for you is perfect.

. . . . . . . . . . . . . . . . . . . . . . . . . . . . . . . . . . . . . . . . . . . . . . .

# Anavay Taffe

Ms. Anavay Taffe is a fearless warrior of God and a mum to three teenage daughters. She lives in Washington state, where she is an Army reservist, model, author, life coach, and a full-time student online at Liberty University, majoring in Christian counseling.

In her free time, Anavay enjoys writing, studying Scripture, taking photos, spending time with family, being out in nature, and doing God's kingdom work.

Anavay designs Christian apparel discipleship-apparel.creator-spring.com, with part of the proceeds going toward Rising Up Ministries and Children Of the Night—a safe haven for boys and girls who have been trafficked. Her life's mission is to help others, showing them the love of God and how beautiful a relationship can be with Father God and Jesus Christ, our Lord and Saviour.

To connect with Anavay, you can email her at operationletstalk@gmail.com

www.risingupministries.org
https://www.childrenofthenight.org/
https://www.instagram.com/ms_anavay/
https://www.facebook.com/msanavay

# The Warrior Within

By Anavay Taffe

*The thief comes only to steal and kill and destroy; I have come that they may have life and have it in full* (John 10:10 NIV).

Addictions have a ripple effect—they not only impact the individual struggling with them but also affect others around the afflicted person. Many of the choices I made while in my addictions caused pain to the souls of those I loved the most.

Personally, my first addiction was of a sexual nature. While my past misfortunes do not excuse my behavior, they do provide insight into why I engaged in unhealthy, selfish, and sometimes irrational behaviors shaped by my upbringing.

Starting at the age of three, I was sexually molested by my mother's boyfriend. By the time I was four, my mum had died in a car accident, and shortly after, my twin and I went to live with our father. The learned aspects of being preyed on sexually stayed with me, and I, unfortunately, projected that onto some of the children in the neighborhood where I lived, becoming the predator myself.

When we were eight, my twin sister and I were adopted by our grandmum on our father's side because my father's wife gave him an ultimatum: either get rid of us or divorce her. After the adoption, my life transformed into a new paradigm where I learned how to be a child and experienced what it felt like to be safe. The adults in my life respected my personal boundaries, allowing me to avoid compartmentalizing so I could stay strong and just survive.

That safety lasted for just a short period of time. As the saying goes, history repeats itself. The revolving door of sexual violence found its way back into my life when I reached my teen years. I believe the life-changing circumstances I was put in at various stages in my life are what ultimately led to my sexual addiction.

When I was fourteen, my grandparents uprooted us, taking us from Rainier, Oregon, to Naples, Idaho. That is when that revolving door again swung open. Even though my grandparents provided for my basic needs, they were not there for me or my sister emotionally, so I eventually sought attention and validation from other people.

Within the first year of living in Idaho, I became good friends with a girl at my school. One day, an opportunity to go home with my new friend for a sleepover presented itself. I called my grandmum and asked if I could go; she said no because it was a school night, but I went home with her anyway. What happened after I got to my friend's house is a blur. It wasn't until recently, during a Holy Week pilgrimage that I took with the LORD in 2024, that I came to understand the extent of what happened to me that dark night.

My friends' parents had gone out of town. Initially, just me, my friend, and her eighteen-year-old brother were in the house. What I remember is fragmented, at best; the memories that have surfaced are like a movie being played on repeat. In one scene, there is a man giving me a drink. In another, that same guy is taking advantage of me.

The next day, I went to school and acted like nothing had happened because

I remembered very little of that night. I thought maybe I had too much to drink—I had never drunk before, and I remembered having only one beer. During recess, I passed out and was taken to the hospital. I was given various tests; a certain type of drug showed up in my system, which confused me because I didn't do drugs, and I didn't remember being offered them when I was with my friend.

Over the years, I tried to make sense of what happened. Deep down, I knew there was something more. At times, it was frustrating because it was like trying to put a jigsaw puzzle together, but the puzzle pieces seemed to be eluding me. It wasn't until I went on one of my intense healing journeys in September 2024 that the reality of what happened was brought to the surface.

I rented a cabin for a few days in the same Idaho town where I had lived as a young teenage girl. While I was isolated among the thick forest of western red cedars and Douglas-fir trees, I spent my days driving to the places that held both strong and faint memories and praying to Yahweh about what happened.

The LORD revealed to me that my fragmented memories of that night weren't some delusion. These memories that I blocked out were of four men from the Ku Klux Klan, and they were very much real.

Over the years, I had a fear of white men who looked anything like the men who attacked me that night. I always wondered why I was so terrified of anyone who resembled them. I just assumed it was because the majority of men I encountered when I was sexually trafficked were Caucasian. When the LORD showed me what happened that night, I felt like I had been violated all over again, and I struggled with coming to terms with it.

I fought against feelings of anger toward the men who hurt me because I was just fourteen years of age. Until then, I was living a life of somewhat normalcy. I didn't even have a boyfriend at the time; I was going to school and doing the things a typical teenager does. Out of everything that has happened to me throughout my life, the events of that night anger me the most. Thoughts of finding the men and making them suffer in horrible ways played out in my mind, but Yahweh has reminded me that vengeance is His, not mine.

> *Beloved, do not avenge yourselves, but rather give place to wrath; for it is written, "Vengeance is Mine, I will repay," says the LORD* (Romans 12:19 NKJV).

Indeed, our heavenly Father knows best, and repaying evil for evil is not the answer, no matter how someone has wronged us.

> *Finally, all of you be of one mind, having compassion for one another; love as brothers, be tenderhearted, be courteous; not returning evil for evil or reviling for reviling, but on the contrary blessing, knowing that you were called to this, that you may inherit a blessing* (1 Peter 3:8-9 NKJV).

I'll admit—it's hard to accept this teaching sometimes, but I know that one day Yahweh's judgment will come, and those who think they have gotten away with harming a child, or anyone for that matter, will not go unpunished.

I have to remind myself that we are called to love one another as Christ loves us...

> *A new commandment I give to you, that you love one another; as I have loved you, that you also love one another. By this all will know that you are My disciples, if you have love for one another* (John 13:34-35 NKJV).

...and to forgive them just as Christ has forgiven us...

*Be kind to one another, tenderhearted, forgiving one another, even as God in Christ forgave you* (Ephesians 4:32 NKJV).

*For if you forgive men their trespasses, your heavenly Father will also forgive you. But if you do not forgive men their trespasses, neither will your Father forgive your trespasses* (Matthew 6:14-15 NKJV).

*Judge not, and you shall not be judged. Condemn not, and you shall not be condemned. Forgive, and you will be forgiven* (Luke 6:37 NKJV).

Sometimes, following this teaching is easier than at other times. But at the end of the day, I choose forgiveness because the shackles of unforgiveness are like poison to the blood. When I choose to forgive someone, the mental anguish I'm feeling is extinguished, and the sorrow festering inside like a disease evaporates. When we choose forgiveness, peace and healing occur, and the Holy Spirit abides even closer.

After being assaulted by those men at my friend's house, I went into a downward spiral of promiscuity. An older couple who lived not too far from me had an adult son with a daughter my age. I would visit the couple, and when their son would come to their house, I would have sexual encounters with him.

I also met twin boys who were the same age as me. We became friends, and I developed a relationship with their dad, which turned sexual. He groomed me over time; in my naivety, I believed his attention toward me meant that he cared for me and that I was special to him. My grandmother allowed me to hang out with him and his boys because he gave her cigarettes and alcohol. Not only did we hang out, but there were many nights that I would sleep over at their house, travel in their RV with them, and go snowboarding. I was vulnerable and desperately in need of a father figure, and I saw that in this man. When the relationship started with him, I thought it was normal, despite me being a young teen and him being nearly fifty years of age.

By the age of fifteen, I left Idaho to live with my biological dad. I was only there for a few months before moving to Portland, Oregon, where my eldest sister, whom I hadn't grown up with, lived. I ended up on the streets, smoking marijuana and mingling with the hippies. This ultimately led to me being trafficked just shy of my sixteenth birthday. It wasn't until I was nearly eighteen that my trafficker was arrested. I tried to get my life back on track, but the reality was that I was too far gone and broken. I didn't know what normal was. I felt like I was barely hanging on.

Over the years, I attempted to reshape the narrative of all the pain inflicted upon me into a story where I could control the outcome. It was easy to adopt this mindset because I had suppressed so much and became an expert at recalling only the "good" that I crafted in my mind. I convinced myself that the things that happened to me weren't as bad as the haunting flashbacks that lingered throughout the years, telling myself I was merely imagining things. But deep down, I knew I wasn't.

By the time I was 27, I had ended a nine-year marriage that had driven me to the brink of taking my own life. To cope with the PTSD stemming from the physical, mental, and religious abuse I endured during my marriage, I turned to alcohol and marijuana, trying to fight the demons of my past as best as I could. Alcohol, random sexual encounters, and drugs became my means of numbing the pain and escaping the memories that haunted me. Not a day went by when I could go without one or the other.

During this long season of addiction, I struggled to be the best mother I could be for my girls. I had no idea how to cultivate healthy relationships with anyone, which left me feeling alone, isolated, confused, hopeless, and worthless. It was nearly impossible to envision a future for myself, and more often than not, I wished for my life to end. Yet, it was my girls who kept me going.

Despite not having a traditional relationship with the LORD, I prayed to Him constantly, believing that He would deliver me from the hell I was living in. Glory HalleluYah! He did! Deep down, I knew He would come through for me. In 2018, I surrendered my life to Him and was freed from alcoholism and drug abuse. My crippling depression, social anxiety, and panic attacks no longer confined me to isolation at home or led to breakdowns in public.

After I submitted to King Yahshua, the past I had been running from began to surface. The nightmares and flashbacks of the hurt I had endured started to make sense as the Holy Spirit gradually unveiled my tumultuous past. He began a transformative work within me, peeling back the many layers of trauma and revealing the truths of my younger years. This process helped me understand why I had become the woman I was before giving my life to Him, ultimately guiding me to a deeper understanding of my identity as a child of Elohim.

> Therefore, if anyone is in Christ, he is a new creation; old things have passed away; behold, all things have become new (2 Corinthians 5:17 NKJV).

I also believed that I had been freed from my sexual addictions, having remained faithful throughout my second marriage, which I entered into just a few months after giving my life to the LORD. Unfortunately, in 2022, my second husband divorced me because of my calling from the Holy Spirit to join the military. Shortly after graduating from job training, I stumbled. I left AIT (Advanced Individual Training) in Fort Lee, Virginia, and moved back to Florida. For a season, I found myself succumbing to moments of weakness, giving in to my fleshly desires for intimacy with men I was not physically, spiritually, or emotionally attracted to.

Throughout this struggle, I never stopped praying, repenting of my sins, or believing that Yahweh would continue to heal me and help me become a woman of purity. And He did. In 2023, while I was in the mountains of Virginia during Sukkot, He finally broke the chains of my sexual addiction. The Holy Spirit revealed to me that I had soul-tie attachments, something I had previously dismissed as mere New Age nonsense.

Oh, how wrong I was! Soul ties are very real, and if left unaddressed, they can keep us chained to past behaviors and people who no longer serve a purpose in our lives.

When I released the soul ties that were attached to me, it became a beautiful ceremony that ultimately set me free.

> Now the LORD is the Spirit, and where the Spirit of the LORD is, there is freedom (2 Corinthians 3:17, NIV).

I am beyond grateful that my heavenly Father and Saviour has been so loving and merciful throughout this journey I've been on. For some people, the LORD takes away their addictions seemingly overnight, and for others, like myself, it's a process that takes immeasurable faith. The kind of faith that lets us know without a doubt that, in His time, He will free us from our addictions. If you are struggling with addiction of any kind, it is essential to remember to die to your old self daily and pray for the LORD's will to be done in your life.

> Give us this day our daily bread. And forgive us our debts, as we forgive our debtors. And lead us not into temptation, but deliver us from evil: For thine is the kingdom, and the power, and the glory, for ever. Amen (Matthew 6:11-13 KJV).

Dear sister, we will encounter moments of temptation and weakness that may lead us to stumble, but know that Yahweh is always here to lift us up and refine us into the warriors He has called us to be. Perfection may elude us, but we can strive each day to fulfill His will for our lives by turning away from evil.

Remember to stand strong in the midst of the storms of adversity and take heart in knowing that the LORD has made us overcomers. He has prepared us for a time such as this, and our past can be transformed for good; it does not have to define us or shape us into someone we are not.

I love you all, and I pray that my testimony inspires you and fills you with hope, reminding you that tomorrow can be a better day. You are special. You are loved. And you are an overcomer in Christ Jesus, our LORD and Savior.

*A man's heart plans his way, but the LORD directs his steps* (Proverbs 16:9 NKJV).

# Breaking the Chains of Shame

By Connie A. VanHorn

> *Therefore, there is now no condemnation for those who are in Christ Jesus, because through Christ Jesus the law of the Spirit who gives life has set you free from the law of sin and death* (Romans 8:1-2 NIV).

Shame can keep us stuck in our past mistakes. It can keep us from our true purpose and make us feel trapped in a life that isn't what God wants for us. Shame whispers lies, making us believe we don't deserve love, forgiveness, or the grace that God freely gives.

But through Christ, we can break free from the chains of shame and start living a new life full of freedom and completeness with the one who made us.

In the Bible, we read about Mary Magdalene. She was considered an outcast in her society. She lived in a world that labeled her by her past. But when she encountered Jesus, everything changed. He saw her not as a woman defined by her shame but as a precious daughter of the King, worthy of healing and redemption.

After her transformation, Mary became one of the first witnesses of Jesus' resurrection, trusted with the task of sharing the good news. Through her story, we learn that our past does not define our future; our past can be a stepping stone to God's greater purpose in our lives.

When I first gave my heart to Jesus, I was struggling with chains of shame.

My life was far from picture-perfect when I committed my heart to Christ. I was lost and broken. The messiness of my past weighed heavily on me, creating a shadow over my new faith.

I remember thinking, *I am made new. Why don't I feel new?* I kept replaying the mistakes I had made, feeling unworthy of God's grace and of being in the Christian community. The shame felt suffocating. It was keeping me from truly being free and finding my God-given purpose.

But God, in all His goodness, gently reminded me of my new life and the truth found in Romans 8:1-2. When I accepted Christ, I was no longer bound by my past or the mistakes I had made. His sacrifice on the cross shattered the very chains that held me captive for so many years.

I began to surrender my shame to Him, and I experienced the incredible reality of His goodness and forgiveness. Just as He did for Mary Magdalene, Jesus started to replace my shame with His truth: I am accepted, loved, and made new in Him.

You, too, can break the chains of shame in your life. This is not a one-time event but a lifelong practice and relationship with God. Each step you take in faith brings you closer to the freedom that is yours through Jesus.

Jesus has come to set you free. Allow that truth to light every step you take towards your new life and freedom.

. . . . . . . . . . . . . . . . . . . . . . . . . . . . . . . . . . . . . . . . . . . . . .

# Jaime Cowhick

 Jaime Cowhick graduated with a Bachelor's Degree in Psychology and a minor in Christian Ministry in 2016, followed by a Master's in Mental Health in 2020 from Trinity International University. She founded the YANA Recovery Center in Fort Lauderdale, which provides therapeutic support for sex trafficking survivors and women transitioning out of the adult entertainment industry.

Jaime has also worked as a Primary Therapist in various drug and alcohol treatment centers. Currently, she is employed at Camillus House in Miami, where she provides therapy for human trafficking survivors.

As a survivor of sex trafficking herself, Jaime was trafficked for over eight years by her boyfriend in Miami, Florida. She grew up in Springfield, Illinois, born to two drug-addicted teenagers, which resulted in her being placed in foster care before being adopted.

Throughout her teenage years and into adulthood, Jaime faced struggles with suicidal attempts and drug addiction. On June 2, 2017, she surrendered her addiction to Jesus Christ.

Jaime is a member of Calvary Chapel Fort Lauderdale and attributes her survival to her spiritual path, which empowers her to help trafficking victims.

Today, she finds encouragement in the success stories of the women she assists and is driven by her love for Jesus.

# Brokenness Redeemed

By Jaime Cowhick

*But because of his great love for us, God, who is rich in mercy, made
us alive with Christ even when we were dead in transgressions—it is by
grace you have been saved* (Ephesians 2:4-5 NIV).

No darkness is beyond God's grace, no past too broken for His redemption.
God doesn't turn away from us but invites us to bring our afflictions to
Him. My story is heavy, but it is also one of hope, a testament that His grace
is enough and His power to redeem has no limits.

I was born Melanie Ann Clifford-Dillinger on December 2, 1977, in
Quincy, Illinois, to teenage parents, just kids themselves. They were both
addicts and deeply broken.

Everyone has a story, and my biological mother's was one of profound pain
and darkness. She endured years of sexual abuse at the hands of her own
father; there was even uncertainty about whether he was my actual birth
father. I was taken from the hospital straight into foster care—my mother
never even got to see or hold me.

On January 13, 1978, my adoptive parents picked me up from the
Department of Children and Family Services. For six weeks, I had been in

the care of a stranger. Although my birth family couldn't care for me, God had already written a greater purpose for my life. Even in abandonment, He had a plan—one of redemption, hope, and a future.

> For my father and my mother have forsaken me, but the Lord will take me in (Psalm 27:10 ESV).

I was blessed to be adopted, but my experience was far from perfect. People often say adoption is a gift from God—and while that's true, not everyone's journey is easy.

I attended the daycare and preschool where my adoptive mother worked. Since I looked nothing like my adoptive family, kids often teased me, asking, "Who are your real parents?" Each question deepened my uncertainty, sparking an identity struggle that followed me through life.

I believe God's grace was with me early on, gifting me with a love for dance to cope with childhood anxiety and uncertainty. From three years old, I found freedom beyond words when I stepped onto the dance floor or flipped across the gymnastics mat. Movement became my refuge; loneliness faded, and joy took its place. For over thirteen years, dance and gymnastics gave me purpose, healing, and a way to turn sorrow into something beautiful.

> You have turned for me my mourning into dancing; you have loosened my sackcloth and clothed me with gladness (Psalm 30:11 ESV).

At seven years old, I was sexually abused by the son of a family friend. Since his sister babysat me, I was often at their house. I kept silent, unsure of what to do. When I finally told my parents, they didn't believe me.

At eleven, a similar incident happened with a neighborhood boy near a park I often visited. I rode my bike home in tears, but instead of receiving comfort from my parents, my father said I looked ugly when I cried. From that moment, I hid my face when upset, ashamed of my tears.

My adoptive father, a Vietnam veteran, refused therapy for his Post Traumatic Stress Disorder (PTSD), believing it was a sign of weakness. Instead, he carried his trauma into our home, where I bore the weight of his verbal and emotional abuse.

After the sexual abuse, my isolation deepened, and depression took hold. At twelve, I attempted suicide for the first time and discovered self-harm. I began cutting myself as an outlet, slicing my skin like paper, desperate for the emotional pain to stop.

Not long after, I found another escape. Severe menstrual pain led me to painkillers, and I instantly fell in love with how they made me feel. What started as relief quickly became addiction. Later, I was diagnosed with endometriosis and prescribed opiates. Having unlimited access to painkillers fueled an addiction that lasted nearly 30 years.

However, my substance use had begun long before the pills—it started with alcohol.

At five years old, I had my first drink. My adoptive parents were heavy drinkers, and when my dad asked me to grab him a beer, I didn't just take a sip, I took gulps. From that first taste, I was hooked.

Alcohol was always present at family gatherings. As kids, we were allowed to drink as long as we weren't going anywhere. Whenever I could, I self-medicated—drowning emotions, numbing anger, and burying the pain I carried.

At thirteen, I began having questions about my birth family; I was searching for a sense of identity. The lack of answers left me struggling with low self-esteem.

High school only made life more difficult. I kept to myself, only socializing with close friends, and was teased for being quiet. Letting people in felt impossible—I didn't know how to be vulnerable. Frustrated with public school, I transferred to a private one, where I made friends and joined clubs.

Yet, despite the fresh start, I still struggled to open up.

Before switching schools, my parents had taken me to a psychiatrist for attention issues, and I was prescribed Ritalin for Attention Deficit Hyperactivity Disorder (ADHD). However, the guidance counselor at my new school questioned the diagnosis. After hearing about my trauma, she told me I needed counseling, not medication. After multiple meetings, she concluded I had PTSD. My parents said they had already spent enough on therapy. They failed to see the difference between psychiatric medication management and actual counseling and dismissed the suggestion for counseling.

Through it all, I continued getting my prescriptions for pain medication and relied on them more and more.

At 16, my dream of dancing professionally and attending Juilliard was shattered. My knee suddenly collapsed at school, leaving me unable to stand. Rushed to the hospital, I was diagnosed with a torn ACL, torn meniscus, and patellofemoral syndrome. My addicted mind welcomed the pain meds, but my dreamer's heart was devastated. Dance had been my escape, my therapy—and now, it was gone. I delayed surgery as long as I could, but reality hit hard when I had to quit gymnastics and dance.

When I graduated high school, I didn't just leave home—I left the church too. My relationship with God was nonexistent. Church had been an obligation, not a refuge, and deep down, I resented God. If He was real, why was my life filled with so much pain?

I moved to Kentucky to heal from broken relationships and another suicide attempt, but within a week, I met a man from Brazil. Something in me knew I would marry him.

For two years, things felt stable, but then his immigration status became uncertain. He failed his interview, lost his work permit, and faced deportation. We hired an immigration attorney, had a quick courthouse wedding, and entered the process together. When he finally received his green card, we moved to Miami, hoping for a fresh start. But instead of growing closer, we drifted apart.

I took a job as a legal secretary, where I met police officers, attorneys, and judges—many of whom loved to party. So, I joined them. What I thought was a fresh start became another downward spiral. My marriage began to suffer. My husband was sleeping on a futon and constantly chatting online with people in Brazil. I grew increasingly angry, so I sold both the computer and the futon. The next day, while I was at work, he left. I came home to an empty apartment, abandoned once again.

Despite my failed marriage and heavy partying, my life seemed to be on an upward trajectory. I had been promoted and was working alongside police officers and attorneys. But beneath the surface, I was unraveling.

One weekend while partying, I tried cocaine and felt an escape stronger than anything before—even what I experienced with opiates. Experimentation became addiction. I used regularly, spiraling into drinking, drugs, and empty relationships, mistaking control and manipulation for love.

One night, speeding down I-95, I decided I wanted to end it all. With cocaine in my system and chaos in my mind, I didn't care who I hurt—not even myself. But when I got home, something unexpected happened. I cried out to God, the God I didn't even believe in, to help me. And He did.

> In my distress I called upon the LORD, and cried unto my God: He heard my voice out of His temple, and my cry came before Him, even into His ears (Psalm 18:6 KJV).

I called 911 and went to a psychiatric hospital for 72 hours. There, I discovered I was pregnant. For a moment, I had hope, but when I told my boyfriend, his first response was abortion. Wanting to keep the baby, I moved back to Illinois for a fresh start.

My boyfriend's pressure to terminate the pregnancy and my addiction didn't stop. At 15 weeks, I walked into Planned Parenthood and ended my pregnancy.

I didn't realize how deeply that decision would scar me—emotionally, physically, and spiritually. It created a wedge between me and God that I didn't know how to repair. The moment it was over, shame, guilt, and regret consumed me. I sank deeper into sorrow, numbing the pain any way I could, giving myself away for my next high. My life felt worthless.

But even in my darkest moments, God wasn't done with me. I couldn't see it yet, but He was already writing my redemption story, patiently waiting for my surrender.

Instead of surrendering to God, I ran—just as I always had—drowning my pain in drugs and alcohol. I moved back to Miami—where my past quickly caught up with me. My old boyfriend found out I was back in town, and I fell into the same toxic cycle with him. He kept me high while sex trafficking me, subjecting me to rape, threats, and constant degradation. I was numb to the nightmare I was living. Addicted to Xanax, Percocet, and crack cocaine, I was trapped—not just physically but emotionally—in a trauma bond with my abuser. Every time I tried to escape, he found me.

For eight years, I lived this horror, even recruiting other girls into the same life. When I finally broke free, I thought I was safe, but the trauma still controlled me. Seeking help, I went to therapy and was placed on antidepressants. I tried 12-step programs but would relapse within weeks. My therapist told me I couldn't return unless I got sober.

Desperate for something more, I found myself drawn to a church with the same name as the one I had attended as a child. I resisted, but the Holy Spirit kept pulling me to it. God was working—preparing to meet me. *"You will seek me and find me when you seek me with all your heart"* (Jeremiah 29:13 NIV).

I was ready for surrender and change. A pastor referred me to Forgiven and Set Free, a post-abortion Bible study. It took me a long time to make the call—I didn't want to take the class, but I knew I needed help. As I went through the study, I slowly felt God working in me. Though I was still partying, something inside me was shifting. I looked into Celebrate Recovery, a Christ-centered 12-step program.

Around that time, I was diagnosed with cervical cancer. I needed a partial hysterectomy due to having abortions and Human Papilloma Virus. The night before surgery, I cried out to God—the God I still wasn't sure I believed in—and promised Him I would change.

A few months later, I walked into my first Celebrate Recovery meeting at Calvary Chapel Fort Lauderdale. My past still had a grip on me. My trafficker always found me, no matter how hard I tried to escape. But then, I made the choice that saved my life—I moved, changed my number, and cut ties with everyone from my old life.

At Celebrate Recovery, I met a woman who became a pivotal part of my healing. For over a decade, she was my sponsor, guiding me when I couldn't guide myself. I loved how the program addressed all struggles, not just addiction. I often wanted to quit while working the 12 steps, but my sponsor kept me on track. She saw my potential before I did, prayed for me, and reminded me of God's grace. She became the mother figure I never had, showing me unconditional love—even when I felt unworthy of it.

On December 31, 2010, I committed my life to the Lord at Calvary Chapel Fort Lauderdale.

Determined to build a new future and fueled by God's strength, I went back to school, earning my bachelor's degree in Psychology with a minor in Christian Ministry from Trinity International University. I became a Certified Addictions Counselor and a Certified Recovery Support Specialist with the State of Florida. God was not just restoring my life—He was giving me purpose.

Before long, my life started to unravel again. Believing my new successes were enough, I stopped going to meetings. Friends reached out, worried, but I ignored them. Before I knew it, four-and-a-half years of sobriety were gone. Shame consumed me. I started using heroin again, injecting it into my feet to hide my relapse.

Even in my darkest moments, the Lord was convicting me. He was stirring something in my spirit, calling me back. *Fight the good fight of the faith. Take hold of the eternal life to which you were called when you made your good confession in the presence of many witnesses* (1 Timothy 6:12 NIV).

As my fall semester ended, I focused on finishing my graduation application. I tried desperately to get sober, knowing this wasn't what God wanted for me, but withdrawal left me violently ill.

On December 23, 2015, everything changed. I was using, surrounded by the wrong people, when my phone rang. My best friend, prayer partner, and biggest encourager—Bobby—had died from a fentanyl overdose. I couldn't believe it. Bobby was gone.

The night before, he had called me but, lost in my addiction, I didn't answer. I knew he wanted to talk, but I never called him back.

Christmas Eve and Christmas Day passed in a blur. Friends urged me to change my number and asked, "What lengths are you willing to go to for your sobriety?" With their help, I trusted them to help me find my way back—to recovery and to God.

I ended up detoxing on my own. I was extremely sick, but God was with me the entire time.

After Bobby's funeral, I walked into Celebrate Recovery, picked up my blue chip, and broke down in tears. I knew this was it. If I didn't stop, I would die—just like Bobby. But more than that, I knew God still had a plan for my life. I had to live out the purpose that Bobby and I once dreamed of together. It was time to step into the calling God had been preparing me for all along.

Through this journey, God revealed so much and freed me from the pain I had carried for years. I finally forgave my parents for the trauma they caused. I've forgiven my adoptive parents and found peace with my past. Before my biological mother passed, I built a relationship with her and her family. Despite her struggles, she made the brave choice at fourteen to give me life. Losing her to suicide brought deep guilt, but through God's grace, I focus on gratitude and trust we'll reunite in heaven.

I have limited contact with my biological father, who remains in active addiction. Though we've never met, I pray for the chance to share God's love and the hope of recovery with him.

As part of my steps, I wrote a letter to Bobby. Although I was anxious, God protected my heart as I wrote eight incredibly healing pages. Letting go of the guilt I carried over his death wasn't easy, but today, I have an incredible relationship with his parents, who now think of me as a daughter.

My relationship with the Lord is growing stronger every day as He continues to shape me into the woman I was meant to be.

> *Now all glory to God, who is able, through his mighty power at work within us, to accomplish infinitely more than we might ask or think* (Ephesians 3:20 NLT).

I recently celebrated seven years of being sober. In 2020, I earned my Master's in Mental Health Counseling and now work as a primary therapist at JC's Recovery Center. I founded YANA Recovery Center of Fort Lauderdale—a ministry providing therapeutic services for sex trafficking survivors. We are currently working to open a safe house to support their healing.

God has given me opportunities to give back and share my testimony, and two years ago, James Kennedy Ministries featured my story on TBN. It was an incredible honor that humbled me beyond words.

I face daily health challenges and chronic pain, but that doesn't stop me from serving the Lord and fulfilling His purpose. Grateful for those who have walked with me, I thank Jesus every day for His grace. I trust He has a beautiful plan for my future, including a husband who will love me unconditionally.

No matter how broken you feel or how many times you've fallen, you are never beyond God's grace. He sees you, loves you, and has a purpose for your life. Freedom isn't easy—there will be moments when you stumble—but what matters is that you keep getting back up. When you trust the Lord, He will break every chain, heal your heart, and lead you into a life of purpose and love. Surrender your past, embrace His grace, and step into the future He has for you. You are never too lost to be found, never too broken to be made whole. *"Come to me, all of you that are weary and carry heavy burdens, and I will give you rest"* (Matthew 11:28 NIV).

# Breaking Chains from Abuse

By Melissa Gissy Witherspoon

Abuse—whether physical, emotional, verbal, or spiritual—destroys lives by shattering trust and inflicting deep wounds. Thankfully, the Bible speaks powerfully about God's desire for our freedom, healing, and restoration. He is a God who breaks chains, setting captives free (Isaiah 61:1). If you or someone you know has suffered from abuse, know that God is not silent, nor is He distant. He offers healing, justice, and a new life beyond the pain.

Abuse is an evil distortion of the authority and relationships God intended. Scripture consistently condemns the oppression and mistreatment of others. Psalm 11:5 states, *The Lord tests the righteous, but his soul hates the wicked and the one who loves violence* (ESV). Abusers often manipulate others into silence, but God does not tolerate injustice. He sees every wound inflicted and will bring judgment upon those who harm others (Romans 12:19).

Jesus came to set the captives free. The good news of the gospel is that Jesus came to rescue and heal the brokenhearted. In Luke 4:18, He declares, *"The Spirit of the Lord is upon me, because he has anointed me to proclaim good news to the poor. He has sent me to proclaim liberty to the captives and recovering of sight to the blind, to set at liberty those who are oppressed"* (ESV). Abuse creates captivity, fear, and shame, but Jesus offers freedom. He restores dignity and identity to those who have been crushed.

God calls us to step out of the darkness. Many abuse survivors (I am one of them) wrestle with fear, self-doubt, and guilt. Some are afraid to leave abusive situations because of manipulation or threats. But God calls His children to live in truth and freedom, not fear. Ephesians 5:11 teaches us to *Take no part in the unfruitful works of darkness, but instead expose them* (ESV). As Jesus' followers, we are empowered to break the silence, seek help, and trust that God will provide a way out. Abuse thrives in secrecy, but healing begins when light is brought into the situation.

> He heals the brokenhearted and binds up their wounds (Psalm 147:3 ESV).

God heals the brokenhearted. Healing is a journey that takes time, but we can trust that God is present every step of the way, caring for our wounds. Your journey to restoration may include, among other things, biblical counseling, community support, and learning to replace lies with God's truth. God assures us that what the enemy meant for destruction, He can use for our redemption (Genesis 50:20).

Walking in freedom is more than escaping a harmful situation; it is embracing the life God has for you. He has more for you than you could think or imagine (Ephesians 3:20)!

> For freedom Christ has set us free; stand firm therefore, and do not submit again to a yoke of slavery (Galatians 5:1 ESV).

You are not defined by your past. You are not defined by what someone else has done to you. God alone defines you. And in Him, you are loved, valued, and victorious.

God is a chain-breaker. Trust Him to lead you to healing, safety, and freedom.

. . . . . . . . . . . . . . . . . . . . . . . . . . . . . . . . . . . . . . . . . . . .

# Natalie Keith

Natalie Keith is a Jesus-loving, fast car-driving, coffee-obsessed wife and mama of two amazing kids. She lives by wild faith with a "yes, Lord!" heart, on a mission to advance God's kingdom through media, business, and community—dreaming big with Jesus every step.

Alongside her husband, Natalie is an entrepreneur who builds businesses with heaven's blueprint and bold kingdom purpose. She is the founder of Brideside Life and the creative force behind *Dare to Be Great*—a raw, real media series (coming soon to Amazon and Netflix, in Jesus' name!) filled with miraculous stories that stir the soul and challenge believers to rise up and walk boldly in their God-given greatness.

Whether writing for ministries, building an orphanage in Uganda, planning retreats in Costa Rica, or capturing supernatural God stories on camera, Natalie is all in for kingdom work—and loving every second of the wild, beautiful ride.

When she's not working on passion projects, you'll find her dating her hubby, hanging with her crew on the water, working out, loving on her animals, or walking the beach, talking with God about what's next in their adventure together!

Follow the journey:
TikTok: @brideside.life
Facebook: Natalie Brocato Keith
Email: natiekeith@gmail.com

# A Marriage Redeemed by Faith and Grace

By Natalie Keith

*Above all, love each other deeply, because love covers over a multitude of sins* (1 Peter 4:8 NIV). This verse reminds us that love—true, godly love—has the power to bring healing and restoration, even in the face of deep wounds and brokenness. When we choose to love as Christ does, offering grace and forgiveness, we open the door for His healing work in our relationships and marriage.

Faith—real, raw, unshakable faith—rarely makes sense. It defies logic, moves mountains no one thought could be moved, and speaks life into situations that seem beyond hope. Faith isn't about having all the answers; it's about trusting in the One who does, even when everything around says otherwise.

The world tells us to believe in what we can see and rely on what makes sense. But faith? Faith asks us to step out onto the water when the storm is raging. Faith tells us to trust in God's plan when life feels like it's falling apart. Faith whispers, "Keep going," when every part of us wants to give up. Faith tells you to trust when you cannot see.

I was never the type to use dating apps. But feeling bored and frustrated after a few long, unsuccessful relationships with local guys, I thought, *Why not try something different?* On a leap of faith, I signed up for a three-month subscription to Match.com. And guess what? The first and only guy I met from the site, Mike, is now my husband.

Mike lived about an hour from me, but after our first date, we saw each other literally every day. He would make that hour-long trip into New Orleans every night just to see me. We met on July 8, 2005. Just seven weeks later—on August 29, 2005—Hurricane Katrina hit. In those short weeks before the storm, we had already grown incredibly close¬—spending every day together, talking for hours, learning each other's hearts, and building a connection that felt effortless.

It took Mike three whole days to kiss me, which was almost unheard of! I actually started to wonder if he was even into me. But then, on our third date, while we were in a pool, he finally leaned in for that first kiss. And it was amazing. It wasn't just a kiss but a moment that shifted something deep inside me. It was as if time slowed, and in that instant, I knew. I knew he was different. I knew he was the one.

Looking back, I see that God was already weaving our stories together. That kiss wasn't just the start of a romance—it was the beginning of a God-written love story filled with faith, trials, redemption, and purpose.

Things moved quickly after that. Mike invited me to meet his grandparents in North Louisiana. Taking that trip felt like an exciting next step, but I had no idea how much life was about to change.

While we were visiting, Hurricane Katrina devastated New Orleans. At first, it didn't feel real. But it was clear this was serious. I couldn't return home— roads were closed, and the city was shut down. I was stuck with people I barely knew while my family and friends were back home scrambling to escape.

I felt hopeless. For the first time in my life, I experienced real depression. Lying in his grandparents' home, I was overwhelmed with anger, confusion, and desperation. I just wanted to go home, but there was nothing left to return to. New Orleans was uninhabitable. Everything I had known, my routine, my security, my sense of normalcy, had been washed away in an instant.

I ended up moving in with Mike, his brother, and another roommate. Not exactly my dream situation, but I was grateful to have a place to stay. And then reality hit hard. Just because a hurricane wipes out your home and job doesn't mean the bills stop coming. Life didn't pause to let me grieve the loss of everything familiar. I had to find work fast.

A few months later, we decided to get an apartment together—right across the street from my new job in orthodontics, which I loved. Things seemed to stabilize, but the storm that had displaced me physically was nothing compared to the storm about to hit our relationship.

In living together, our true selves began to emerge. I learned that he lied, watched pornography, and had terrible communication skills. He learned that I was strong-willed, feisty, and had major anger issues. And yet, by this point, we were already engaged. Yes, less than a year into our relationship. And then came the moment I had to make a choice. I loved him, but I also knew my worth.

I told him plainly that I would not marry him if pornography and lying were part of his life. I couldn't build a future on a foundation of deception. With a heavy heart, I took off my ring and gave it back to him, unsure what would happen next.

It was a defining moment for both of us. Would we walk away or fight for something deeper—something real?

Of course, like any dramatic love story, we found a way to work it out the best we knew how. It wasn't easy, and it wasn't perfect, but we chose to move forward. We chose to fight for our love, to believe in something greater than our brokenness. And so, with hope, faith, and a willingness to grow, we stepped into the unknown and went through with the wedding.

Our wedding day was truly a fairytale. We were married at St. Louis Cathedral in New Orleans, one of America's oldest continuously running cathedrals.

My uncle drove us away in his classic 1937 Buick Special—she was called Miss Daisy—and honestly, it felt like something straight out of a 1930s movie. Can you picture it? Pulling out of the oldest cathedral in the U.S., in the heart of the French Quarter, riding in an old-timey, classy gangster car with my handsome husband by my side. I truly felt like a princess.

I had originally wanted to get married under a huge oak tree, but the family tradition was to marry in a church, so I chose the most breathtaking and significant one I could. And there I was, April 27, 2007, madly in love, walking down the aisle, barely able to breathe from the excitement.

Mike and I spent the first few years of our marriage doing all the things you would expect: finding a home, working, and growing our family. But there were choices also being made that were leading us into destruction. Even though we were growing our home, little did we know our love was growing cold.

Our marriage unraveled around the seven-year mark. Ever heard of the phrase "the seven-year itch"? People throw it around like it's just a saying, but I remember wondering, *Is this a real thing? Is this really happening to us?* Every time Mike would bring up the saying, I'd get so frustrated. But looking back, I realize we were speaking destruction over our marriage without even knowing it.

Now that I know God, I realize how powerful our words really are. Can you curse your life by speaking things over yourself or your marriage? Yes, you totally can! The world throws around phrases so loosely, thinking they're just harmless sayings, just careless jokes. But Scripture says otherwise.

> The tongue can bring death or life; those who love to talk will reap the consequences (Proverbs 18:21 NLT).

Let me tell you: we reaped those consequences.

The truth is, at that time, God had no place in our marriage. We had no foundation in Him. I was raised Catholic, but I wasn't practicing any faith, and my prayer life had dwindled dramatically. Mike was raised Baptist, yet he wasn't practicing his faith either. We didn't attend church together and never prayed with each other. In fact, we rarely mentioned God in our day to day. We lived without conviction or accountability, saying and doing things as if consequences didn't exist.

At one point, our marriage was completely destroyed because we didn't have God in our lives. When I say destroyed, I mean everything you can do to wreck a marriage besides physical abuse. You name it, it was there. Lies? Yes. Adultery? Yes. Pornography? Yes. Drugs? Yep. Drunkenness? Absolutely. The list goes on...

Because my husband's communication was lacking and my anger was intense, we couldn't function as a team. We drifted apart. He didn't trust me enough to share his struggle with pornography because of my anger, and my anger deepened because of his secrecy. I was lost, lonely, and desperate—handing control of my life over to the enemy without even realizing it. In my weakest moment, I ran into the arms of another man. Yes, I was already sleeping in my son's room, and we were living like we were divorced—but in God's eyes, I was still married.

After that decision, I knew I had no control over my life. Even when I wanted to choose right, I couldn't. That's when I realized I was in bondage. The enemy had a grip on me. I saw and heard things I knew were lies. I knew this was spiritual and that I needed a Savior. I cried out to Jesus for 24 hours—begging for Him to bring me forgiveness, healing, and rescue. And He did just that. My first step was honesty and repentance. I told Mike what I had done. We separated for a year and a half.

During that time, I grew strong in the Lord. I learned to forgive—myself, Mike, and others. I discovered the power of spiritual warfare and how to partner with God to break the enemy's hold. I learned obedience and trust. I didn't know that God was working on Mike's heart, too—and He planned to lead us back to each other.

Sometimes, it takes hitting rock bottom to turn to Jesus. I'm grateful that's what happened to me. I finally met Jesus—not just knowing about Him, but inviting Him and the Holy Spirit to live in my heart and mind. Everything changed.

Since then, it's felt like walking blindfolded, holding tightly to Jesus' hand, and trusting He's leading me with love, purpose, and my best interest at heart.

That's what it means to be born again—when your spirit comes alive through the power of the Holy Spirit. As Jesus said in John 3:3 (NIV), *"Very truly I tell you, no one can see the kingdom of God unless they are born again."*

My born-again life in Jesus has been a wild ride—full of faith steps, leaps, and jumps! I don't live for myself anymore; when I was in control, I was destroying myself. I handed the reins over to the enemy without even realizing it, allowing him to rule my life. I didn't have the Holy Spirit in me—guiding, leading, and convicting me—so I lived in anger, unforgiveness, and bitterness.

I made choices that should have changed the course of my life forever—and not in a good way. I didn't face my problems; I ran from them. I was like a wild, untamed horse, restless and reckless, chasing after things that only left me empty. Romans 8:6-8 (NIV) says, *The mind governed by the flesh is death, but the mind governed by the Spirit is life and peace.* And that's the truth. It's easy to see whether we're walking in our flesh or His Spirit.

I learned to reflect on questions such as: Am I anxious, or am I at peace? Am I worried about outcomes, or am I resting in the assurance that God is in control? Am I constantly striving, chasing, and exhausting myself, or am I waiting patiently on the Lord to lead the way?

The enemy always works to plant seeds of doubt about God's goodness, mercy, and provision. He is the author of confusion, the father of lies, and the master accuser. And do you know his favorite trick? He doesn't have to speak the lies himself—he gets us to do it. He gets us to believe and repeat them and live as though they're true. But they're not.

We must treat the enemy like a robber in our home—an intruder with no right to be there. We can't sit back and let him steal our peace, joy, or faith. We must speak out against him, using the power of God's Word, especially when our faith feels weak. We must surrender control—not in fear, but in faith. Trusting God's work doesn't mean sitting back and doing nothing; it means actively stepping forward in obedience. Faith requires action.

*As the body without the spirit is dead, so faith without deeds is dead* (James 2:26 NIV).

Getting back together with my husband after a year and a half of separation—just two weeks before our divorce was finalized—was nothing short of a miracle. Our marriage had been torn apart by adultery, pornography, drugs, and compulsive lying. We had moved across multiple states, knowing no one and unsure how to navigate the challenges ahead. He left jobs without a backup plan while we had two small kids to care for. Then, he walked away from a well-paying industrial job, dropping everything to step out in faith into something completely new—commercial real estate, an industry he had never worked in before.

Looking back, every leap of faith and step together into the unknown led us exactly where God wanted us to be. What started as job changes and state-to-state moves turned into something far greater than we ever imagined: a marriage restored with God at the center, allowing us to birth ministries, create series for Amazon and Netflix about the power of God, build orphanages, and write books. It has been a journey of faith beyond our understanding, but God knew. He had a plan all along, even when we couldn't see it. Even when we were struggling to have faith.

We did what the Bible instructs in Proverbs 3:5-6 (NIV): *Trust in the Lord with all your heart and lean not on your own understanding; submit to Him, and He will make your paths straight.* God made our paths straight—through every uncertain step, risk, and moment when we thought we wouldn't make it. Faith doesn't always make sense, but obedience to God's call has led us to a life far greater than anything we could have planned on our own.

If we had leaned on our own understanding, our marriage would have been over the moment adultery and pornography reentered the picture. That's what most people do, right? When betrayal shatters trust and pain cuts deep—divorce seems like the only way out. And after all the job losses, wouldn't it have made sense to scramble, stress, and fight to get back into the same familiar patterns? That's what the world would say. But God's ways are not our ways.

Leaning on our own understanding wouldn't have meant forgetting what lies behind and beholding that He was doing something new (see Philippians 3:13). If we had listened to family and friends who told us we were making a mistake, we would have never moved forward. But we went for it anyway, trusting God. We ignored the doubts, fears, and voices telling us we were crazy; we chose faith. We trusted God to do the impossible and stayed obedient when we felt Him calling us.

He took our brokenness and placed us on solid ground. He healed our hearts. He delivered us from the enemy's trap. Together, we trusted Him—fully, completely—and allowed Him to work out the unrighteousness in our lives. And because of our faith and obedience, He made beauty from ashes. He always does.

I wasn't taught early on to live a holy and righteous life. I didn't know the Holy Spirit is always at work in me. But now I do—He is constantly transforming me, molding me into His image, shaping me for His purpose.

*And we all, who with unveiled faces contemplate the Lord's glory, are being transformed into His image with ever-increasing glory, which comes from the Lord, who is the Spirit* (2 Corinthians 3:18 NIV).

This is faith—knowing that we are being changed! When God is transforming us, conviction will come. He will show us what to turn away from, who to let go of, where not to go, what not to watch, and guide us and direct us every step of the way. These are all signs of the Spirit's work in our lives.

Romans 14:7-8 (NIV) says, *For none of us lives for ourselves alone, and none of us dies for ourselves alone. If we live, we live for the Lord; and if we die, we die for the Lord.* That alone is a complete faith walk—choosing to live not for ourselves but for God. It's about trusting Him completely, knowing that every step we take is part of His greater plan.

Being in relationship with God fuels my faith in ways I never imagined. I pray that sharing my faith story with you encourages you. No matter where you are, no matter what you've been through, know that God has a plan. Maybe we just need to lean in a little closer, listen a little harder, and step out in faith. Rest assured, we are never alone on this journey. God is with us, waiting patiently on us to call on Him and follow Him in faith!

# Breaking Chains of Toxic Relationships

By Melissa Gissy Witherspoon

On our faith journey, few things are more critical than discerning which relationships build us up and which break us down. Scripture is clear that God desires us to live in unity, but not all relationships are rooted in love, respect, or truth. Some are chains that bind us rather than bridges that connect us.

One of the most vivid examples of an unhealthy relationship in the Bible is found in the story of Samson and Delilah (Judges 16). Samson, chosen by God from birth, was gifted with supernatural strength to deliver Israel from the Philistines. But despite his divine calling, Samson's weakness for Delilah led him into a toxic relationship. Delilah's love was conditional and manipulative—she was more committed to silver than to Samson's soul. Each time she tried to betray him, Samson ignored the signs, eventually revealing the source of his strength. *She made him sleep on her knees. And she called a man and had him shave off the seven locks of his head* (Judges 16:19 ESV). Because of Delilah's actions, Samson's strength left him, and he became a prisoner to those he was meant to defeat.

Like Samson, we, too, can be blinded by relationships that don't honor God. We may hold onto those relationships, hoping they'll change, but if we listen to the Holy Spirit, He will tell us when to destroy those harmful chains that bind us and pull us away from God and His purpose for our lives. *Do not be deceived: "Bad company ruins good morals"* (1 Corinthians 15:33 RSV). God calls us to love others, yes. But He also calls us to walk in wisdom, guard our hearts, and release what hinders us from growing in His grace.

My own understanding of love has been transformed through my friendship with Gary Chapman, author of *The Five Love Languages*. His insights helped me realize that love isn't just something we give—it's also something we must learn to receive. For years, I poured into others from an empty cup, confusing self-sacrifice with holiness. However, as Gary teaches, effectively loving others requires knowing how to love ourselves. Jesus commanded: *"You shall love your neighbor as yourself"* (Mark 12:31 ESV). That means setting healthy boundaries, recognizing red flags, and understanding that true love never manipulates or wounds.

My marriage was destroyed during active addiction. Over time, and by God's grace, we healed and corrected many unhealthy patterns. Along the way, I learned to discern which relationships could be restored and which were only meant for a season. Through prayer, Scripture, and wisdom from the Holy Spirit, I've come to understand that broken or damaged associations can chain us to damaging and ungodly practices. God gives us the grace to repair our connections with others through conversation, forgiveness, and/or counseling. But sometimes, He asks us to let go. This release should not happen out of hatred but out of obedience. God doesn't guide you to release another because He wants you to give up on them but because He loves you and wants to protect your purpose.

Jesus came to break every chain—even those disguised as friendships, relationships, or obligations that the devil uses to keep us from following His plan for our lives. Take time to discern God's will, and then, in His strength, choose to walk in the freedom He alone can offer.

> For freedom Christ has set us free; stand firm therefore, and do not submit again to a yoke of slavery (Galatians 5:1 ESV).

. . . . . . . . . . . . . . . . . . . . . . . . . . . . . . . . . . . . . . . . . . . . . . . . . . .

# Stacy Thomas

Stacy Thomas is a dedicated wife and mother of three adult children. She has 30 years of experience as a pediatric and adult Occupational Therapist.

Stacy has proudly served as the Ministry Leader at her local Celebrate Recovery for seven years and has played a vital role in establishing community-based nonprofit ministries, including Backpack Blessings and Protect Our Preemies.

As a contributing author in Women World Leaders' 7x bestseller, *Surrendered: Yielded With Purpose,* Stacy has also published multiple articles in a local Christian magazine and in Voices.

In her free time, Stacy enjoys traveling with her husband, visiting her children, hiking, and engaging in other outdoor activities. She has a passion for writing and sharing her testimony.

*I will say of the Lord, "He is my refuge and my fortress, my God, in whom I trust"* (Psalm 91:2 NIV).

# From Self to Surrender

By Stacy Thomas

Our God is a god who sees all, hears all, and knows all. He is not the God of chance; He is the God of absolute. He does not create anything for "no good reason," though I have always wondered, *What is the purpose of those pesky gnats?*

So, if God created a gnat, and He creates everything for a purpose, then what is my purpose? What is your purpose? Can we know our purpose without knowing our Lord and Savior, Jesus Christ? Oh, I sure thought I could. Until one day...

The day God stepped in on my behalf. The day He helped me realize I have NO control.

> *For I know that good itself does not dwell in me, that is, in my sinful nature. For I have the desire to do what is good, but I cannot carry it out* (Romans 7:18 NIV).

My mind swirled. *What should I do? Where do I go? I cannot live like this anymore.* For countless years, these thoughts and, at times, audible statements colored my attitude with darkness, discontentment, and pain.

They buried me under the heavy burdens of my young life and chained me to every wrong choice I had ever made as I attempted, under my own power, to gain freedom and contentment.

Though I stood before the world believing I would never measure up, I worked overtime to portray strength, importance, and success. I fervently stuffed my hurts, habits, and hangups to appear "fine." Perfect.

Oblivious to my wounded inner self and still blaming others, I precariously dangled on the edge of a proverbial cliff. Anchored to perfection, I continued to fight for the comfortable fantasy life at the other end of the rope—the life that had been my self-ordained purpose. The one that said, "If I just get it all perfect, then I will be ok." For years, I continued to believe I was in absolute control, all the while denying my part and my irrational, insane expectations.

Subconsciously, the battle weapons I had in my arsenal were steeped in old wounds and fueled by pain. My internal war exploded outwardly when the protective, impenetrable walls around my heart were threatened. The walls prevented the discovery of overwhelming guilt and shame and the revelation of past failures and hidden hurts. With artillery consisting of offense and pride, life circumstances rerouted my focus and shifted my target toward the ones I loved most.

In these many moments of defense, simultaneously fueled by the promptings of my unrecognized insecurities, I launched verbal and emotional attacks while unknowingly fulfilling the enemy's plan to kill, steal and destroy.

Now facing heaping mounds of continued wrong choices and irrational thought patterns, life was swirling out of control. No matter how hard I tried using my own power, there was no way to correct the trajectory before me. Stationed in overthinking, I wondered, *How did I ever get to this place?*

In retrospect, sure, I had lost my dad too early. However, that pain was buried deep in my heart and had no bearing on life today. Or did it?

I got divorced after the birth of my two beautiful children, yet I hid the wounds of my relationship, excused my immorality, and denied that there were any feelings worth dealing with. I picked myself up and moved on to marriage number two and the blessing of his young son. A new life. A new focus.

Yet I carried a suitcase of old wounds, including pain, denial, avoidance of reality, brokenness, bitterness, and unmanageable anger. I held this locked suitcase tightly while continually stuffing more hurts, irrationally exploding, and manipulating a sort of dysfunctional normalcy.

It was time! Time for action. Time to "fix." Isn't that what I do best? As a healthcare provider, that's my specialty, my role, my purpose. Though I was exhausted and the old rope of control was frayed and unraveling, my pride refused to give in to defeat. *Who will I be if I quit? Nothing. Nothing but a failure.*

> For it is God who works in you to will and to act according to His good purpose (Philippians 2:13 NIV).

## JANUARY 2011

In February 2010, our church launched Celebrate Recovery. Thinking it was a program for people with addictions, I took no interest because I was not one of "those people." However, there was a prick in my heart as I began to hear about the stories of transformation and freedom.

Being a new year, I had vowed that my marriage would not continue as we were, though I had no idea what to do to fix our long-standing issues. I had head knowledge of the principles lived out by Jesus; however, my damaged heart continued to lock out the truth, blaming my husband for our dysfunctional living.

With a very young faith and an unwillingness to look within, I ignored that I attempted to control every aspect of our lives and our children's lives. Simultaneously, I battled with questions such as, *Why am I so easily discarded and ignored?* Feelings of rejection consistently beat on the door of my heart, further rooting a belief system that my life was unimportant.

As an only child, my heart always craved acceptance and adoration. My young parents loved me dearly, yet I recorded their busyness and responses to my age-appropriate emotional needs as rejection.

Over time, I grew to believe that my performance and perfection drove my approval ratings while gaining me little morsels of attention. I was driven to be independent, required to be self-controlled, and expected to do what was "right." When I missed the mark, I banked correction as criticism and disapproval as rejection. I perceived my worth and value by others' approval.

Almost 40 years later, I continued to carry that habit of people pleasing into every relationship, which played unknowingly into the hand of codependency, a poison to every relationship and devastating to my own physical, emotional, and spiritual life.

> *Therefore, I urge you brothers and sisters, in view of God's mercy, to offer your bodies as a living sacrifice, holy and pleasing to God—this is your true and proper worship* (Romans 12:1 NIV).

In January 2011, the Holy Spirit used a dear friend to prompt me toward Celebrate Recovery as I learned the actual basis for the program. Celebrate Recovery is a faith-based recovery program that professes Jesus Christ as the higher power and expands the traditional 12 steps of recovery to include relevant scriptures and biblical living principles based on the beatitudes from Matthew 5. I learned the program is helpful for anyone struggling with any hurt, habit, or hangup.

My friend had attended for the past year and shared her testimony of recovery from alcoholism. I was floored by her story, in awe mostly because my self-absorbed thoughts couldn't believe she had any struggles. I perceived her life as perfect. She had a successful career and was happily married with two well-behaved sons. As a faithful church volunteer and leader, she was accepted and adored. I measured my successes against her and even harbored jealousy toward her.

After our conversation, despite my best efforts to ignore the frequent whispers in the depths of my heart, I attended Celebrate Recovery. Armed with doubt and cynicism, I confidently walked through the doors, believing I was attending for the sake of my family—to gain strategies to "help" my husband. All the while, I was privately experiencing the initiation of surrender to the idea that I was completely powerless in my circumstances.

I followed along as the meeting progressed, struggling to hide my unending tears as we worshipped. Though there were a hundred people in attendance, my soul connected to the warmth and love of someone beyond the physicality of that room. I had attended church in that room for years, yet I had never experienced such overwhelming emotions. My heart was being prepared for the healing yet to come.

Following the lesson, I met with the ministry leader. In my mind, it was clear that my next move should be step study—an in-depth study on the 12 steps completed in a confidential, same-gender small group, typically lasting a year. I was determined to dig in and get through it quickly for the sake of my marriage and family.

As I stepped out of denial, God revealed my powerlessness. He required me to look deeply into my past and identify all those I had hurt and all who had hurt me. He required me to admit this all, both in the quiet of my prayer time and openly to another person.

Well, the rubber met the road there! I had always been concerned about what others think; now God was requiring me to admit all my mess and mess-ups to someone I saw every day! Though I got stuck for a bit in rebellion, God, in all His wisdom and patience, provided the perfect timing for me to confess to another.

The chains of fear immediately fell away as I spoke. Providing an example of Jesus' love, my sponsor sat quietly and listened. If not for her familiar face, I would have believed I was in the presence of God. No judgment; just love.

God used this study to remove the scales over my eyes, reveal my hardened heart, and begin the process of a layer-by-layer recovery journey. He stripped me of my old coverings and would not let me move any faster than He planned, walking me through some of the most difficult conversations as I moved forward to offer amends and request forgiveness. The fear of rejection threatened, yet my God saw fit to walk with me through these steps while providing incredible love, mercy, and grace.

In the beginning, I believed I would not be in recovery long. In reality, I now know I will be in recovery until I cross heaven's threshold.

> So if you think you are standing firm, be careful that you do not fall (1 Corinthians 10:12 NIV).

## JANUARY 2012

I finished the first step study with a newfound peace and understanding of codependency. I began to reconcile the anger I had carried for so many years as forgiveness brought a salve to my fractured heart. Realization and understanding created opportunities for me to start a transformation that only God could orchestrate.

Confession swung open the prison doors as the bondage of guilt and shame was unshackled. Healing poured in and washed away unresolved grief, unforgiveness, and suppressed anger. Peace flooded my soul as I began to learn the power of surrender.

For the first time in a very, very long time, I could breathe. Not just body-sustaining breaths but cleansing, refreshing, and peace-giving breaths. Life was looking up. I thought, *I'm doing pretty good*. Until...

Typically, we are not notified of incoming trials; being in recovery does not change that fact. Following my first step study, I became "comfortable" with my CR family and a bit complacent regarding my relationship with Jesus. Without warning, the rock of self-assurance where I confidently perched let loose.

On February 25, 2012, I relapsed and fell into the old control habits and wrong thinking. I reacted in anger. No! More like rage. Irrational, crazy, seemingly psychotic rage. My tongue destroyed any healing achieved over the past year. I unraveled any newfound trust as the old control freak monster raised its head from the pit of insecurities. I had heard about relapses, but NOBODY prepared me for the gut-wrenching and astronomical guilt and shame that followed in the days to come.

I experienced suffocating regrets and unbearable aches because I had let my family and myself down, and even more devastating, I had failed Jesus. Once again, my performance weighed my worth. My failure to trust God and turn to Him in that moment cost me everything.

Though we had many separations in the past, this time, my marriage was over. My children distanced. The biggest fear that fueled my rage and control—abandonment—was realized. I was truly alone.

I begged God for forgiveness. While at my very worst, I began to understand His unending grace and mercy.

> *Blessed are those who are persecuted because of righteousness, for theirs is the kingdom of heaven* (Matthew 5:10 NIV).

> *Brothers and sisters, if someone is caught in a sin, you who live by the Spirit should restore that person gently. But watch yourselves, or you also may be tempted* (Galatians 6:1 NIV).

## JANUARY 2025

It has been 14 years since God led me through the doors of Celebrate Recovery on that cold, dark night in my broken world. Since then, God has continued to show me His faithfulness. At Celebrate Recovery, God brought people along my path that encouraged me toward the Truth, held me in my darkest nights of relapses, and celebrated with me as I experienced God's mercies.

Today, I find true freedom as God continues to grow my faith and unlock the chains that bind me to lies and misconceptions. Celebrate Recovery provided a safe place to experience the good, the bad, and the ugly of my journey while God continues to show me His grace and mercy.

The Lord used Celebrate Recovery as a platform to grow me in various ways. I became a teacher, which frightened me because I still believed that my sin was obvious and everyone would see me for who I thought I was. However, I discovered that God had made me new. He equipped me and used my successes and failures to help others. Today, it is my joy to bring the Good News to anyone I meet. It is with confidence that I admit my faults so that others may see the work of the Lord in my life, not by my power but His.

Today, I am driven by the truth that I am created for a purpose—not mine but His.

During my journey, the ministry was seeking an interim leader. Because of my growing confidence and pride, the Lord allowed me to step into the role, although I was still self-seeking and not truly surrendered to Him. For seven years, He used that leadership role to humble me, mold me into His image, and help me recognize the stumbling blocks of codependency.

I will forever be grateful for those lessons, the support of our church staff, and the amazing Celebrate Recovery team God positioned me to serve. If not for the grace of God and those He surrounded me with, I would not know the true meaning of humility. I would not understand the beauty of boundaries and the concept of servant leadership.

Today, I apply these lessons as I continue to learn to love others and allow God to do all the fixing.

In 2020, following COVID and on the heels of returning to in-person meetings, I was diagnosed with chronic Lyme disease. God required me to step down from leadership and focus on my health. I battled again with perfectionism and performance as my mind entertained the idea that I had not done enough or could have done better as the ministry leader.

God used this situation to remind me Whose I am. He provided me peace to step away and hand the reins to His next leader. Though I battled with the release of control, God reminded me that, in that instance, I had completed His purpose, and my service for His kingdom would continue in other areas.

I am thankful for God's guidance, compassion, and patience. I am grateful that Celebrate Recovery's biblically based lessons continue to help me walk out the recovery steps daily as I journey into a healthy, faith-filled, and free life.

God reconciled my marriage and continues to restore my relationships with my husband, children, and family. Most importantly, with each year, I see God continue to influence deeper healing, growing my faith, trust, and dependence on Him. He has shown me how, at times, I fall back into self-reliance and control and has used Lyme disease to teach me the importance of seeking Him first in all things.

Even in the frustrating moments of dealing with medical care, health insurance, negative side effects, painful flare-ups, and just good ol' treatment fatigue, God is with me. He is in control. He is my maker and my healer. He will bring good from this disease just as He did with every other trial I have ever faced.

Celebrate Recovery, its mission, and its biblical teachings were used by God to change the trajectory of my life. Today, I have a biblically based arsenal to fight every spiritual battle as I intentionally choose Jesus as my Lord, provider, healer, and Savior.

Today, I walk in the light and freedom only found in a relationship with Jesus. I feel certain I would still be living a self-focused, self-reliant, dark, broken, miserable, and lonely life if it were not for Jesus and the courageous and honest service of the precious souls at Celebrate Recovery.

If you don't have true peace or struggle with any hurt, habit, or hangup, I encourage you to check out Celebrate Recovery at www.celebraterecovery.com. This website can point you to a Celebrate Recovery ministry in your area.

I hope and pray you will give yourself a chance by looking into the depths of your heart. Allow Jesus to reveal the amazing, important, creative, and strong individual He specifically created you to be. Be courageous and strong, for the Lord is always with you. And please remember...

YES! We all are one of "those people." Jesus and Celebrate Recovery is for EVERYONE!

We are all sinners in need of a Savior. Let go and let God bring light to your darkness, peace to your storm, and beauty from your ashes.

> *Be on your guard; stand firm in the faith; be courageous; be strong. Do everything in love* (1 Corinthians 16:13-14).

# Breaking Chains of Resentment

By Connie A. VanHorn

Recently, I heard someone say that resentment is a strong poison for the soul. We all know what it's like to carry the weight of hurt feelings—whether from broken relationships, strained family ties, past trauma, or unfulfilled dreams. But holding onto resentment can drag us down and rob us of happiness, destroy our health, and, most importantly, harm our relationship with God.

I can definitely relate to this, as I held onto resentment toward a certain woman for several years. She was unkind to me, which, over time, created feelings of resentment within me. It wasn't until someone shared Joseph's story (Genesis 37-50) with me that I found the strength to see God's heart and let go of the resentment holding me captive.

Joseph was the son of Jacob. His brothers were very envious of Joseph and sold him into slavery. Then, they deceived their father into thinking Joseph was dead. Imagine the deep hurt and anger Joseph experienced as he was wrestled from everything he loved and sold.

Years later, Joseph found himself in a position of power in Egypt. His brothers came to him, desperate for food, but they didn't recognize that it was Joseph whom they were petitioning for their very survival.

It would have been easy for Joseph to seek revenge and punish his brothers for what they had done. Instead, Joseph responded with grace and forgiveness. When his brothers understood the situation, they feared Joseph's wrath, but the scorned brother reassured his betrayers: *"Don't be afraid...You intended to harm me, but God intended it for good"* (Genesis 50:19-20 NIV).

Joseph's ability to forgive inspired me in a big way. He accepted the pain that came from his past but refused to let it trap him. By choosing forgiveness, Joseph reclaimed his power and transformed his tragedy into a story of strength and healing.

Joseph teaches us that forgiveness doesn't mean we forget the wrongs done to us; it means we decide not to let those wrongs define us. We choose to love even when it's hard. When we allow ourselves to love this way, we unlock the door to healing and open our hearts to God's goodness.

We open the door for God's miracles!

God wants us to bring our pain to Him and trust in His plan. Just as Joseph understood his suffering was part of a bigger plan, we can also find purpose in our struggles.

When I surrendered my pain to God, He allowed me to see this particular woman through His eyes. I recognized the childhood trauma she had experienced, and I loved her in a way that brought healing to our relationship.

God had a bigger plan!

We hold the power to break free from the chains of resentment and live life filled with fulfillment and joy. When we do, we not only free ourselves, but we also inspire those around us. Your story of courage and grace can encourage others to love in a way that changes lives.

Just like Joseph, who turned his pain into a message of hope, you, too, can find beauty in your pain and live a life free from resentment.

· · · · · · · · · · · · · · · · · · · · · · · · · · · · · · · · · · · · · · · · · · · · · · ·

# Amber Olafsson

Amber Olafsson is a Bible-loving, Jesus-following, coffee-drinking kingdom dreamer with a heart full of fire for God's Word and His people. She's a passionate Bible teacher and speaker, and the founder of *The Light Conference*—a national event where women and teenage girls of every background gather to worship, get refreshed in God's presence, and remember who they are (and Whose they are). She co-leads United House Ministries and directs the Charlotte region for ARMI (Association of Related Ministries International) alongside her husband and best friend of over 20 years, Andrew.

Amber is also the founder of United House Publishing, where she helps believers turn their God stories into books that impact the world. She's the best-selling author of *I'll Say Yes: and Trust God With the Rest,* as well as *The Awesome One,* and co-author of *Armor Up: A 40-Day Spiritual Bootcamp.*

Somehow, in between ministry, teaching, speaking, and book launches, Amber and Andrew also run Allegiance Coffee, a franchising dream brewed to help others launch their own coffee shops. They're raising three bold, slightly wild kids and a growing farm full of chickens and chaos. Amber loves to travel, write songs, bake sourdough, talk about Jesus, and drink as much coffee as a person legally should.

# Overcoming Depression's Grip

By Amber Olafsson

*But everything exposed by the light becomes visible—and everything that is illuminated becomes a light* (Ephesians 5:13 NIV).

If we take a moment to contemplate the struggles we've faced in our life, tracing back the pain points, we might find a pattern—a common way the enemy of our souls attacks us.

When I was around eight years old, my best friend sat me down and told me she didn't like me anymore and was never "really" my friend. It shattered my little world. I loved this girl. She was at each of my birthday parties, and I attended all of hers. From Sunday School to sleepovers, playing with dolls, and adventuring in the woods, we had done everything together. I couldn't believe she didn't like me—and never had. I was stunned but held it together as she told me how she really felt. I spent that evening bawling in the lap of my mother, who was a great source of comfort. She was there for me when my little heart needed it, and she always has been.

I got over that heartbreak pretty quickly, learning that not everyone wanted to be my friend. That was okay.

But though that was the first time I experienced rejection, it certainly wasn't the last. Relationship problems became the primary way I experienced discouragement.

Years later, I was hit with turmoil again, and although I was an adult, I couldn't keep it together. As my "friend" shared harsh words about me, a steady stream of tears trickled down my face. I could not believe what I was hearing. Completely caught off guard and utterly shocked by another friendship breakup, crying was the only response I could muster. *Was this seriously happening again?!* The feelings of rejection and hurt from past relationship trauma all collided and pushed me into a place I'd never been before.

The arrow that struck my heart was not only from my best friend but from a family we did life and ministry with. When the rejection came from this unexpected direction, I was DEVASTATED. I didn't just cry for a moment or a night. I experienced over a year of sadness. A deep darkness descended on my bright and joy-filled personality.

"Is Amber depressed?" An avid reader of my blog detected a change in my normally hope-filled words and inquired of someone close to me about how I was doing. Because of this question, I was told to be more careful about what I shared because it could reflect poorly on me or my family. Not only was I experiencing the lowest of lows, but I was also being shamed for being open and honest. One can imagine the effect. As a writer and person, I sunk deeper, withdrawing even more.

This was the first time I considered that maybe I was depressed. Instead of hearing, "Are you feeling down?" or "How can I help?" I got the impression that as a Christian, I was to keep it quiet, never admit I was struggling, and face this sadness with a "fake-it-till-you-make-it" attitude. You know, mask up and give off the perception of perfection—as pride always prompts.

But hiding it won't heal it. Depression is a debilitating disorder that is one of the most common mental illnesses in the United States. It is a big deal and often gets overlooked, swept under the rug, or offered a quick but often unhelpful "just pray about it, and you'll be fine" statement from someone who cannot relate. Some people like to think depression isn't real or isn't a big deal, but I am here to tell you, as someone who has lived through the nightmare of depression, it is both real and paralyzing.

A person can be depressed and not even be aware of it—that was the case for me. From the outside, my life was picturesque. I was married to my best friend, had two beautiful toddlers, and was growing in my relationship with God and pouring into others through ministry—I was literally living my best life. As the quintessential optimist, nothing got me down, and I had no real problems. Then, out of nowhere, a traumatic relationship experience hit me like a ton of bricks, and I crumbled under the weight.

Depression can be set off by something traumatic, and trauma is relative. What may be devastating for me might not be for another. It is essential to listen with empathy when someone opens their heart to us. While another's situation might not bother us, it may trigger something unhealed in someone else or play on their insecurities or fears. Compassion, never judgment, should always be our response.

When I walked through depression, I went from being the normally happy-go-lucky Amber to the girl who cries at the drop of a hat, is dismal about her calling, and is unaccountably quick-tempered. Discouraged to my core, I allowed self-doubt to creep in. The boldness I once had completely left the building. Damaged by the hurt, I didn't know who I was anymore, wondered if God was against me, and considered never trusting anyone ever again.

Like a broken record, I re-lived the scene over and over and over. No matter what was on my daily agenda, I found myself constantly coming back to what happened. Not a day went by that I didn't think about the hurt. The wound went so deep that I doubted my soul would ever recover.

It was dark. It felt hopeless. I was in the pits. The nightmares I routinely experienced of being paralyzed and having my mouth held shut by a demonic force felt like they were happening to me in real life. I didn't know how to find my footing, and I was unaware of how to battle the formidable foe of depression. It felt taboo to talk about it in church circles, so I suffered alone. Questions plagued me day and night: *Who am I? What am I here for? Are there people who want me around? Should I ever let anyone get close again?*

Throughout my dark days, I continued reading the Bible daily. I was no longer on fire for the Lord as I had been, but I stayed consistent in my efforts. Sometimes, that is all we can do when we've lost our passion—keep opening up the Bible and allow the words of God to sprinkle over us. Eventually, that constant drip will add up.

One morning, I found myself reading Psalm 23. I've read it countless times, so when I began perusing the familiar passage, I didn't expect anything extraordinary to happen. But I was wrong. I started reading:

*The LORD is my shepherd;*
*I shall not want.*
*He makes me to lie down in green pastures;*
*He leads me beside the still waters*
(Psalm 23:1-2 NKJV).

But then I got to verse three:

*He restores my soul.*

I felt it, like the warmth of the sun breaking through the dreary clouds of an overcast sky. Those words jumped off the page and did something inside me. They lifted my spirit. They filled me with life. They offered HOPE!

Those were the first Bible verses I ever memorized as a six-year-old, and I have probably recited that passage hundreds of times. But as a kid, my soul didn't need restoring, so I just said the words that were devoid of meaning. But not this time. Now, when my soul had been shattered into a million pieces, I needed to know this promise. *God is not a man that He should lie* (Numbers 23:19 NKJV). So, if the Bible declares, *"He restores my soul,"*

I knew He would. I took God at His Word. I anchored my faith in that Scripture and repeated it anytime I felt broken. It was my first glimmer of light in the darkness, and I knew this broken-hearted season would be coming to an end. If you find yourself with a soul that needs restoring, let this Scripture be a promise for you to cling to and fill you with fresh hope.

Even though I had a breakthrough, the battle raged on. Unstable emotions, discouragement, and nightmares still plagued me. *What is this? And why can't I shake it? I know what the Bible says— my soul will be restored. But how?! How do I see the full victory?!*

Life went on; I made my quiet time with the Lord a priority. During those precious moments in the "secret place," as Psalm 91 calls it—the safest place in the world—I processed my pain with God. I would weep as I recounted what had happened and what was lost. I discovered what David meant by, *Trust in him at all times, you people; pour out your hearts to him, for God is our refuge* (Psalm 62:8 NIV). Surely, God had become my refuge; as I spoke out my hurt, the weight became lighter. I learned the meaning of "pouring out my heart;" I got the words out, speaking them even if it was between sobs—audibly unloading the words from my mind.

Not only did I learn to lay everything bare before God, but He also began nudging me to forgive. Naturally, forgiving was something I didn't want to do. But the alternative was to stay bound by chains in a prison of bitterness. Finding it impossible to forgive in my own strength, I called on Christ's strength to fill me. He walked with me, hand in hand. What began as a begrudging, "I forgive her—there, I said it!" eventually grew into genuine forgiveness from my heart. And as that happened, more of the depressive fog began to lift.

I still had wounds. Things weren't all sunshine and rainbows. Darkness continued threatening me, trying to pull me back down—but I was making progress. They were baby steps, yes, but they were in the right direction—toward God's light.

Spending time in God's presence through prayer and reading the Word was my constant source of hope and light. Singing praise music also immediately alleviated any lingering negative thoughts.

One morning, everything changed. I was listening to "Overcomer" by Mandisa, and as I sang along—something shifted in me. I felt the Spirit of God breathe on those words. The lyrics arrested me in the very best way. I immediately thought, *That's right, I am an overcomer. I am not going to stay down. I am going to overcome this season of depression!*

That was the moment I put on my spiritual boxing gloves. It was time to fight! I made a decision: Depression was not going to beat me—I would conquer it! And I committed to finding Scriptures to bolster my resolve.

I needed a massive mind shift before I would be able to see a change in my emotions, reactions, and life. The change had to begin in my thinking. We cannot defeat a thought with a thought; we can only defeat thoughts with spoken words. If we want to beat negative thinking, we must begin speaking the truth found in God's Word over our lives.

I started taking back the fight with every Bible verse I discovered! I found Scriptures about living as a champion, rising above our circumstances, overcoming, and being a conqueror. I put my faith in what God's Word said, not what my negative thoughts screamed. No longer was depression overcoming me. I was overcoming it with truth!

These verses became my lifeline:

> *In all these things we are more than conquerors through him who loved us* (Romans 8:37 NIV).

> *But thanks be to God, who in Christ always leads us in triumphal procession, and through us spreads the fragrance of the knowledge of him everywhere* (2 Corinthians 2:14 ESV).

*But thanks be to God! He gives us the victory through our Lord Jesus Christ* (1 Corinthians 15:57 NIV).

*And they overcame him by the blood of the Lamb and by the word of their testimony* (Revelation 12:11a NKJV).

*No evil will conquer you; no plague will come near your home* (Psalm 91:10 NLT).

The Bible tells us that when we are in the battle of our lives, to withstand the attack, we must take up the sword of the Spirit—which is the Word of God (Ephesians 6:17). This doesn't mean we merely think about a Bible verse; we must speak Scriptures out loud and ask God for the faith to believe them so we can dismantle the lies and negative thoughts.

Proverbs 18:21 (NIV) says *The tongue has the power of life and death,* meaning our words affect everything. They carry the ability to bring either life or death to our thoughts and our lives.

As I fought depression, I had to use my words wisely if I was going to overcome it. Every time a discouraging thought came my way, I declared one of these Scriptures out loud—and I could feel every chain of bondage begin to break. Little by little, the dark talons of depression finally loosened their grip! I constantly reminded myself that depression was not the victor—I was. Because God said so!

It took less than a month of consistently speaking out the truth of who the Bible says I am before I was completely freed. Halleluiah! God took me on this incredible journey from wounded warrior to victorious champion. Together, we worked on mending my soul, actively forgiving those who hurt me—freeing my hardened heart from bitterness and finally learning to speak the Word of God to fight and win every battle!

Fast forward a few years. One hot summer afternoon, I was catching up with a close friend over an iced coffee. As she poured her heart out, I picked up on the familiar darkness of depression. She had been pursuing help in various forms but was still stuck. I knew the feeling all too well, but I also knew the way out.

After listening, relating, and meeting her where she was, I eventually asked her, "What Bible verse are you putting your faith in right now? What promise from the Lord are you standing on for your victory?"

She looked at me as if I was the first person to suggest this, then slowly responded, "I don't have one..."

In a split second, the conversation took a sudden turn. Holy anger and flaming passion rose up in my heart against depression! That was it—I was tired of watching depression take people out left and right. My heart began to beat faster as the fire in my soul started to burn. I couldn't stop the words from pouring out of my mouth—telling her about the power of the sword of the Spirit and declaring Scriptures that speak to being a conqueror over depression. I shared from personal experience how God set me free as I processed my pain with Him, placed my faith in His Word, and spoke Scripture out loud over my circumstances.

As I spoke, I watched her countenance shift from downcast to hope-filled. I saw the light grow in her eyes. Then I realized what day it was: July 2nd—just two days before July 4th, the day we Americans celebrate our independence. In that moment, the Lord impressed upon me to share this prophetic truth with her: "Do you know what today is? July 2nd. That means in two days, we'll be celebrating our nation's independence. But this year, July 4th is going to have a whole new meaning for you—because you'll be celebrating freedom from depression. It's your Independence Day! Today, we are serving depression an eviction notice. Let's find Scriptures for you to speak and begin taking back the fight!"

We spent the rest of our time together in Scripture, finding promises of freedom, breakthrough, and victory. The Word of God came alive to her, and through it, she became alive. She put her faith in what God said and began defeating depression! She called me a week later to announce her full deliverance! After trying multiple things over the past year with nothing working, finally, the Word did! She was truly free!

When we face a trial and allow God to lead us out, we are anointed with the ability to lead others where we have been. It is now my joy to minister to those who have battled depression. I've witnessed breakthrough after breakthrough.

When we experience victory, we must stay on guard for additional attacks. It's not that we don't actually get free—we do—but the enemy wants to test whether we'll hold our ground. To be honest, every once in a while, that little stinker called depression tries to make an appearance in my life. When it does, I find that holy anger rising again, and I get a little feisty, maybe even a bit indignant.

In response to those depressing thoughts, I declare, "Excuse me?! Depression? I don't think so! I beat you once, and I'll beat you again. No weapon formed against me will succeed. Further, I condemn every tongue that is accusing me in judgment. This is my heritage as a servant of the LORD. My vindication is from God!" (from Isaiah 54:17).

It's our job to refute negativity. If we give depression an inch, it will take a mile. Stand your ground, speak out the Word, and know—you are a victorious child of God!

In the darkest time of my life, I found something to put my faith in: my God, what Jesus did, and His Word! The chains of depression and discouraging thoughts lost their grip on me once I knew the truth:

Because I am in Christ, I am an overcomer!

And so are you, my friend! May God bless you on your journey. And may the Word of God bring you strength and peace.

# Breaking Chains of Depression

By Melissa Gissy Witherspoon

King David—a man after God's own heart—knew the weight of sorrow, the sting of isolation, and the dark pull of depression. In Psalm 42:11, David cries out, *Why, my soul, are you downcast? Why so disturbed within me? Put your hope in God, for I will yet praise him, my Savior and my God* (NIV). These words reveal that even God's anointed king wrestled with emotional and mental heaviness.

David's journey speaks to mine. For years, I used substances to self-medicate the highs and lows of bipolar disorder. I didn't understand that my brain was wired differently. I only knew that the mania gave me moments of drive and confidence, but it always came at a cost. The crashes afterward were brutal. Addiction promised relief, but instead, it deepened the valleys and made the chains of depression tighter.

But God did not leave me there...

Through recovery, I found new ways to live—ways that honor both my healing and my diagnosis. Dialectical Behavior Therapy taught me how to manage the extremes: how to calm the storm of mania and find light in the depth of depression. One of my greatest outlets has been writing. Like David, who poured out his soul through the Psalms, I pour mine out through words—and in that, I find peace and purpose.

The key for me has been staying connected to God. He is my lifeline. I used to live in fear of the "lows" that came after my energetic seasons of success. But now, I live in acceptance. I understand that both the mountain and the valley are part of my walk with Him. On the days I'm full of energy and goals, I serve Him. And on the days all I can do is breathe and hold on, I still serve Him—because even rest and stillness can be holy.

God is not surprised by my ups and downs. He made me. He knows that some days will be a battle and others a breakthrough. And yet, He walks with me through all of it. Psalm 23:4 reminds me, *Even though I walk through the valley of the shadow of death, I will fear no evil, for you are with me* (ESV).

Depression tries to convince us that there's no way out—that the valley will last forever. But God says, "I am the way." With Him, I have learned to embrace every part of the journey. My good days are a gift. My hard days are a testimony. And every day is an opportunity to walk in freedom. In His presence, the chains are broken, and hope is always ahead.

. . . . . . . . . . . . . . . . . . . . . . . . . . . . . . . . . . . . . . . . . . . . .

# Amanda Frick

Amanda Frick is the founder of New Roots Recovery, a pioneering organization dedicated to empowering individuals on their journey to recovery and healing. As a first-time published author, Amanda is proud to share the pages of *Faith Unchained* with influential women and world leaders, inspiring others through their shared stories of resilience and hope.

In addition to her professional endeavors, Amanda serves as a dedicated youth leader at Marcus Point Baptist Church, where she fosters the growth and development of young minds, instilling in them the values of faith, community, and perseverance.

As a mother, wife, sister, aunt, and daughter, Amanda values the importance of family and the lessons learned through love and commitment. Balancing her roles, she embodies the belief that faith is a powerful catalyst for transformation and unity. Through her work and personal life, she aims to inspire others to break free from their chains of silence and embrace a life of purpose and fulfillment.

# A Journey of Faith, Healing, and Redemption

By Amanda Frick

*For it is by grace you have been saved, through faith—and this is not from yourselves, it is the gift of God* (Ephesians 2:8-9 NIV).

Faith often appears when you least expect it, especially in life's most difficult moments. Ephesians 2:8 reminds us that faith is a gift from God—and it is one that entered my life unexpectedly.

When I was seven, my two brothers and I were adopted into a loving Christian family. I was introduced to Jesus and embraced by a church community that nurtured my faith and sense of belonging.

Those early years were filled with wonder. I eagerly absorbed everything about my faith, leading to the pivotal moment I accepted Christ as my Savior. I still cherish my memories from Marcus Pointe Baptist Church— singing in the choir, attending church events, and experiencing the joy of fellowship.

The church became my refuge, where I felt safe, loved, and accepted. Some of my happiest memories were the magical lock-ins, filled with laughter, singing, and dancing to Christian music. The church gym pulsed with joy, offering a much-needed escape from life's struggles.

In those worship rooms, I built unbreakable friendships. Wednesday nights became my sanctuary, a time to leave my worries behind and embrace faith and fellowship. Coming from a life of struggle, discovering faith felt like a long-awaited victory.

Just as life seemed to be improving, darkness fell. At thirteen, my world was shattered by unimaginable betrayal—sexual abuse by the very person meant to protect me. My adopted father, a federal firefighter, stole my innocence, shaking the faith I once clung to. The safe haven I had trusted now felt fragile, and I questioned everything I believed.

Haunted by the question, *How could a loving God allow this?* I felt torn between faith and reality. Instead of seeking help, I withdrew, burying my pain beneath layers of silence and shame.

My siblings were often locked outside, left to play while chaos unfolded inside. It was a cruel reminder of our fractured family and the harsh realities I endured.

With my adoptive mother preoccupied, I was left vulnerable, my sense of safety disappearing. I longed for a mother's love but instead faced an aching void of struggle and despair. The absence of stability distorted my understanding of trust and relationships in ways I wouldn't fully grasp until much later.

Fear consumed my nights, and days were shadowed by an unshakable sense of doom. Trauma became my constant companion, shaping a world I couldn't escape. I learned to survive amid the chaos, yet beneath it all, I was slowly breaking.

I stayed silent—he said if I spoke, everyone would die. I can still smell his coffee-laced breath and feel his finger jabbing between my eyes as he made his threats. Carrying the unbearable burden alone, I believed my silence kept my family safe.

I dreaded waking up each morning. I was trapped in a reality I couldn't escape. I longed to speak up, but who would believe me? Who would care?

As my faith wavered, doubt consumed me. *Why did God allow this suffering? Why was I so alone?* These questions haunted me, especially during my years in the Department of Children and Families. Every cold, unwelcoming placement felt like a betrayal—a reminder that I was unworthy of love and safety.

Life was a whirlwind of confusion and heartache, leaving scars that shaped me. I bounced between homes—living in a tent with my parents, staying with relatives, and ultimately being removed from my parents' custody.

Foster care felt more like a prison than a refuge. Those meant to protect me saw me as nothing more than a paycheck, and the abuse continued. Trust became a luxury I couldn't afford.

I built walls, keeping the world at arm's length. My only solace was escape— sneaking out, fading into the background, doing whatever it took to disappear. I no longer turned to God; survival was my only guide.

What haunts me most is that no one in authority recognized I was mirroring the dysfunction I had been exposed to—what I believed was normal. No one saw the signs. No one intervened. Had just one person looked deeper, I might have been spared from what was still to come.

Growing up in a broken system left me grappling with loneliness, rejection, and fear. Dark days were filled with psychiatric treatment and medication, but unknowingly, I was building resilience—piece by piece, forging a spirit that refused to break.

*God has not given us a spirit of fear, but of power and of love and of a sound mind* (2 Timothy 1:7 NKJV).

The weight of suppressed pain led to a mental health breakdown. I hit rock bottom, powerless to protect myself or my family. Stigma made seeking help difficult, but when the burden became unbearable, I entered a psychiatric unit, forced to confront the trauma, loss, and abuse that had shaped my life. There, I was diagnosed with PTSD and other conditions—finally putting a name to my pain.

My faith felt distant, but even in despair, a flicker of hope emerged—a promise of transformation through love and understanding. Healing was neither quick nor easy. Sharing my story was terrifying yet liberating, and with each truth I released, the burdens that had held me captive began to lift.

Sitting in that psychiatric unit, I realized this wasn't just a place for treatment—it could be a turning point. I had taken the first step toward reclaiming my voice, understanding that while my past shaped me, it didn't have to define me.

The most profound shift came one night in yet another foster home after I revealed my deepest, darkest secret. Consumed by hopelessness, I reached a breaking point—I could no longer live in fear. Darkness surrounded me, but within it, a small spark remained—a fighting spirit refusing to be extinguished. I resolved to break free from the chains of silence that had bound me for so long.

Repeated escape attempts failed, and only when I was placed in a maximum-security facility did I realize—there was no more running. Trapped behind high walls and electric-wired gates, something inside me shifted. I was forced to look inward and confront the pain I had buried for years.

As my 18th birthday and release neared, I stood at a crossroads. Fear of the unknown loomed, but for the first time, a desire for healing pushed me forward. In that moment, I made the hardest yet most crucial decision—not just to survive, but to truly heal.

Forgiveness was a double-edged sword. I longed for freedom from resentment, yet anger kept me bound to my pain. In therapy, I wrestled with the idea until I realized that forgiveness wasn't about excusing the past—it was about reclaiming my freedom.

With each act of forgiveness, I released a piece of the past, creating space for healing and the slow rebuilding of my faith.

My breakthrough came unexpectedly during a therapy session when I finally understood that to move forward, I had to stop letting my trauma define me. My forgiveness wouldn't just benefit others—it would free me.

Despite my realization, I became trapped in a cycle of poor choices that led to incarceration. Surrounded by others carrying similar turmoil, the weight of my past clung to me, refusing to let go.

I occasionally attended chapel, searching for a glimmer of hope, but I struggled to approach God in my brokenness. Deep down, I felt unworthy, as if my past disqualified me from His love. Yet, looking back, I now see that was when I needed Him the most.

Upon my release, the hope of starting over was clouded by fear and uncertainty. Reintegrating into a world I no longer understood felt overwhelming. I had once been entrenched in a life of drugs, guns, and violence, but I was determined to create a new path—one that looked nothing like my past. With nowhere else to go, I moved back in with my adoptive mother, torn between gratitude for her support and the heavy weight of my trauma.

Despite my resolve to heal, I slipped back into old habits. Marijuana became my escape, numbing the anxiety that consumed me. Then, I met the father of my children—a man I believed would bring love and stability. But that illusion quickly shattered. He was unfaithful, leaving me alone to raise our two beautiful children. His betrayal reopened deep wounds of abandonment, but this time, I wasn't just fighting for myself—I had two little lives depending on me.

Determined to be the best mother I could be, I did what I knew best—I ran.

I left Florida and headed to Oklahoma City, reuniting with my biological mother for the first time in 20 years. It was something I had longed for my entire life.

More importantly, I became determined to do my best ensure the abandonment I'd experienced at different times in my childhood would not become a generational pattern. Every day, I worked tirelessly to create a loving home, determined to keep them out of the child welfare system. But in my struggle to survive, I neglected my relationship with God. Consumed by the demands of motherhood and healing, my faith became an afterthought. Within a year, life's circumstances led me back to Florida. I was still searching for something more but was uncertain what awaited me.

Amid the chaos of daily life, something incredible began to unfold. My children found their way into the very church I had once attended in my youth—the same place that had once given me security. Their joy and excitement mirrored what I had once felt, stirring something deep within me.

I couldn't ignore the gentle nudge in my heart, echoing my adoptive mother's words: "Get them in church." As I watched their faith grow, I reflected on the spiritual lessons that had once shaped my own life. Perhaps, after all this time, God was calling me back.

> "Even now," declares the LORD, "return to me with all your heart, with fasting and weeping and mourning" (Joel 2:12 NIV).

As time passed, I gave birth to a baby girl—this time with a different father, a man I was not married to. The moment I held her in my arms, I felt an overwhelming surge of love, hope, and faith. She was a reminder that, despite my past, I had the power to create a new legacy—one built on love, resilience, and faith. Holding her tiny life, I felt God's gentle whisper, inviting me to return to Him.

Through my journey, I have learned that it is never too late to reconnect with God. As I embrace my role as a mother and wife and recommit to my faith, I am learning to trust that every challenge is an opportunity to draw closer to Him. With each step, God is unchaining my faith—opening my heart to healing and hope.

When I joined New Roots Recovery, a community supporting healing from addiction and trauma, my faith was fragile—a delicate thread hanging by a whisper.

The weight of grief pressed heavily on my spirit after losing my roommate and my husband's best friend, Brendan Koper, to fentanyl poisoning.

During this difficult season, I came across Melissa Gissy Witherspoon on Facebook. Her story resonated deeply—here was a woman who had walked through the fire and emerged transformed, just as I longed to be. When she invited me to reconnect with my faith, I felt both daunted and invigorated.

For weeks, I wrestled with doubt, afraid to reach out. But when I finally did, Melissa's warm response dissolved my fears of rejection. Through our conversations, I rediscovered the power of connection and the strength that faith provides. She encouraged me to explore Women World Leaders, where, for the first time in years, I felt truly accepted. *Had God been shaping me into the strong, resilient woman I was meant to be all along?*

As the quiet stirring in my heart grew stronger, everything changed on September 5th, 2024. During a call with Kimberly Hobbs from Women World Leaders, a realization struck me: *I recently married the man of my dreams—my life can change today!* In that moment, I recommitted my life to the Lord, inviting Jesus into my heart. Instantly, a weight I had carried for decades was lifted, and Kimberly vowed to walk with me in strengthening my faith.

I knew I was on the right path, but almost immediately, the enemy attacked my family. It was as if stepping back into God's grace triggered a battle for my faith. But this time, I was different—standing firm on the foundation I had once lost but now reclaimed.

This time, God had prepared me. Armed with renewed faith and His strength, I faced challenges head-on. Instead of being overwhelmed, I surrendered to Him, turning to prayer and scripture for guidance. God worked through my faith sister, Connie VanHorn, and my faith community, surrounding me with wisdom and encouragement. He also strengthened me through my children and husband, who became my motivation to stand firm.

As I reflect on this portion of my journey, I see more clearly than ever that life is a tapestry woven by God's hands—each thread, both joyous and painful, has contributed to a larger story of grace, redemption, and love. Through every storm, He was there—shaping me, refining me, and preparing me for something greater. I now understand that, even in suffering, I can rise again—not by my own strength but through the power of God's transforming love.

On my journey of faith, I've found that it is never too late to reconnect with God. As I embrace my role as a mother and wife and recommit to my spiritual journey, I'm learning to trust that every challenge can bring me closer to Him, unchaining my faith and opening my heart to the possibilities of healing and hope.

Was God shaping me into this beautiful, strong woman all this time? The very woman I had long neglected? Gradually, I've found myself opening up to the concept of a loving God once more.

Community has become a lifeline during my darkest hours. When I aligned with New Roots Recovery, I encountered a supportive network of individuals who shared their struggles and triumphs. We became a family. Through this community, I began to realize I wasn't alone.

The act of sharing my story in such a safe space gradually chipped away at the walls I had built. The encouragement and understanding from others in recovery became a mirror reflecting back the love and hope I desperately needed. I began to see how faith could manifest through relationships and not just in solitary moments of introspection.

Faith isn't meant to be a solitary journey. Faith thrives in community—among those who share both the joys of recovery and our future and the burdens of our pasts. The lessons I gained through this community transformed my faith into something tangible and alive.

Embracing the ups and downs of life, I found guidance from spiritual mentors and the stories of those around me. Each testimony of resilience, each shared struggle, added depth to my understanding of what faith could be: a vibrant tapestry woven from diverse threads, each with its unique color and pattern.

Marrying Zack marked a profound new chapter in my life. As a wife and mother, I saw faith in action, guiding me through love, support, and growth. With Zack by my side, I finally felt the stability and partnership I had always longed for.

Amid the beautiful chaos of family life, I discovered a new purpose. Though the daily demands could feel overwhelming, the love we shared became my foundation. Stepping into marriage brought immense joy, but it also challenged me to reconcile my past with the future I wanted for my family.

Being a stay-at-home mother and wife often feels like a relentless tide—homeschooling my 9-year-old autistic daughter, managing meals, laundry, doctor's appointments, and still making time for God. The hustle can cloud my spirit, but I've learned that faith isn't just in big moments; it's found in the small, everyday ones.

Faith reveals itself in the quiet connections—holding my children close, sharing a laugh with Zack, or pausing to reflect on how far I've come. In these moments, I see God's presence, reminding me that my journey is not just about where I've been but about the love, resilience, and grace shaping my future.

As I reflect on my journey, I am filled with gratitude. Every experience—painful or triumphant—has been a stepping stone toward deeper faith and God's unwavering love. Faith is not stagnant; it grows as we navigate life's struggles. Faith calls us to seek, question, and trust in His grace. Through it all, I have clung to these powerful verses, reminding me that my journey has always been in God's hands, not my own.

*"For I know the plans I have for you," declares the Lord, "plans to prosper you and not to harm you, plans to give you hope and a future"* (Jeremiah 29:11 NIV). Even when our path feels uncertain, God has a purpose for our life.

*I can do all this through him who gives me strength* (Philippians 4:13 NIV). Through every challenge and triumph, this verse is an anchor, reminding us that our strength comes not from ourselves but from God.

I pray that my journey inspires you to embrace your own path of faith. It won't always be easy, but even in the darkest moments, remember—you are never alone.

Through the unity of the Holy Spirit, we can break free from our past and step boldly into a future filled with purpose and love. Your past does not define you; it is simply a chapter in a greater story of faith, resilience, and self-worth.

# Breaking Chains of Abandonment

By Melissa Gissy Witherspoon

There's a deep ache that comes with abandonment. It lingers in the soul like a shadow that won't go away. For years, I chased worldly things—status, people, substances, achievements—trying to quiet that ache. But no matter what I reached for, I always ended up feeling alone, empty, and unseen.

But twelve years ago, at the very beginning of my recovery journey, I was sitting in a treatment center when a guest speaker stood up and said words that hit me like lightning: "You will never have to feel alone again." I still get chills thinking about it. It was as if God Himself spoke through that man, reaching directly into my broken heart and planting a seed of hope.

The truth is, I was never alone. God had always been there. Even in the pit of my addiction, even in the moments I felt tossed aside, God never left.

When I think of abandonment and redemption, I think of Hagar in the book of Genesis. She was a servant, used and discarded by people who should have cared for her. She ran into the desert pregnant, scared, and completely alone. But in Genesis 16:13, something beautiful happens. God shows up. And she gives Him a name: El Roi, "the God who sees me."

Hagar's story reminds me that even when the world casts us aside, God sees us. He meets us in the wilderness—when we're raw, hurting, and trying to hold ourselves together—and He speaks life into our hearts.

That day in treatment was my desert moment, and God showed up. Through the unity of the Holy Spirit, that promise the speaker gave me has come true. I have more meaningful relationships and deeper connections today than I ever imagined possible. I've learned that God often heals our abandonment wounds not just through His presence but through His people—His authentic, Spirit-led community.

I'd be lying if I said feelings of undesired isolation never creep back in. There are days I still feel a twinge of loneliness as that old wound tries to reopen. But when that happens, I pause. I remember that man's voice. I remember that God sees me, just like He saw Hagar. I whisper a quiet "Thank You." And I let the Holy Spirit remind me that I am never truly alone.

> *For the Lord will not forsake his people; he will not abandon his heritage* (Psalm 94:14 ESV).

God is faithful. He never abandons us. And through Him, we are never alone again—chains of abandonment are broken!

. . . . . . . . . . . . . . . . . . . . . . . . . . . . . . . . . . . . . . . . . . . . . . . . . . . . .

# Veronica Isaacs

Veronica Isaacs, originally from Salem, Ohio, now resides in Stuart, Florida. She is the Executive and Marketing Assistant at Freedom Support Solutions, LLC, a bookkeeping and daily money management firm that serves busy executives and small businesses. Additionally, she holds the role of Marketing Manager for the Association of Christian Business Women, a networking group dedicated to empowering businesswomen, entrepreneurs, and ministry leaders through faith-centered connections.

A 2022 graduate of Charleston Southern University, Veronica earned a Bachelor of Science in Psychology and is currently pursuing her MBA. She is passionate about deepening her faith, growing professionally, and embodying values such as kindness, empathy, and empowerment. Inspired by her mother, Stacy Jo Coffee-Thorne—founder of both Freedom Support Solutions and the Association of Christian Business Women—and her stepfather, Allen, author of *Unbound* and founder of Reviving Recovery, Veronica is committed to making a positive impact and values the importance of storytelling and perseverance.

Outside of her professional endeavors, Veronica enjoys photography, writing, and immersing herself in history and the arts. An animal lover at heart, she cherishes her cat, Tink. When she's not working or studying, you can find her engrossed in puzzle books or indulging in some retail therapy.

# Breaking Free from the Storm

By Veronica Isaacs

Have you ever felt like you were drowning in the middle of a storm? Like nothing you do can save you? You keep flailing your arms in hopes that someone will rescue you, but the water keeps hitting you. Relentless. This storm is relentless. No reprieve in sight.

And suddenly, it takes you under. You are drowning in the water. The water burns your lungs as you try to scream out. It's hopeless. You stop fighting it, letting it chain you to the ground. With every inch of resistance you give, the chains tighten on you. Holding you in their unforgiving grip. They keep you there hopeless, joyless, and broken.

I never imagined things would look as they did at the end of 2023. I was single-handedly destroying my life. I was in a relentless storm that had fully taken me under, stuck in a storm of hopelessness and pain. It felt like I had nothing to live for. I just wanted it all to end.

Many times, I tried to save myself, crying out and praying that it would all stop. I truly didn't care what I lost first—my life or my pain. I attempted to end my life to no avail. It felt like I would never see the sun again. For almost eight years, my life felt like this. But for some reason, I was still living. Still breathing.

By the power of God, I was saved. I was truly saved.

At fifteen, my storm began. I was an active volunteer in my church's kids' ministry, went to church every Sunday and Wednesday, was an honor roll student, and had a plan for my life. Nothing was going to stop me. The storm started slowly, and then, all at once, it took over my life. I had just transferred to a new high school, which was much different from the performing arts school I had just come from. Relentlessly, I was told I needed to kill myself.

In this same year, I was assaulted—the extent to which I kept hidden. I couldn't understand what had happened. It was the true catalyst that the enemy knew exactly what to do. The enemy used this to his advantage. He was impeccable at getting me alone and whispering how unworthy I was to have this life I was gifted. He taunted me ongoingly with what and who I thought I was.

My self-worth was at an all-time low. *Who would want me now?* I was damaged. One thing I cannot make clear enough: the devil is a liar and a thief who only wants to rob, kill, and destroy. But I listened to him. The depression that I had managed to keep in check overtook me. It went from a storm to a sea of hopelessness. Hand in hand with depression, anxiety came. It grasped at my body, clawing its way into my soul. I would cry and scream out to God to take it away.

The pain felt unbearable. I wanted it to be gone. I felt so alone. So epically alone. Although a house full of family and friends loved me, I became more distant. First Peter 5:8 warns us that the enemy is like a lion looking to devour. He got me alone, and the mental beating I took from him was intense.

On the outside, I still looked like the same girl who attended church and Wednesday youth group and was an honor roll student. But I was a shell of who I once was. Depression and anxiety had their claws so deep in me, shackling me and holding me in an unbelievable state of self-hatred, fear, and any negative emotion you can have about yourself. I was not good enough; I wasn't worthy of anything—of this life, being loved, chosen, cherished, or valued.

The truth is I didn't have the strength to fight anymore. My soul was tired. I just wanted a reprieve from the chains that had changed me. I no longer had plans for my life, and I certainly did not know God's plan for me. I began to think that maybe He didn't have a plan for me. I was going through the motions of life and losing my faith in God, which was slipping away fast. By the time I was eighteen, I felt like God was abandoning me. And in my mind, that's just what fathers did. My father was never consistent in my life. We went years without speaking.

*If I wasn't enough for my earthly father, how could I be enough for a heavenly Father?* This type of question fueled my confusion and contradicted what I had been taught my whole life. The enemy was having a field day in my confusion and playing on my weakness, making my restraints even tighter.

As I submitted college applications, I thought, *What is the point of this?* I truly had no direction for my life. My friends knew what the next few years would look like for them, but I felt so lost. My mom, a strong warrior of faith, always told me, and still tells me, that the Lord has a plan for my life. She encouraged me with Jeremiah 29:11, *"For I know the plans I have for you," declares the Lord, "plans to prosper you and not to harm you, plans to give you hope and a future"* (NIV).

I knew God's plan was not to harm me, but I wondered what the plan was. I thought maybe I would find it at college. My mom had convinced me to leave for college instead of staying home and attending community college. She would tell me I needed to take a step of faith. So, we packed up her car with my things. She and my stepdad dropped me off with a tearful goodbye, and for the first time, I was truly alone. I was now five hundred miles from home, alone in Charleston, South Carolina, where I would live for the next seven years.

The storm just kept growing, making me feel forever trapped. I was lost in the sea that it had created. The depression seemed to take a break, but my anxiety was fueled by my fear of being in the unknown, well outside my comfort zone. You wouldn't think you could lose your faith at a Christian College, but it happened to me.

My life was changing so fast I couldn't keep up. The anxiety would keep me tossing and turning at night, clawing at my throat and making me want to scream, but nothing would come out. It consumed me, pulling me deeper into its grasp. Fear, dread, and inner turmoil grew, furthering the enemy's grasp on me.

The next time I saw depression, it grasped me by my wrist and dragged me down, though I didn't know why I let it take hold of me. I had this feeling of complete powerlessness. I had no control of anything. The enemy would begin to whisper that no one wanted me here. He would whisper I wasn't enough. These were the same tactics he had used before, but this time, I didn't pray. I didn't cry out. I didn't fight back, which gave the chains more power to hold me.

I had a great friend who would tell me, "When you have nothing to live for, live for me." That is great for the short term, but what about the long term? It is not sustainable because I was placing my life in the hands of fallible people. People can, and often will, fail you. But I didn't know who else to turn to. I wanted to be done with being a Christian. I was tired of asking for deliverance from the pain I had—the pain that kept me in chains.

Looking back, I wish I had more trust. I wish I had declared Proverbs 3:5-6 over my life, which says, *Trust in the Lord with all your heart and lean not on your own understanding; in all your ways submit to him, and he will make your paths straight* (NIV). I should have believed that the Lord was consistent in His promises, unlike my earthly father. But anxiety tugged on its chain and told me, "He's the same." I was letting my father here on earth dictate my relationship with my heavenly Father, furthering the torment of my inner turmoil.

I was done.

I mentioned I was an honor roll student in high school. What I did not mention is that my worth and value were wrapped up in my grades—it was the one thing I felt I was genuinely good at. In my junior year of college, I walked away from my relationship with God and almost failed out of college. Anxiety attacked me, telling me nothing would come of my life if I didn't get good grades. Depression told me how my failing would let everyone down. I tried, but it wasn't enough.

It wasn't enough.

Finding my worth in anything but Jesus was detrimental. I spiraled, feeling even more lost. I still didn't know what I was doing at college. I had never planned on making it that far in life. I had walked away from everything I had known with no intention of ever walking back.

Around this time, I got a job hostessing at a popular chain restaurant. I liked it, but the pain from having been assaulted re-manifested whenever I was touched, even just tapped on the shoulder. Despite having pushed down the pain, shame, paralyzing fear, and brokenness, the emotions now spiraled even deeper. I tried to bury my turmoil in school and work, hiding the brokenness that reached the depths of my soul. I didn't realize the torment I was causing myself.

I got good at my job. It kept me busy and shielded me from worrying about the inner workings of the anxiety, depression, and overarching brokenness that seemed to be chained to me. I grew numb to it and learned to keep it at bay, and the enemy stopped rearing his head in my direction so much. I lived fully for the world.

At twenty-one, I got into my first relationship. We took a trip together that stands out—visiting my mom and stepdad for their vow renewal. My oldest sister asked if we would want to go to church with her. I was hesitant, but something in me told me to say yes. That was the first time I actually wanted to attend church, and I enjoyed it. I knew who the pastor was, and something about it made me want to return.

Looking back, I believe the Holy Spirit was giving me a much-needed nudge in the right direction—but I didn't acknowledge it.

At the end of that relationship, I didn't like the person I had become. I was even more broken but hid it by drinking with the intent to overindulge. My mornings were spent wondering what happened the night before. I wanted to be numb again. I truly did not want to be me. I did not want to feel like the person I had become—I didn't like her. In fact, I hated her. I felt so lost. It had been four years since I walked away from my relationship with Christ, and I couldn't go back.

I was running.

That same year, my father passed away. I had recently gotten back in touch with him and was looking forward to much-needed reconciliation. He had a heart attack and passed away two days after being released from the hospital. I broke. That time, I truly broke. It shattered every being of my body. The depression and anxiety came full force back into my life. I felt so lost; I kept telling my mom how I felt. My job at the restaurant was becoming too much for me to manage.

I started a relationship with a new guy, which was horrible; I knew it, but I was too stubborn to admit it. My life was falling completely apart, and yet again, I couldn't stop it. I called my mom every night to talk to her, most times sobbing. She would listen as I told her everything going on in my life. She slowly started to breathe life into me. When I would tell her that I was lost, her simple answer was, "You're not lost, simply wandering." Though I was broken, beaten, and battered, I started to see a little hope.

The chains of depression were loosening their grasp on me. My mom would pray over me, and I would listen. I was slowly letting God back into my life. During this time, I was reminded of Psalm 34:18, which declares, *The Lord is close to the brokenhearted and saves those who are crushed in spirit* (NIV). I felt so spectacularly broken. I thought God had left me, but the truth is I had been pushing Him away for years. I had wandered away.

It had been years since I entertained the idea of moving back home, but there I was, telling my mom I needed to come home. I needed rescuing. I needed saving. I needed something that couldn't be found where I was. December 30, 2023, my two sisters, twin brother, mom, and stepdad came and packed up my belongings to move me back to the life I had been running from.

I was rescued at last.

Stepping into church the following week after leaving Charleston, I remember a feeling washing over me. It was like a sense of relief. Like my soul was finally able to rest. The storm was breaking, and I could only think of it as a miracle. All the glory goes to God. Over the next few weeks, I listened intently to the pastor's messages. I slowly felt the chains that had held me captive release their grip on me.

I began praying for peace. And, WOW! Did that change my life. Thankfully, the relationship I was in that I knew wasn't good for me ended. I wasn't heartbroken; it felt like a blessing from God. Life started to change quickly; although the storm was breaking, I still felt a heaviness. That changed one particular Sunday.

My sister volunteered at each of the four church services each Sunday. That week, I sat through every sermon. There was one service remaining—the six o'clock service. Throughout the day, I had been thinking, *I don't remember saying the salvation prayer when I was younger. I remember raising my hand in elementary school, but I don't remember repeating a prayer.*

As we headed back to the church for the last service, I had this internal dialog about whether I should raise my hand and say the prayer. It was getting down to the last second to raise my hand. A nice woman was sitting beside me running ProPresenter. I had known her for just a few weeks but didn't know her well. She looked at me and said, "Ronni, raise your hand." I looked at her, dumbfounded, as tears started welling up. Then, I raised my hand.

The chains broke. I was free. Suddenly, I knew beyond the shadow of a doubt that I have a heavenly Father who loves me, I have been chosen, I am redeemed, and I have hope and a future. I had been made whole.

Now, I remind myself daily that I am set free and delivered in Jesus' name. As I said earlier, the devil is a liar and a thief and, quite frankly, is redundant in his tactics. When he comes rearing his nasty, little head, I repeat Ephesians 1:4, which declares, *Even before he made the world, God loved us and chose us in Christ to be holy and without fault in his eyes* (NLT).

Through Christ, I have been made worthy. I have value. I don't have to be afraid; the Lord is with me. I will walk in strength given to me by the Lord. I will walk past the chains that held me for so long with a changed demeanor of victory and completeness.

I can now use the chains that once caused me so much pain to tell the story of success made possible only by God. I know who I am through Christ. The enemy really thought he could have me, but I am a child of my heavenly Father; He says I am His.

Have you ever been in the middle of a storm that felt like it would take you under, but you knew it wouldn't? Have you ever felt as if you have an impenetrable armor protecting you? Do you have a peace that you know will guide you through the storm you know won't last forever?

With God as your guide, you can have faith that empowers you to look at the menacing clouds head-on. You can know who you are through Jesus Christ.

Through God, you can survive your darkest nights, knowing that the joy found only in Him *will* come in the morning.

# Breaking Chains of Guilt

By Connie A. VanHorn

*"Call to me and I will answer you and tell you great and unsearchable things you do not know"* (Jeremiah 33:3 NIV).

Do you ever wish you could dial God's number when you need Him most?

Jeremiah 33:3 is like an emergency phone number we can call anytime we feel overwhelmed by guilt. God doesn't want us to live in guilt and encourages us to reach out to Him.

When we "call" on God through prayer, worship, or simply turning our hearts to Him. He promises to answer us, revealing His love, grace, and understanding, even in our weakest moments.

Guilt can weigh us down with so much regret, and the shame of that regret can keep us from God's blessings. It's easy to dwell on all our past mistakes, believing we are unworthy of God's love and forgiveness.

Here's the good news: God doesn't want us to live in guilt; He invites us to come to Him in repentance and find freedom.

Repentance is a powerful step towards our healing. It requires honesty and humility as we acknowledge our wrongs and turn away from them. When we repent, we're not just expressing remorse; we're making a commitment to change our hearts and behaviors.

God wants our sincere repentance and is ready to shower us with His forgiveness and mercy. While guilt may try to cling to us, we cannot allow it to define who we are. Instead, treat guilt as a catalyst that drives you back to the Father.

We can never make a mistake that is too big for God's forgiveness. The moment we give our hearts to Jesus, He files away the things in our past and never brings them up again.

He makes us new!

> Therefore, if anyone is in Christ, the new creation has come. The old has gone, the new is here (2 Corinthians 5:17 NIV).

This Scripture changed my life after I was saved. The first time I read it was the moment I realized that God had made me a new person. This is the power of faith in Jesus. God's grace allowed me to move forward, leaving behind the weight of guilt and breaking the chains keeping me from my new life.

Now, my renewal through repentance is a constant reminder of God's love and mercy that encourages me to live in a way that reflects His goodness and grace.

When guilt attempts to hold you back, turn to Jeremiah 33:3 as a reminder to call on God, trusting that He will provide the peace and wisdom you need. As you trust Him, He will help you understand the truth: you are loved, valued, and forgiven.

Take time to pray and seek His guidance and forgiveness. Embrace the journey of repentance as an opportunity to grow closer to God. Allow His forgiveness to wash over you, renewing your spirit and setting you free from guilt so you can walk in His light.

Let's break the chains of guilt and live in the freedom God intended!

. . . . . . . . . . . . . . . . . . . . . . . . . . . . . . . . . . . . . . . . . . . . . . .

# Leah Starr Harris

Leah Starr Harris is a dedicated counselor based in Texas, committed to nurturing the well-being of children and families. Her work centers around fostering healing and strengthening relationships within the family unit.

Currently pursuing her PhD at Liberty University, Leah will graduate in May 2026. She is a proud mother of three young children and has a loving and wonderful husband. They live on their small farm in East Texas, embracing the joys of rural living.

Leah's passion for health and wellness shines through her role as a certified Pilates instructor, where she inspires others to embrace fitness.

Leah is also an accomplished author with three published books—*The Tempest and the Rescue, Hidden Treasures,* and *When Papaw Went to Heaven*—each available on Amazon.

As a gifted songwriter and musician, Leah has released two CDs, both of which can be enjoyed for free on her YouTube channel, LeahHarrisThroneRoomMusic. She has an upcoming single set for release in the summer of 2025.

Most importantly, Leah loves Jesus and does it all for His glory in and through her life!

To learn more about her music and family ministry,
visit ThroneRoomMusic.org!

# Overcoming Fear by Faith

By Leah Starr Harris

Since I was a little girl, fear has tried to haunt me. I grew up in a house where my dad never locked the doors. That was more common than it is now. But even as a child, having unsecured doors felt like an open invitation to something unwanted.

At night, I would be plastered in the middle of my bed, staring at the bright lights hanging from my ceiling fan with wide eyes, not wanting to break a stare in case something happened while I blinked. That was me trying to fall asleep.

I remember this image vividly. I was all alone, and I was in fear—fearing death by murder when I was six. I even had a detailed escape plan. If someone came for me in the dead of night, I would crawl through my window and hide under the trampoline in our backyard. Thus began my fear of early death.

But I also feared life.

As I aged, fear threaded its way through my existence. In my twenties, a counselor asked me what I was afraid of. I don't know if it was meant as a rhetorical question, but I answered it—my list was long. I said that not only was I afraid to die, but I was also afraid to live. (As in Shakespeare's *Hamlet*, "To be or not to be.") So many aspects of truly living scared me...to trust or not to trust...to love or not to love...to be loved or not to be loved. Existing was paralyzing.

Up to that point, most of my life had been limited by fear's grip on me. It suffocated my relationships, my God-given talents, and my opportunities by spinning webs of worry, doubt, isolation, and anxiety. It kept me bound. I was constantly eating the fruit of a poisonous tree. Seemingly, fear would have won had it not been for the testimony of Jesus Christ in my life and the demonstration of His power time and time again.

When I recommitted my life to the Lord in my mid-twenties, I was introduced to Jesus as my friend. Although I grew up going to private school, a personable, intimate relationship with God and the guidance of His Holy Spirit in everyday moments was something I was missing. But I encountered Him radically during a season of pure spiritual confusion that, otherwise, would surely have had a perilous end.

When I recognized Jesus' presence, I immediately followed. He set my feet to walking. We started at a brisk pace, and quickly, our walk turned into a run. I became enfolded by the truth of who God is. I fell in love with Him.

Overcoming fear by faith is a part of my testimony that the beautiful God of the universe has walked me through—hand-in-hand, side-by-side, and step-by-step.

His power has continued to carry me into victory, across one mountain at a time. In Matthew 17:20 (NKJV), Jesus told his disciples, *"If you have faith as a mustard seed, you will say to this mountain, 'Move from here to there,' and it will move; and nothing will be impossible for you."*

Throughout my journey, God has been weaving a beautiful tapestry of faith in each mountain-moving experience. All to the glory of His name.

Through the intimacy of our relationship, God allowed me to begin to confront fear. Although I do believe in instant deliverance from demonic influence, my experience of choosing faith over fear has been present in the deep crevices, valleys, and mountaintop moments. I've constantly been presented with a choice of whether or not to believe God amid trials and tribulations of life while fear was vying for my attention and old scripts were whispering in my ear.

But God came for me. Time and time again, He has come valiantly, swooping in to save me.

For example, overcoming fear in my marriage has been an ongoing process, one that I continue to lay at the feet of Jesus in surrender. In a past relationship, I had a horrific experience of unfaithfulness by a significant other, which hurt my ability to trust freely. I was blindsided by the act. Shortly after the betrayal, I could feel the walls go up, and I made an inner vow never to let my guard down again.

Almost a decade later, I can testify that the Holy Spirit has showered my husband and me with miraculous signs and wonders confirming our union. It has truly been heavenly. God's presence has been continually undeniable in our marriage from day one.

However, for a while, I struggled to trust our love and the strength of commitment we had to one another. I was deathly afraid of a betrayal. The fear all but consumed me. I was triggered easily by anything I perceived as unfaithful. It was easy for me to find ways to validate my distrust. I searched for him to look or glance in another woman's direction, noticed every comment or gesture, and questioned his past or anything I could find that might draw a question mark beside his integrity. I was extremely insecure and kindling a rage from past hurts.

My husband became part of the vicious pattern as I pushed him away in my anger and then accused him of wanting to leave me.

All the while, I was confirming the script fear had written on my heart: My husband couldn't be trusted, didn't love me, and would eventually abandon me—just like others had done. I feared I wasn't lovable and I wasn't good enough.

During this time in my life, I addressed God with the same question time and time again: "Can I trust this man?" And time and time again, God silenced the enemy's voice by reminding me that my husband was a promise He had fulfilled. I clung to God's words as I sought to overcome the fear that seemed to be all around me, waiting for an opportunity to pounce.

Looking back, I brought my fear to God too many times to count. I was desperate under the weight of fear's constant barrage. I worried that God would tire of answering my need for confirmation and reassurance; I often said I was sorry for my lack of faith. When my knees failed me, I looked to God for the strength to carry on.

Although this exchange and encouragement from God was something I looked to constantly, one specific day, the Lord came to my rescue and delivered me from fear's grip.

My husband and I were at a national park, and the enemy was rampantly trying to cause division. The violent attack of familiar lies threatened to ruin our weekend getaway, and I was crumbling under the pressure of it. As we continued to walk in the heat of our argument, I stumbled upon a mound of feathers under a huge oak. They were cardinal feathers!

To give you some background, I collected feathers long before my husband and I met. When I found a cardinal feather, it was a special treat—I treasured it as a symbolic reminder of God's promises. So, in the park that day, I felt the Lord ministering to my heart with a strong impression from His Spirit, saying I could trust my husband and assuring me, "I will answer your call for help—time and time and again." It was a beautiful moment that sticks in my mind and brought freedom to my heart. I kept those feathers on display as a reminder of God's promise.

Since then, I have continued to grow in trust with my husband and confidence in our relationship in our eight years of marriage. It has been a continual process of choosing faith over fear—a beautiful walk.

Not long after we were married, I was faced with another mountain. I had gotten pregnant and was part of a church community in which many other women about my age had become pregnant within a couple of months of each other. Some were carrying their first child like I was, while others had previous healthy pregnancies and deliveries.

Being pregnant was all very new to me. I didn't know what to expect! It was one of those beautiful seasons in which I experienced a lot of firsts. I hadn't even been around pregnant women before, so I was unprepared for the intensities of pregnancy, such as morning sickness, the emotional rollercoasters, and the quick changes my body would undergo. Even in that, I did my best to embrace this as a precious gift.

Sadly, many of the women around me began to miscarry within weeks of each other. This was heartbreaking to witness, as many of them were dear members of our church and close friends. Some were almost full-term when it happened. It was devastating.

I was suddenly concerned that I might also miscarry, as so many others had done. The enemy capitalized on my weakness, and it fed my own fear like gasoline to a fire. The enemy came almost every day to plant seeds in my heart and find an opening to entrap me.

I felt helpless to overcome it.

It was an ongoing battle. I was so scared to lose the baby growing inside of me. My heart was pleading for security in the life of my child. I needed to know she would be okay and we would make it through until the end with a healthy delivery. I cried out to God for an answer and assurance.

One morning, as I was going about my usual routine, I was halted by the voice of the Holy Spirit rising from my heart, "You will carry your child to full term and deliver a healthy baby girl."

The statement stopped me in my tracks as it interrupted my train of thought seemingly out of nowhere. God had spoken. These were not my own thoughts. God's promise left me with peace and the fruit of His Holy Spirit; it was even more reassuring that I *heard* His voice.

Now, I had a word to stand on. Every time the enemy came to steal, kill, and destroy, every time he came to whisper in my ear and provoke me with fear, I was reminded of what God had spoken and the truth of my circumstances. He had *told* me I would carry my child full term into this world. I would *not* miscarry. I would deliver a healthy baby girl.

And so, I used God's words as a weapon against the wiles of the devil, thanking Him for what He had spoken to me and for the life of my baby. I partnered with relevant scripture in prayer, declaring it over the child in my womb. I began wielding the sword of His Word to cut through the temptation knocking at my door.

Again and again, I had to choose not to give in to fear. God and I overcame a mountain together, and He built my faith in the process.

Even now, as I remember that time, I am awed by His faithfulness in completing that which He had spoken. Regardless of what life brings and how my thoughts and feelings are affected, this remains true.

Picture this: A young maiden is working in the fields harvesting a crop and spending time in the sun without a care in the world. Suddenly, the storm clouds of life start to roll in, the presence around her darkens, and she feels afraid. She can sense the evil trying to penetrate her mind, searching to discover any weakness in the armor of her soul. Before she can think to stop it, she is under siege. The "what ifs" and "hows" of fearful trepidation are whispered, reminding her of past pains. The dark storm clouds start swirling, beckoning her to give in to their chains.

As her stature starts to cower under the heaviness, she feels desperation coming from her spirit. "God, help me!"—a plea uttered in her time of need. And He hears her. Just then, her eyes are drawn upward; her gaze lifts above the fog of deception that had begun circling her. She sees what had been so near her all along. It is a tall tower, its stature strongly visible over the dark, hovering clouds. Instantly, she turns. Dropping everything in her hands, she runs to it.

She knows she is running to Him, her fortress and safety. When she arrives, He is already waiting to embrace her. He speaks softly, reminding her of who she is and His truth. He provides the waterfall of fresh perspective, revitalizing her in His words and promises.

Rescuing her once more.

*The name of the Lord is a strong tower; the righteous run into it and are safe* (Proverbs 18:10 NKJV).

There is a dance in the process of overcoming fear by faith. Faith accounts for the anticipatory span of time—when victory in the natural realm has not yet been, and you wait for the promise to become a tangible reality! There you are, waiting for the tide to change, having to believe before the promise is revealed.

The precipice in which you are awaiting the climactic release of tension and force that comes anticipating an answered prayer. It is the threshold. According to Oxford Languages, threshold means: "1. A strip of wood, metal, or stone forming the bottom of a doorway and crossed in entering a house or room. 2. The magnitude or intensity that must be exceeded for a certain reaction, phenomenon, result, or condition to occur or be manifested."

Interestingly, both definitions apply here. The threshold of our faith crosses us over into answered prayers by our belief in God. The threshold accounts for the moments before we walk through the doorway to blessing—the process of stepping over. It is also the magnitude or intensity that must be exceeded (the activation of our faith despite circumstance) for a certain reaction, phenomenon, result, or condition (answered prayers and promises fulfilled) to occur or be manifested.

Hebrews 11:1 (NKJV) reminds us of this by explaining, *Faith is the substance of things hoped for, the evidence of things not seen. For by it the elders obtained a good testimony.*

Faith is required to believe what is unseen or has not yet been manifested. Likewise, the threshold is the span of time where our faith in God's Word must carry us. It is the time we must press in and declare over our lives that which God has spoken. When fear is lurking at our door, trying to master us, we must gird up the loins of our minds and believe by faith all that is unseen, declaring in prayer with thankfulness what God has spoken.

> Be anxious for nothing, but in everything by prayer and supplication, with thanksgiving, let your requests be made known to God; and the peace of God, which surpasses all understanding, will guard your hearts and minds through Christ Jesus (Philippians 4:6-7 NKJV).

We can edify our souls by recalling all God has done and thanking Him for always being true to His Word. If He said it, it will be.

> If we are faithless, He remains faithful; He cannot deny Himself (2 Timothy 2:13 NKJV).

By choosing faith over fear, the beautiful garment of faith is woven through our lives.

It is a process that continually strengthens us as we are overcome by the power of God's Spirit in us and in His glorious name. We can abide in Him in the waiting, knowing He is building our faith and refining it as gold (1 Peter 1:7).

The Bible says Jesus is the Son of God and that He came to earth as man to fulfill the ultimate sacrifice. As the spotless Lamb, He was the unblemished payment for our sins and became the ransom for our lives. He reconciled us back to God the Father so we can have restored communion and relationship with Him.

Jesus died and rose again as the first of many brethren to overcome spiritual death so that we may walk in the garden of life and be restored to our rightful place as the sons and daughters of God.

Our faith in Jesus and His Word, as the substance of things hoped for and believed for in our lives here on earth and in the life to come, carries us through each day. Belief in Him as the Son of God, our Lord and Savior, is the gate, door, or threshold that grants us access to His eternal kingdom.

Hebrews chapter 11 references the biblical patriarchs who were counted as righteous by their faith in God and the fulfillment of His promises. They were clothed in robes of righteousness by their faith! The book of John refers to Jesus as the Word made flesh:

> *And the Word became flesh and dwelt among us, and we beheld His glory, the glory as of the only begotten of the Father, full of grace and truth* (John 1:14 NKJV).

This scripture encompasses the testimony of Jesus in my life. By standing on the rock of my salvation—my precious Jesus—I will continue to cross over the threshold with faith and claim victory over fear.

We must remain rooted and grounded in Him and look to the daily bread of His Word to sustain us as our ultimate source of truth.

No matter what.

# Breaking Chains of Anger

By Connie A. VanHorn

*Get rid of all bitterness, rage and anger, brawling and slander, along with every form of malice. Be kind and compassionate to one another, forgiving each other, just as in Christ God forgave you* (Ephesians 4:31-32 NIV).

When I became a new Christian, I thought everything would be easier. I expected God to protect me from difficulties. So, when I faced hard things and was attacked, I felt very alone. *Why isn't God protecting me? I thought that as a new believer, I would be protected.* I became angry at God.

But the truth is, God never promised that life would be easy. He promised to be with me through every storm. And He held to that promise; He never left me. Our God never leaves His children stranded. I didn't understand this right away, so anger became another heavy chain I needed to let go of, which I was able to do step by step by learning to trust God and His presence.

Anger often comes from deeper hurts and pain we haven't addressed; it can spill out of our mouths when things aren't going our way. Words are so powerful and have the power to heal or to hurt. I often say that hurt people tend to hurt people. Our buried feelings can turn to anger and end up hurting us and those we love.

Personally, I had to dig really deep to allow God to heal me so I wouldn't lash out in anger and hurt those closest to me. Our God is so clever. He drew me to Him and gave me time to heal. And in my waiting—and sometimes despite my whining, He pruned my anger.

Here's the good news! God wants to heal you, too. He invites you to bring your anger and hurt to Him. In response, He will unchain you. You can trust that God can and will heal your broken places and turn your anger into peace—if you let Him. Instead of allowing anger to take over your heart, God's kindness and love can take over your life.

God promises to walk with us, and when we trust Him, we can break free from the chains of anger. I always tell my kids that it's easier to be kind than to be anything else. That's because God will always give us His strength to share kindness.

Something very powerful happens when we take time to be with God. He heals us, removing anger and loneliness and replacing them with His peace and joy so we can experience the life He wants for us.

God is with you in every struggle, and if you let Him, He will take your pain and anger and turn it into something good.

> The Lord said…"Have I not commanded you? Be strong and courageous. Do not be afraid; do not be discouraged, for the Lord your God will be with you wherever you go" (Joshua 1:1,9 NIV).

. . . . . . . . . . . . . . . . . . . . . . . . . . . . . . . . . . . . . . . . . . . . . . . .

# Amanda Joy Lane

Amanda Joy Lane is from Palm Beach Gardens, Florida, and is a devoted mother to her beautiful 7-year-old daughter. As a healthcare recruiter, she is passionate about connecting talented professionals with meaningful opportunities in the medical field. With an understanding of the industry's needs, Amanda works hard to ensure that candidates and healthcare facilities thrive.

Outside of her professional life, Amanda finds joy and grounding in her faith. She attends church every Sunday at Christ Fellowship, where she embraces the strength and community that her church provides. This connection helps her reinforce her commitment to living with purpose.

In her spare time, Amanda enjoys playing pickleball, which keeps her active and also fosters friendship and camaraderie. She cherishes family time and is dedicated to creating special memories with her daughter, who inspires her daily to lead with love, resilience, and hope.

Amanda lives by the scripture, *"For I know the plans I have for you," declares the Lord, "plans to prosper you and not to harm you, plans to give you hope and a future"* (Jeremiah 29:11 NIV).

Never give up!

# The God Who Never Lets Go

By Amanda Joy Lane

*"I took you from the ends of the earth, from its farthest corners I called you. I said, 'You are my servant'; I have chosen you and have not rejected you. So do not fear, for I am with you; do not be dismayed, for I am your God. I will strengthen you and help you; I will uphold you with my righteous right hand"* (Isaiah 41:9-10 NIV).

Rejection has a way of shaking us to our core, of making us question our worth and place in the world. But even in that pain, God's truth never wavers. He has chosen us, not forsaken us. Isaiah 41:9–10 reminds us that no matter how cast aside we may feel—by people, circumstances, or even our own brokenness—God's hand is steady, His love unchanging, and His purpose for us unshakable.

My journey has been marked by rejection—times I craved acceptance, wrestled with self-worth, and drifted from the God who never let go. From childhood changes that left me feeling out of place to relationships that chipped away at my value, I searched for belonging in all the wrong places. But through every heartbreak, betrayal, and lonely season, God was working—refining me, drawing me back, and redeeming what was lost.

I was born in Palm Beach Gardens, Florida, and lived in Jupiter until about the age of eight. During that time, I attended church regularly with my family. I remember Sundays at Cathedral of Life, where Pastor Damin would preach, and afterward, a sweet lady would sell mini shepherd's pies. I enjoyed going to Lighthouse Elementary with my best friend Jackie and found learning fun.

Most of my family lived in Florida—they still do. My dad often took me to my grandparents' house after school. They ran a business called Cochran Storage and lived above it. We'd ride around on the golf cart while my grandmother made spaghetti in the kitchen. My grandparents laid a strong foundation rooted in love for Jesus, which shaped how they raised their kids and has carried through generations. As a mom now, I'm so grateful for that.

When we moved from Florida to Ohio, starting a new school was rough. I went from a place where talking about God and being kind was "cool" to a school where I got made fun of for following rules and not cussing. I hated it. Feeling judged at school made me feel judged in general, so I avoided being the center of attention. I missed my grandparents and cousins. I just wanted to go home. Looking back, I spent many years feeling upset over that move. Deep down, I knew Florida was home, and I felt a constant pull to be there.

Shortly after we moved, we started attending a new church. It was much smaller and very different from my old church—the one with the sweet pie lady I missed so much. I didn't want to go to the kids' service like before, so I'd sit with my parents in the pew, bringing things to entertain myself until it was over.

Looking back, I realize I was already starting to drift from God. As a child, I couldn't grasp faith as an adult does. I needed to learn at my level and build friendships with peers who were walking with Christ. Instead, I gravitated toward friends who didn't go to church, pulling me even further away from Him.

At the age of nine, I got baptized. I didn't fully understand what I was doing, probably because I never attended Sunday school.

Eventually, we moved to what I consider my childhood home. At the front of the neighborhood was a community pool where we spent our summers. My mom would take my two younger sisters and me there all day, and we made some of our best family memories. I also started at a new elementary school, where I formed wonderful friendships—some of which I still have today.

Skipping ahead to high school, I had my first real boyfriend during my sophomore year, who asked me to homecoming. Since our middle schools had just merged, that year was all about meeting new people and blending friend groups. That's also when I was first introduced to drinking and partying. I was further from God than I even realized, finding any excuse not to attend church. Fitting in and having lots of friends mattered more to me than anything else.

After a year and a half together, my high school boyfriend broke up with me. I was crushed. He was my first love and best friend—we spent nearly every day together with our shared group of friends. The next day, those same friends showed up wearing or carrying things I'd given him and dumped them all in the trash after school. It was brutal. I'll never forget how deeply that broke me—but I'm also thankful for what came next. It forced me to start fresh, discover who my real friends were, and be with the people God knew I truly needed.

I reconnected with two girlfriends who had strong relationships with God. At first, I hung out with them separately, but soon, the three of us started going to church together. I felt so close to God in that season. I was in church twice a week, hungry for more of Him, taking notes during every service, slain in the Spirit, and fully involved in youth nights. I learned a lot about myself during that time. I still went to parties, but I made much better choices. Most importantly, I realized it's not about how many friends you have—it's about the value of the ones you have that truly matters.

Then my high school boyfriend came back. Long story short, we dated on and off for ten years. A lot happened during that time, and I allowed things I shouldn't have because I didn't value myself. I stayed because I had gained weight, believed the things he said, and tied my worth to his words. Most of our friends were off at college or in relationships, and I felt stuck.

But then God stepped in. Out of nowhere, something shifted. I wanted to take care of myself. I started waking up at 5:30 each morning, excited for life like never before. My favorite part of the day was heading to work. I worked at a nursing home and loved helping the residents start their mornings—getting them up, encouraging them, and making them feel good. I cut carbs, started fasting, and began exercising. I was learning to love and value myself. And with that came clarity. I began to see my worth and reflect on everything I had allowed in that relationship.

I spent the next few months going out with my girlfriends, slowly drifting from God again. Then I met my husband. We kept running into each other at a local bar and became friends. Over time, he became my best friend. We spent so much time together having fun—playing sports at the park, goofing off, day drinking, making giant water blobs, camping—never a dull moment.

At the bar, we became regulars. We'd dance for hours and laugh nonstop; people would say they envied our relationship. I had blinders of excitement on. We dated for two years and had plenty of fights; his drinking became an issue. I remember wondering, *Is this all our life will ever be? Just the bar?* I'd ask him often, and his answer was always the same: "We're just having fun."

One night, after an argument at the bar, I left and started walking home—we lived just around the corner. I told him I was done and wanted to break up. When we got home, he pulled out a ring and proposed. Looking back, I wonder if that would've happened if I hadn't been walking away.

In the days leading up to our wedding, questions kept circling in my mind: *Are we ever going to stop living at the bar? Does he believe in God? Will we ever go to church regularly?* On our wedding day, I still had doubts. My mom asked if I wanted to back out. She saw things I couldn't—or maybe didn't want to.

About two months after the wedding, I had a gut feeling I couldn't shake. I went to spend the morning with my parents and happened to check my husband's location. At 11 am, he was in a rough part of town, 30 minutes from home—and I just knew. I called him at least 20 times. When he finally picked up, he said he was at a friend's house. But I knew where that friend lived, and it wasn't anywhere near there.

When I say God brings all things to light, I mean all things. And He gave me no peace about it. A friend suggested I check an escort site. I told myself, *No way—not my charming, funny, nerdy, kind husband.* But then I found a post from a woman listing a meeting spot at a gas station at the end of her street—the same street he was on that morning.

I confronted him, but he wouldn't be honest. So, I reached out to the woman. To my surprise, she was kind—she talked to me on the phone and even sent me their entire conversation. I was in shock. I had married a complete stranger. I never imagined someone I loved could be capable of that.

But I stayed. I felt so much shame at the thought of leaving right after getting married. I told myself I'd give it six months. I was embarrassed. Then I found out I was pregnant—a moment that should've been filled with joy but was instead clouded by the reality that I was contemplating leaving my marriage.

There was deep sorrow in realizing I was married to someone I no longer recognized. But that pain pushed me closer to God. I chose to live my life for myself and my baby. Even though I was still married, I had to choose me—because my actions were the only ones I could control.

I started listening only to Christian music, doing daily Bible studies, and rebuilding my relationship with the Lord. I needed Him more than ever. I was pregnant, living with a husband who yelled at me to drop him off at the bar, who constantly had porn on his phone, and who told me I was worthless and that my body looked weird.

Then he got the call—he was being deployed for a year. I have to admit, part of me felt relieved. Our baby would be turning one when his deployment began, and I told myself I'd use that time to figure things out.

But the year leading up to his deployment was brutal. His drinking got worse. He'd leave for the bar and not come home. He tore me down constantly. Women started messaging me, saying they'd been with him the night before. It got so bad I'd lock myself in another room out of fear during his drunken rages—or pack up in the middle of the night, baby in my arms, and sneak out the back door to my parents' house. I'd call my mom, and she'd gently remind me, "Just a few more months—you'll have space to figure things out."

I was torn. I never wanted to be divorced. I felt like, biblically, I was supposed to stay married. But by the time deployment rolled around, I had lost all respect for him and the desire for our marriage to work out.

That year of deployment ended up being the best year of my life. I found a home church we attended every week. No chaos, no walking on eggshells— just peace. I made real friends and finally felt like I could breathe. I'm still so grateful for that time. Being home with my daughter was a gift I'll always cherish.

My husband returned on January 10, 2020. Almost instantly, the drinking and destructive behavior resumed. To him, I hadn't lost enough weight, so I was worthless. I did the only thing I could—I met with a divorce attorney, told him I wanted out, and packed my things. But when he agreed to go to rehab, I left my bags where they were... and stayed.

Then COVID hit—just days after my husband returned from rehab—and I was terrified. I had a toddler and a husband I couldn't rely on—no real partner in the chaos. I went into full panic mode, spent $600 on groceries three days before lockdown, then went to bed with a prayer.

That night, I asked God to humble me. I knew I had married for the wrong reasons. I'd gotten comfortable—the new car, the big house—all things I didn't want to lose. But deep down, I knew comfort wasn't the same as peace.

Have you ever had a back thought while praying? I did. As I asked God to humble me, part of me pushed back: *No, actually, I'm humbled enough. COVID has already shown me a lot.* But I went to bed uneasy.

Then, at 1 am, the dogs started barking. After a year alone during deployment, I was used to random noises and almost rolled over to go back to sleep. But something inside me said, Get up. I listened. I heard sounds— like someone breaking in. But when we followed the noise, we realized our home was on fire. In that moment, I knew God was saying, "I'll tell you when you're humble enough."

We lost almost everything. I was able to save our important documents, but anything tied to memories was destroyed in the fire. We had to start over. I was terrified, displaced with a small child in the middle of a deadly pandemic. Thankfully, we found a rental and stayed there until our home was rebuilt.

I was scared of God. I didn't want to pray out of fear I'd say the wrong thing. I was angry and kept asking myself, *How did this become my life?* I felt distant but stayed as close to Him as I could manage. Looking back, I should've started therapy after the fire. I developed daily anxiety and constantly convinced myself I was dying from whatever I could Google.

Meanwhile, my husband had slipped back into his old ways. And this time, there was no escape—we were quarantined.

Eventually, we moved back into the newly rebuilt house. It was beautiful— something I had poured my heart into. I worked so hard on every detail, hoping it would feel like a fresh start. But after just a week, I knew I had to leave.

My husband was out of control too often, and the environment wasn't safe. He'd drink and try to "play" with the kids, not realizing it felt more threatening than fun. What he saw as harmless chaos felt dangerous to us. I had to make the hardest decision—not just for me, but to protect my daughter.

Then my dad called and said, "I'm bringing a U-Haul. Pack your stuff. I'm moving you and Emery to Florida." He felt terrible that it had come to this, but he knew I was no longer safe. I stayed for two more weeks, packing and trying to hold it together.

During that time, my ex-husband asked to sign over his parental rights. I was heartbroken—*How could you?* But I called my attorney, she drew up the papers, and he walked in and signed them. By the grace of God and because of that decision, my daughter is safe and thriving today.

That was it. Emery and I were on our way to Florida. I'll never forget that drive. It's so hard to leave someone you don't want to leave, but when addiction takes over, it leaves you with no choice. My parents found me an apartment and paid for it—something I'll always feel guilty about but forever grateful for. They gave up so much so that Emery and I could have a fresh start.

I spent the next few years healing. I'd wake up every day feeling worthless, haunted by the words he had used as weapons. My anxiety got so bad that I could barely leave the house. I'd sit at home and play with my daughter all day because even stepping outside triggered panic. But little by little, I healed.

Every day, I reminded myself: God, *You know the plans You have for me* (from Jeremiah 29:11). My village surrounded me and helped me get plugged into a church. I landed my first good job, my daughter started preschool, and I began therapy and learned to fight my anxiety without medication.

Now, we are healthy and happy. There's so much good in our lives.

Looking back on the heartbreaks, the fire, the fear, and the rejection, I see the fingerprints of a loving God who never let go. When I felt cast aside,

He whispered, "You are my servant; I have chosen you and not rejected you." When fear gripped me, He reminded me, "Do not be dismayed, for I am your God." And when I had no strength left, He upheld me with His righteous right hand.

The rejection I once thought defined me was really a redirection—toward something better. Toward Him.

Through every broken chapter, God is writing a story of redemption.

On the other side of pain, I can say with full confidence that healing is real, God is faithful, and the best is still ahead.

Every day, I keep moving forward in faith. No matter what you have gone through or are going through, you can keep moving forward in faith, too. God's got you. And He will never let you go.

# Breaking Chains of Rejection

By Melissa Gissy Witherspoon

Rejection is one of the most painful experiences a person can endure. When someone turns away, it cuts deep, leaving wounds that can shape our identity, distort our self-worth, and hinder our ability to receive love. Many people walk through life shackled by the chains of rejection, struggling with insecurity, fear, and a constant need for approval. But the good news is that Jesus Christ came to set us free from these chains.

Rejection can come from multiple sources—family, friends, relationships, or even the church. Perhaps you were abandoned by a parent, excluded by peers, or betrayed by someone you trusted. The enemy uses these moments to plant lies in our hearts: "You are not good enough." "You are unlovable." "You will always be alone." If we accept these lies, we begin to live in bondage, seeking validation from people instead of finding our identity in God.

However, Scripture reminds us that when we give our lives to God, He will never reject us. In Psalm 27:10, David declares, *Though my father and mother forsake me, the Lord will receive me* (NIV). Human rejection is painful, but God's acceptance is eternal.

Jesus Himself experienced rejection. *He was despised and rejected by men, a man of sorrows and acquainted with grief* (Isaiah 53:3 ESV). Jesus' own people turned against Him. Even His disciples abandoned Him at His lowest moment. Yet, Jesus never allowed rejection to define Him—He remained rooted in the Father's love.

And when He died on the cross, Jesus took our rejection upon Himself, making a way for us to be fully accepted by God. Ephesians 1:6 says, *To the praise of His glorious grace, by which He made us accepted in the Beloved* (ESV). Through Christ, we are no longer rejected—we are chosen, loved, and secure.

Recognizing the lies of rejection is the first step to freedom from this debilitating chain. Identify the false beliefs you've embraced about yourself and replace them with God's truth.

> *You are a chosen people, a royal priesthood, a holy nation, God's special possession* (1 Peter 2:9 NIV).

Forgiving those who have rejected you is essential. Holding on to bitterness keeps you chained to pain. Jesus forgave those who rejected Him, and He calls us to do the same. Ask God for the strength to release resentment and walk in freedom.

Embracing God's acceptance will transform how you see yourself. Spend time in His presence, let His Word renew your mind, and allow His love to heal the wounds of rejection. His love is greater than any human rejection.

Your worth is not determined by those who reject you but by the One who has redeemed you. Walk in confidence! Through Christ, the chains of rejection are broken; you are set free!

. . . . . . . . . . . . . . . . . . . . . . . . . . . . . . . . . . . . . . . . . . . . . . . . . .

# Monica French

Currently residing in Jupiter, FL, with her youngest daughter, who is entering high school, Monica French was born in Japan to a Navy father and a Japanese mother. She spent her early years in Hawaii before growing up in Southern California.

Monica is the proud mother of four wonderful children—three girls and one boy—spanning 14 years from oldest to youngest, and she has one "adopted" son. Her talented children inspired her to embrace the roles of team mom for baseball and taekwondo and support them backstage in theater and pageantry.

Monica loves the ocean and being in nature. She is passionate about people and healthy living, with careers in non-profit work, sales, marketing, teaching, and the medical field. She holds numerous certifications and a degree in Social Work, as well as teaching credentials in two states.

Her specialty lies in networking and empowering others, and she has led a local chapter of a women's networking group for several years.

Following the loss of her mother in 2008 and the passing of her fiancé in early 2024, she is dedicated to raising awareness for suicide prevention.

Above all, she wants her readers to know that there is hope in Jesus, and she is committed to helping others find Him.

# To Fly Again

By Monica French

Suicide. It's a word that carries a heavy weight and one that many would rather avoid discussing.

However, it's a topic that needs our attention and understanding more than ever. Even if suicide hasn't directly impacted your life, I want to offer you an opportunity to gain insight and compassion for those struggling and those who are learning to fly again. I pray my story inspires you and provides hope for healing and the resilience needed to get through the difficult things in life.

When my pastor looked me in the eye and said, "I am so sorry. I have no words," the silence spoke volumes. Moments like this offered peace in the shared struggle of uncertainty.

I responded, "It's okay. I have no words either."

Mutual understanding offered grace.

> The Lord is close to the brokenhearted and saves those who are crushed in spirit (Psalm 34:18 NIV).

In our pain, we can find connection, hope, and healing. When we want to scream out, longing to hear something to help us make sense of it all, we can lean into God and His truths. God's presence surrounds us even in the silence. He offers comfort and understanding and will send people to walk through the struggle with us.

I was in high school the first time suicide touched my life. My new lab partner hung himself in his garage. I didn't know him well, just that he was a year younger and seemed like a really sweet kid. Our school provided counselors, but we were all lost for words, unsure how to process such a tragedy.

The next time suicide affected me was shortly after I got married. One of my mom's clients, a single older woman, chose to take her own life. My mother was heartbroken, experiencing a deep sadness and, because her client didn't know the Lord, a worry about where this woman would spend eternity.

*Cast all your anxiety on him because he cares for you* (1 Peter 5:7 NIV).

Later, my middle daughter tragically lost a friend to suicide. This young woman took her life just a day after her 17th birthday. My daughter was devastated, and I struggled to understand how someone so young, beautiful, and vibrant could feel she had nothing to look forward to.

Then, the unimaginable happened to me.

Scott, my gregarious, intelligent, big-hearted love, decided he couldn't face another day.

The week after New Year's Day 2024, a year that had begun filled with hope and dreams, the rug was pulled out from under me. That Sunday morning, my entire life changed. While worshiping at church with my daughter and two of her friends, I suddenly felt like I had been sucker punched as a wave of sickness washed over me. At that exact moment, my daughter reached out to hug me, something she wouldn't normally do.

Little did I know, that was the moment Scott's soul was ripped from this earth.

As soon as we sat down from worshipping, I sent a flurry of texts to both my son and Scott. They were supposed to meet up that morning to finalize a move. When I heard nothing back, anxiety bubbled up inside me. I needed to get home, but first, I had to drop off the girls. On the way, I received a text that felt like a punch to the gut—a message I wouldn't wish on my worst enemy.

I glanced at it, then quickly placed it in my lap, gripping the steering wheel tightly as I drove. My daughter noticed my change in demeanor and asked what was wrong, but I replied, "I'm not sure," desperately wanting to believe it wasn't as serious as it seemed. I decided to drop the girls off at her friend's house, asking her dad to drive them home.

I didn't scream.

I didn't cry.

I went numb.

My foot pressed hard on the gas pedal. My daughter had seen the text and sensed something was off. I told her I needed to check on something at home, promising to update her once I knew more. As I glanced at her, I saw the tears welling in her eyes, and it hit me that she understood something terrible had happened.

As I drove, I felt utterly lost but clung to the hope that God was with me, holding me together when everything felt shattered.

> So do not fear, for I am with you; do not be dismayed, for I am your God (Isaiah 41:10 NIV).

Once I was finally alone, I sped home, only to pull up to my apartment complex, now transformed into a crime scene. Police cars and people were everywhere. It all felt like a blur. I can't tell you where I parked or who I talked to first—maybe my neighbor. Or my son, who had found him.

I felt trapped in a dream state. It was surreal and disorienting. This couldn't possibly be happening.

I wasn't allowed to go upstairs. I didn't press the issue because I was terrified of what I might see. Instead, I made a few phone calls—to my dad, my pastor, friends, and his mom. My neighbor insisted I sit down on her patio. I felt numb, struggling to comprehend the situation.

Just that morning, we had shared a deep conversation. Then, he texted me his usual <I love you> and <I miss you.> But there had been something more:

<Thank you, thank you, thank you for believing in me. I love you so much!!!>

Followed by four hearts.

He had expressed so much gratitude for my support. So why was I here, dealing with this unimaginable loss? Why did he leave me?

I wasn't hysterical; I didn't scream or cry. Instead, I felt numb, functional, and strangely rational. Survival mode kicked in. I had a child to take care of, someone I needed to be strong for. My son was shattered, and I knew I had to hold it together for him. Like a robot, I moved through the motions, trying not to feel anything. It still didn't seem real.

Once the police finished their investigation, they brought my son over. They kept me from seeing anything, which I was grateful for, but it only added to the surreal feeling. My friend arranged for a cleanup, so I never stepped inside until it was almost back to normal. That first glimpse stayed with me, a haunting reminder of what had happened. I focused on my son, on getting through each moment, knowing that I had to be the anchor in the storm for him.

Somehow, I also had to find a way to process my own grief, even as I held strong for those I loved. I reminded myself that healing would take time, but I wouldn't be alone on this journey.

Life became a blur.

I was on autopilot, only occasionally coming up for air. That's when the pain would hit, bringing tears that wouldn't last as long as I wanted. There was simply too much to do, and everyone depended on me to get it done. I felt as if I were trapped inside a room with a large sliding glass door—able to see the world outside but not quite fully able to engage with it.

I tried my best to maintain my routine, even though it had shifted slightly. Each morning, I made it a point to read God's Word, seeking strength to get through the day.

> The Lord is close to the brokenhearted and saves those who are crushed in spirit (Psalm 34:18 NIV).

Through that hypothetical glass door, I could see so many people stepping up to help me. Friends and family rallied around me, offering their support in countless ways. It reminded me that I wasn't alone in my grief, even if it felt isolating at times. Their kindness acted as a lifeline, pulling me toward the hope I desperately needed.

I held on to those glimpses of love and support, grateful for the community surrounding me, filling the cracks in my heart with their compassion. Even in my numbness, I recognized that healing is a journey, and I would take it one step at a time, leaning on God and those who cared for me.

I could see how God was working things out and providing for us in our darkest moments. Life was hard, but it was as if He were carrying us when we were too weak to walk on our own. Each day, little signs of His presence showed up as friends reached out with meals, neighbors offered support, and unexpected acts of kindness reminded me we were not alone in our grief.

With each passing day, my faith deepened. I began to recognize the ways God was weaving hope into our lives, even when it felt impossible. This really felt impossible. The love and support from those around us were tangible reminders of His grace. I learned to lean into that support, allowing others to help carry the burden.

I found strength I didn't know I had, all while trusting that God would continue to lead me toward healing and flying again. I was incredibly grateful.

Everyone—literally everyone—kept telling me how strong I was. "You're doing great," they said. "I can't believe how strong you are." But inside, I didn't feel strong at all. I knew I had no choice but to keep pressing on, and I realized that my strength came directly from the Lord.

When I felt weak, I clung to the truth of 2 Corinthians 12:9: *"My grace is sufficient for you, for my strength is made perfect in weakness"* (NIV). My mantra became, "I trust You, Lord."

When I couldn't see the way forward, I whispered, "I trust You, Lord." Thoughts raced through my mind nonstop. I thought I had found my forever, but suddenly, I was left without my partner. My daily routine had been filled with his interjections—the little moments that made our life together so special.

*How would I go on without those?*

I could picture him standing in the doorway in the early morning, watching me as I prepared for my devotional time. He would walk over, kiss me on the forehead, and tell me he missed me before heading back to bed.

He helped me choose between pairs of shoes and picked out the perfect necklace to go with my outfit, always telling me how beautiful I looked. When I left, he would text me the moment I walked out the door to say he missed me and loved me.

Yet now, my heart ached as I remembered how he often apologized for not being himself, reminiscing about the things he used to do and dwelling on the past—regrets about when his son was young and what he hadn't followed through with.

I couldn't help but wonder what had happened to my gregarious man who had filled my days with love and laughter. Over time, God came through with visions and dreams. I would wake up and remember something, and God started to reveal the demons that had attached themselves to him. How they relentlessly whispered lies into his mind, increasing over time and eventually overtaking him.

I'm grateful for the vision God gave me that showed Scott being grabbed and dragged into the abyss by the darkest demons, only to be rescued from their grasp by the intense light of Jesus. I saw Jesus proclaiming to the darkness that Scott was His as He pulled him up to heaven, standing before God the Father and showing him as clean and redeemed. It was the most beautiful vision and rescue I could have asked for.

Scott had accepted Christ as his Savior the year before, but God knew I needed to see this vision to be reassured that the man I loved so dearly was safe in the arms of Jesus. I needed to see this so I could learn to truly live again.

To honor Scott, I spent his birthday weekend at my friend's house by the water. I figured it would be a good respite, a place to focus on reading through our texts and my journals. However, I struggled to go through our text messages since they kept scrolling back to the most recent ones. So, instead, I turned my attention to my old journals, hoping to find comfort in the memories.

As I read, I was transported back to the time when I was completely falling in love with Scott. I remembered his beautiful spirit, infectious energy, and attentiveness to detail. He had a genuine interest in people, listening intently as they spoke and drawing them out to share their hopes, dreams, and incredible qualities.

He remembered things about people I often overlooked; he knew my kids' likes and preferences better than I did. But what surprised me as I read through those pages was the realization that I had grieved so much throughout our years together. Even in the joy, there were moments of heartache, and those memories began to surface as I reflected on our time together. It reminded me that love is intertwined with both joy and sorrow and that, even in grief, we can find beauty.

We can learn to dream again.

Scott's depressive state caused him to let go of so many dreams. There were times during our years together I cried over the loss of those dreams. Oddly, I think that helped me in my grief process—I had already mourned significant parts of our relationship. It felt like being in love with something that no longer exists, a painful reminder of what could have been.

Still, the demons of fear often overtook the truths I held dear. I had to remind myself that just because he left me didn't mean he didn't love me. Since his death, I've been able to reconnect with his mom, and we've grown very close. I now support her in ways that Scott could not.

Love is complex, and God doesn't want us to live in fear. He wants us to embrace hope and fulfill our deepest desires and dreams.

I had to find hope again.

I found comfort in God's promises. Psalm 37:4 (NIV) says, *Take delight in the Lord, and he will give you the desires of your heart.* This verse resonates deeply with me because God sees my pain and the dreams I still hold. And pain can fuel our dreams if we believe the One who is in control of them.

God met my vision board with a sense of purpose, filling it with new hopes and aspirations. I started to see a future where healing and joy could coexist alongside my memories.

I began to reclaim those dreams, knowing that God was with me every step of the way. I realized that while I had lost the life I once envisioned, new possibilities awaited. I still have life and purpose. I can still dream! I can still fly until I fulfill my time and purpose on this earth.

Embracing this new perspective of healing has become a way to honor Scott and our love and has helped me find strength in faith and hope for my future. It allowed me to start dreaming again. The road ahead might be challenging, but I trust that God will guide me every step of the way, and Scott will check in from heaven from time to time!

Fly high, Scott! I'll see you soon, my love!

It's time for me to fly again!

There is hope! We can break the chains of depression!

This world can often feel overwhelming and dark, causing deep sadness, despair, and isolation. Depression can feel like a heavy fog that clouds our vision, making it difficult to see the light of hope. For some, these feelings can lead to thoughts of suicide, a tragic outcome that leaves behind a wake of grief and unanswered questions.

But there is hope. This truth is that God does not want us to carry our burdens alone. He invites us to bring our worries and pain to Him.

> *Cast all your anxiety on Him because He cares for you* (1 Peter 5:7 NIV).

God is not distant; He is intimately aware of your struggles and longs to help you break free from the chains of despair.

I'm praying for you!

> *Heavenly Father, I come before You today with a heavy heart for anyone who is struggling with depression or has lost a loved one to its darkness. I know their pain. I ask for Your strength as they step out and break the chains of depression. Help us remember that we are never alone, even when life is dark.*

*Lord, give us the courage to reach out for help, whether through friends, family, or professional support, knowing that asking for help is a sign of strength, not weakness. Give us Your love and comfort, and help us see the light of hope shining through the darkness as we recognize You have a purpose for us. Amen.*

## START HERE

*Reach Out:* If you or someone you know is struggling with depression or suicidal thoughts, don't hesitate to seek help. Talk to a trusted friend, family member, or mental health professional. Remember, it's okay to ask for help.

*Pray:* Make prayer a daily practice. Pour out your heart to God, sharing your fears and anxieties. Allow Him to fill you with His peace and comfort.

*Get Educated:* Take time to learn about mental health awareness and suicide prevention. Understanding these issues can help reduce stigma and encourage open conversations.

*Support Others:* If you know someone who is struggling, be a listening ear. Sometimes, just being present can make a significant difference in someone's life.

God wants you to live in freedom, not in chains. He desires that you experience joy, hope, and purpose. Hold His promises and seek help when needed. Let's support one another on this journey of healing and living. Together, with God's grace, we can break the chains of darkness and step into the light of hope.

Never stop dreaming—you *will* fly again!

# Breaking Chains of Self-Harm

By Connie A. VanHorn

*"Come to me, all you who are weary and burdened, and I will give you rest"* (Matthew 11:28 NIV).

A couple of years ago, I was ordering a sandwich at Subway when I noticed the young girl behind the counter had scars in the shape of horizontal lines going up her arms. I recognized these scars because I had seen them on one of my sisters before. Next to her scars were a few tiny heart tattoos.

This girl was very pretty and kind, and she seemed okay as she continued to make my sandwich. We made small talk, and I loved her bubbly personality. When I left that day, I couldn't stop thinking about her and the pain she must have endured to begin to self-harm.

Self-harm is often a misguided attempt to cope with emotional pain. It can feel like a release and a way to have control when life or circumstances feel chaotic. We all know that feeling in one way or another.

Even though self-harm might provide temporary relief, it ultimately leads to deeper wounds, which are both physically and emotionally painful. Jesus understands your struggles. He sees your pain and the burdens you carry.

In Matthew 11:28, Jesus invites us to come to Him with our heavy hearts: *"Come to me, all you who are weary and burdened, and I will give you rest"* (NIV).

Jesus gives us rest. We don't have to bear our pain alone. Jesus offers us His love and comfort and a love that can break through the chains of self-harm and the pain that leads us to it.

If we look to the world to satisfy us, it will only leave us feeling empty. The pressures, expectations, and emotional chaos that many of us find ourselves drowning in are overwhelming and can lead to self-harm.

Whether it's the weight of expectations, past traumas, the constant comparison to others, or that someone has hurt us, our struggles can create a cycle of pain that is hard to escape. You are not alone in this battle; there is hope for healing. You can trust Jesus to mend the brokenness within!

It's time to break free! Turn to Jesus today and pray. Share your heart with Him; reveal your struggles, fears, and desires for peace.

Allow God to become your coping mechanism and fill the void that self-harm has tried to fill.

Write this vision and ask God to give you faith and specific steps to embrace His promises.

*I am healed.*

*I am strong.*

*Jesus is my comfort and my care.*

Meet yourself where you are. Write down the triggers that lead you to self-harm and pray over each one, asking God to replace harm with healing.

Healing takes time, and it's okay to reach out for help. God has provided an army of support to help you. Reach out to your church, a healthcare professional, or a trusted ministry. To Write Love On Her Arms is one such online resource dedicated to meeting the hurting where they are (twloha.com).

You are not alone. Your Christian family is there for you. Jesus is there for you. He will offer a love that surpasses understanding and the strength to break free from the chains that bind you.

I often think about that young, sweet girl at Subway. I pray that those tiny red hearts represent her own healing and self-love!

Starting today, I pray that you seek your rest in Jesus, knowing you are cherished, valued, and worthy of healing and a beautiful life. Ask Him for His wisdom of who to turn to for help—He will show you.

You are not alone. God's love for you is more powerful than your pain.

. . . . . . . . . . . . . . . . . . . . . . . . . . . . . . . . . . . . . . . . . . . . . . . . . .

# Brittany Weber

Brittany Weber is 37 years young and lives in New Tripoli, Pennsylvania, with her two sons—one is five and the other is two. She is a life coach and a preschool teacher. And her newfound lot in life is her children, her preschool children, the church, and helping others find their purpose in their pain and in life.

Brittany loves her church community, where she sings on the worship team and works with the women's ministry and children's ministry. This is a beautiful way for her to glorify God and thank Him for all He's done in her life. One of her favorite quotes is, "In all that you do, do it in love."

In her free time, Brittany loves to be with her children and the rest of her family. She also loves to work out, is on a deep personal growth journey, and lives a healthy, clean-eating lifestyle!

Email Brittany at beeweb803@gmail.com or find her on Facebook, YouTube, and Instagram.

# From Darkness to Redemption

By Brittany Weber

Throughout my life, God has been present, guiding me even when I was too blind to see Him. Looking back, I recognize His fingerprints on every chapter of my story, even the ones I thought were written in darkness.

As a child, I attended church sporadically, sitting in pews and listening to sermons that felt more like distant echoes than personal invitations. I joined youth groups, learned Bible verses, and bowed my head in prayer. However, my heart remained untouched by true connection.

I had friends, laughter, and moments of joy, but there was always an underlying emptiness I couldn't quite put my finger on. I viewed God as a faraway deity—a powerful, mysterious force watching from the heavens but not someone intimately involved in my life. I imagined Him as a judge, observing from a distance, rather than a loving Father walking beside me. I didn't yet understand that He wasn't just above me; He was within me, omnipresent and longing for a relationship that I had yet to embrace.

It took years of heartache and surrender before I fully grasped the depth of God's love. Yet, even in my wandering, He never let me go. His presence was like the air—unseen but essential. Only when I reached my lowest point, stripped of the illusion of self-sufficiency, did I finally turn toward Him and see the One who had been with me all along.

Jesus' parable of the lost sheep resonates with me so deeply. *"Suppose one of you has a hundred sheep and loses one of them. Doesn't he leave the ninety-nine in the open country and go after the lost sheep until he finds it? And when he finds it, he joyfully puts it on his shoulders and goes home. Then he calls his friends and neighbors together and says, 'Rejoice with me; I have found my lost sheep'"* (Luke 15:4-6 NIV).

At the peak of my addiction to drugs and struggle with mental health issues, I was that lost sheep, wandering aimlessly, unaware that my Shepherd was relentlessly pursuing me with a love that would never fail.

Endlessly scrolling through YouTube, I searched for anything to bring me even a moment of joy. Then, a song came on—"You Say" by Lauren Daigle. At first, I thought it was just another love song, but as the lyrics sank in, I realized it was about a far greater love—the love of the Father. A love that had been pursuing me all along, even when I couldn't see it.

At the very beginning of my addiction, I met my fiancé. Our connection was electric—instant, consuming, and, at the time, it felt like fate. But fate had nothing to do with it. The bond we formed wasn't built on love or trust; it was built on destructive behaviors. We found solace in the same poison—methamphetamine—shooting it into our veins as if it were the answer to every pain, every wound, every disappointment we had ever known.

Within three months, I was pregnant with our first son. It should have been a wake-up call, a reason to change. But addiction doesn't let go easily. Instead of finding stability, my life spiraled further into chaos.

That first year, we lived recklessly, making desperate choices, stealing to survive, manipulating our loved ones, and doing whatever it took to keep the high going while ensuring I had just enough food for the baby growing inside me. It was survival in the most twisted sense—one that revolved around feeding our addiction first while the rest of life came second.

For as long as I could remember, I had chased perfection, striving to be the "good girl" who never failed or disappointed. But the weight of expectation was crushing. When I first tried drugs, I felt a false sense of freedom—an escape from who I thought I had to be. I chased that feeling recklessly, drowning in drugs and alcohol, losing myself in social scenes, and searching for anything to fill the emptiness inside me.

But addiction has a way of consuming everything in its path. The obsession, the relentless pursuit of the next high, or what we in recovery call "the chase," became my master. It ruled my thoughts, my choices, my very existence. Nothing else mattered. Not my body, not my mind, not even the life I was carrying inside me.

Addiction wasn't my only battle. I also struggled with bipolar tendencies, a war waging inside my own mind. The highs were euphoric, almost blinding in their intensity. The lows were unbearable, dragging me into the darkest places where hope felt like a distant memory. I was hospitalized multiple times—each stay a stark reminder of just how lost I had become.

And yet, through every reckless decision, every moment of despair, and every fall, God was there. Even when I ran, shut Him out, and believed I was too far gone, He never left me. He never stopped reaching for me. His love never wavered. *"Fear not, for I am with you; be not dismayed, for I am your God; I will strengthen you, I will help you, I will uphold you with my righteous right hand"* (Isaiah 41:10 ESV).

I didn't know it then, but God was already working behind the scenes, writing a story of redemption that I couldn't yet see. Even in my darkest moments, He was whispering, "This is not the end."

Eventually, addiction took everything. After years of drug use, we became homeless. Just two months after giving birth, I relapsed. Child Protective Services got involved, knowing I had used drugs during my pregnancy.

At the time, it felt like my world was closing in on me, but looking back, I can see God's hand was in it all. CPS wasn't just another obstacle—it was a wake-up call, a divine intervention. What felt like punishment was actually protection. Even in my lowest moments, God was making a way.

We stayed sober for seven months after our first child was born, but deep down, I was still chasing the euphoria that drugs once gave me. An emptiness lingered—a void I didn't know how to fill. Eventually, my parents had enough. Frustrated by our addiction, they kicked us out of the barn we had been living in, leaving us homeless for six months. My fiancé continued to battle severe heroin and methamphetamine addiction. I made a choice—I decided to get sober so I could take care of him and ensure we survived.

We scraped by, delivering food through DoorDash. Toward the end of those six months, we landed jobs together. But the day before our first orientation, everything changed. We were in a car accident—while we were high—and suddenly, what little we had was gone.

Yet, even in that rock-bottom moment, God was already making a way. *"The Lord will fight for you; you need only to be still"* (Exodus 14:14 NIV).

A few months earlier, my parents had discovered The Potter's House, a faith-based program designed to help women rebuild their lives after incarceration and addiction. They saw it as a beacon of hope, a place where I could find healing and restoration. They offered it to me as an option, praying I would accept it. But I wasn't ready. The thought of going without my fiancé was unimaginable. I had convinced myself that we were in this together, that somehow, if I held on long enough, I could save him. I didn't yet understand that sometimes God calls us to step out in faith, even when it means walking away from what's familiar.

By December 2021, after countless attempts to rescue my fiancé from the grips of addiction, I finally reached my breaking point. I had fought, pleaded, and sacrificed—believing that if I just loved him enough, if I just held on a little longer, things would change. But nothing changed. And the truth hit me harder than I was prepared for—I couldn't save him. No matter how much I wanted to, no matter how deeply I cared, the decision to change had to be his.

But God... He showed me in my heart that I could make a change for myself.

The weight of addiction and trying to save someone else while barely holding myself together became unbearable. After years of running—from pain, surrender, and the truth—I finally broke. In my exhaustion, I realized the only way forward was to let go, stop chasing destruction, and seek the Lord. It was time to surrender fully.

With that resolve, my father picked my fiancé and me up from the motel where we had been staying and drove us to The Potter's House. We stayed there for seven months. Even though we weren't living together, we found ways to reconnect. During this time, we conceived our second son—a new life in the midst of what felt like the wreckage of our old one.

Looking back, I can see how, even in my wandering, God was still guiding my steps.

One of the biggest revelations in my journey was realizing that I had put my fiancé on the throne of my life. He had become my idol. But the moment I took him off that throne, God stepped in. When I found out I was pregnant, fear consumed me. I wanted another child, but not like this—not in the middle of my addiction, with my life in chaos. The timing felt impossible. But God knew better. Even when I couldn't see a way forward, He was already making a way.

At that point, I entered another recovery program for women—where I could safely have my child. There, I truly began to know God.

I memorized Scripture, studied His Word, and, for the first time, understood the depth of Jesus—His love, grace, and character. I excelled in my studies, earning perfect scores on most Bible exams. But more than gaining knowledge, I was experiencing true transformation.

When I left the program in 2023, my parents welcomed me home. I had my second son and was reunited with my firstborn, stepping into a life I never thought possible. Adjusting wasn't easy—I struggled to apply what I had learned about the Bible. But as I kept seeking God, Matthew 6:33 became real to me: *But seek first the kingdom of God and his righteousness, and all these things will be added unto you* (NIV).

As the months passed, I enrolled in school to become a life coach, determined to use my experiences to help others. My faith in God, together with the coaching program, gave me purpose and carried me through the challenging transition.

While watching a podcast with Mel Robbins and Sarah Jakes Roberts, something sparked a shift in my mindset. I felt a surge of positivity, motivation, and renewed purpose. But with it came a manic episode. For three days, I didn't sleep. My mind raced nonstop, my energy felt endless, and my emotions were intense. I swung between exhilaration and restlessness, caught in a whirlwind of thoughts I couldn't slow down.

During this time, I started a bipolar journal, determined to document my experiences and regulate my emotions through my relationship with God. It wasn't easy. Manic episodes brought intense irritability, an urgent need to stay busy, and an unstoppable drive to do everything at once. One moment, I felt invincible; the next, I was on the brink of exhaustion, knowing burnout was inevitable.

Even now, I wrestle with the fear of the next depressive episode—it has always been the pattern. The highs never last forever, and the crash can feel unbearable.

But now, I hold onto something greater. I don't have to navigate this cycle alone. Through it all, God is my anchor, my steady foundation in the storm. *"When you pass through the waters, I will be with you; and through the rivers, they shall not overwhelm you; when you walk through the fire you shall not be burned, and the flame shall not consume you"* (Isaiah 43:2 ESV).

During that time, God extended another grace into my life—one that ultimately led me to writing this chapter. While attending a conference, my mother crossed paths with Kimberly Hobbs from Women World Leaders.

Before the event, God had placed it on Kimberly's heart to bring a copy of *Hope Alive*, a newly launched book filled with testimonies of faith and redemption. She carried it, trusting that God had someone in mind who needed to read those stories. That divine appointment happened when she met my mother.

My mother shared my journey. Kimberly, moved by my story, wrote her phone number inside the book and handed it to my mother, saying, "This is for your daughter." She then mentioned another book in the works and encouraged my mother to have me consider sharing my faith story—just as the other women had done.

That moment was no coincidence. It was God's reminder that He was guiding my path, calling me to faith, and using my story for His purpose.

When I received the book, something in me stirred. I felt God reaching out to me again. I was struggling with depression; God felt so distant. But in that moment, I knew He was still there. In the depths of my struggle, I finally found the courage to call Kimberly. For months, I wrestled with doubt, wondering if I was worthy of this faith mission. Could my story truly make a difference? Was I enough? It took three months to accept that sharing my journey could bring hope to someone else.

Everything I endured—the pain, the suffering, the trials that had felt unbearable—now holds a purpose I never could have imagined. I once believed I had to carry my struggles alone, fighting for control. But now, I see the truth.

Jesus already paid the price.

I no longer have to carry the burden of my past or prove my worth—Jesus' sacrifice was enough. His grace is enough. In surrendering my story, I have found the freedom I spent so long searching for.

Scripture reminds us that Jesus spoke of the troubles we would face; He knew that hardship would be inevitable. But when He stretched His arms wide on the cross and took His final breath, He didn't leave us in despair. His last words were not of defeat but of victory: *"It is finished"* (John 19:30 ESV).

The battle I thought was mine to fight had already been won. The burdens I carried—shame, regret, addiction, fear—were never mine to hold in the first place. He took them. He carried them with Him. And when He rose again, He shattered the chains that had bound me for so long.

When doubt creeps in, when life feels overwhelming and uncertain, I cling to His promises. I don't need all the answers. I don't have to control every outcome. I simply need to surrender and trust.

*"The Lord will fight for you; you need only to be still"* (Exodus 14:14 NIV).

Stillness is not weakness; being still is having confidence in the One who never fails. Though the world shifts and storms come, He remains constant.

Now, rather than relying on my own understanding, I choose to lean fully into Him. I've surrendered my life, plans, and future to His hands, trusting He will lead me.

*Trust in the Lord with all your heart and lean not on your own understanding; in all your ways submit to him, and he will make your paths straight* (Proverbs 3:5-6 NIV).

There were many times in my journey when I had no idea where I would go next or how I would survive, but God always made a way. For so long, I relied on my parents as a safety net, leaving them exhausted as they tried to help me navigate life. But now, I understand I must take ownership of my choices and step forward into God's will for me. One day at a time, I am building something greater.

Through faith, free from the bondage of self, I am learning to hear His voice, follow His lead, and walk in His peace. I no longer fear the unknown, seek wholeness in substances, or face my manic episodes alone. Held by the One who knows all things, I move forward, trusting He is always with me, guiding the way.

Today, I am a life coach with a YouTube channel and a professional presence on Facebook, where I share my journey and inspire others. I attend church regularly and serve on the worship team, using my voice not only for song but as a testimony of God's grace. Where I once saw obstacles, I now see opportunities. No matter the struggle or uncertainty, each day, I remind myself that God is in control. This truth keeps me grounded, guiding me in His will.

Life is not always easy. Sometimes, the road ahead seems unfair and burdensome. No matter how difficult the journey, you can trust that God is walking beside you. He is your light in the darkness, your hope in despair, and your strength when you feel weak.

> *Cast all your anxiety on him because he cares for you* (1 Peter 5:7 NIV).

If you are struggling today, I encourage you to surrender your burdens to God. You don't have to carry them alone. He sees you, He hears you, and He loves you beyond measure. Let Him guide your steps, knowing that His plan for your life is greater than anything you can imagine.

> *"For I know the plans I have for you," declares the Lord, "plans to prosper you and not to harm you, plans to give you hope and a future"* (Jeremiah 29:11 NIV).

May God guide you, strengthen you, and bless you for all of your days.

# Breaking Chains of Anxiety

### By Melissa Gissy Witherspoon

Anxiety doesn't always come in shouting or storms—sometimes it creeps in silently, tightening its grip until our peace is replaced with panic. It clouds our thoughts, drains our energy, and distances us from the truth of who we are in Christ. Anxiety can touch every part of us—mind, body, and soul—and, left unchallenged, can become a prison. But when we face anxiety with faith, God will transform it into a path that moves us toward deeper trust, growth, and purpose.

One of the most powerful biblical examples of someone battling anxiety is Elijah. After calling down fire from heaven and defeating the prophets of Baal, you would think he'd be walking in total confidence. But when Queen Jezebel threatened his life, anxiety overtook him. First Kings 19:3-4 (NIV) says, *Elijah was afraid and ran for his life. When he came to Beersheba in Judah, he left his servant there, while he himself went a day's journey into the wilderness. He came to a broom bush, sat down under it and prayed that he might die. "I have had enough, Lord," he said. "Take my life; I am no better than my ancestors."*

Elijah felt crushed under the weight of fear and emotional exhaustion. He isolated himself and wished to die. I, unfortunately, had the exact same conversation with God at my rock bottom of addiction. But Elijah's story reminds us that anxiety doesn't mean we've failed spiritually—it means we're human. And his story didn't end in the wilderness—God met him there, right in the middle of his anxiety and despair. God did the same for me! *And behold, the Lord passed by... And after the fire the sound of a low whisper* (1 Kings 19:11-12 ESV).

God didn't respond with force or loud miracles in that moment—He came gently, speaking peace into Elijah's fear. He reminded Elijah that he was not alone and his purpose was not over.

Anxiety may try to chain us to fear, but God offers us peace and strength.

> *Do not be anxious about anything, but in every situation, by prayer and petition, with thanksgiving, present your requests to God. And the peace of God... will guard your hearts and your minds in Christ Jesus* (Philippians 4:6-7 NIV).

I've personally faced moments of deep anxiety—times when fear made me want to run, hide, or quit everything. But in those moments, when I chose to push through and serve others anyway, I experienced some of my greatest breakthroughs. Shifting anxious energy into service work became my way of telling the enemy, "You will not win."

Revelation 21:4 (ESV) promises us a future where *He will wipe away every tear from their eyes, and death shall be no more, neither shall there be mourning, nor crying, nor pain anymore.* But until that day comes, we press forward, one day at a time, one step at a time.

Anxiety may knock on our door, but it does not have to rule our lives. In Christ, the chains of anxiety are broken.

. . . . . . . . . . . . . . . . . . . . . . . . . . . . . . . . . . . . . . . . . . . . . . . . .

# Afterword

We have reached the summit of our faith journey together. Side by side, we have witnessed the extraordinary strength and faith of so many awe-inspiring women who have shown us that faith is not merely a belief; it is a force that can shatter every chain that binds us. Faith is the courage to climb, even when the path ahead is uncertain and the sky is dark.

Every challenge testified to in this book was more than an obstacle; each was an opportunity to rise, lean into grace, and surrender to the power of the greatest love ever—that of our heavenly Father.

These authors want you to know that, just as they have overcome their struggles, you can also find freedom from yours. You can break free from what holds you back and embrace the beautiful life God has planned for you.

We pray that our stories inspire you to harness that same power, to move ahead with faith that is unchained, and to be a light that shines even in the midst of darkness. Each step you take that is rooted in faith will propel you forward into a future filled with hope.

Whatever chains bind you, know that Jesus Christ has come to set you free.

Whatever fragments of your past you are clinging to, know that you have a Savior who has paid your debt, allowing you to leave those memories behind.

Whatever mistakes or missteps you think define you, know that the Son of God has come to speak truth to all those lies.

God is there for you just as He has always been for us!

*Then they cried to the Lord in their trouble, and he saved them from their distress. He brought them out of darkness, the utter darkness, and broke away their chains. Let them give thanks to the Lord for his unfailing love* (Psalm 107:13-15 NIV).

What are you chained to? What is holding you back from all God called you to be?

Are you chained to your former self? Held captive by the choices you made and the hurt you caused to those closest to you?

Are you trapped in a prison of secrets or haunted by the actions of those who mistreated you—people who should have loved and cared for you? Have you suffered deep wounds yet, somehow, endured the blame?

Do you find yourself living in a prison of abuse? Or are you shackled by the weight of others' expectations of you and feel the burden of people-pleasing that steals pieces of you, leaving you trapped in a cycle of never feeling good enough?

Are you chained by the lie that your worth is determined by your achievements? Or perhaps by the confines of religion that leave you feeling distant from true grace as you try to follow all the rules?

Are you trying to earn your salvation and make your own way into eternity? Or are you chained to your own sin, feeling stuck in the same sinful cycle?

Do you feel held captive in a prison of your own flesh, with depression holding you hostage every single day?

If you are experiencing these or other chains, know you are not alone!

As you've read, many of us have experienced all these chains. But there is hope! We pray you have seen through our stories that God wants to unchain you!

I lived in shackles most of my life, but when I truly understood what Jesus did for me and submitted to Him, my chains were broken—and He's waiting to break yours.

Jesus came to bring you freedom by offering salvation. Through His death and resurrection, He paid the price for your sins and provided a path for you to be with God, releasing you from bondage! By accepting God's free gift of love and forgiveness, you can walk in freedom now and for eternity—free from the pain of your past and all the chains the devil and the world use to try to shackle you from becoming who God created you to be.

When you give your heart to Christ, the same Spirit that raised Jesus from the dead comes to live in you, and the same God who raised Christ also gives life to your body. Hold tight to Him, and He will set you free from every chain.

Let the chains fall to the floor! Hear the shackles break away and shatter so loudly that all will know you are free.

You were once a prisoner, but you are bound no more. You are alive and free because you are a daughter of the King.

Together, we have climbed to freedom by God's grace, and our faith is unchained. So rise up and continue the climb with confidence. You are now equipped with the tools of grace, love, and courage.

The summit awaits, and with *Faith Unchained,* you are destined to soar!

> *Therefore, if anyone is in Christ, the new creation has come: The old has gone, the new is here!* (2 Corinthians 5:17 NIV).

# More WPP Anthologies!

The stories and teachings in *Restoration* will fill you with hope as you witness God's steady and sure hand at work. Although we may feel like we've lost everything, we can stand strong, knowing God will bring beauty from the ashes of our lives. There is no need to despair—God's restoration will begin the moment you give your heart and circumstances to Him.

Men, families, communities, and countries must be on guard as courageous and battle-ready warriors. Men of God are each commissioned to be vigilant conquerors, prepared to lead the fight to overcome evil. The valiant authors in *Fit 2 Fight* share how they have overcome using the weapons that ensure victory no matter what we face.

God longs for you to have ferocious faith grounded in His unwavering love. Get ready to be encouraged as you open the pages of *Unshakable: God Will Sustain You.* Through true stories written by faithful and resilient women, you will witness God's sustaining power available to those who rely on Him.

The authors of *Unseen: You Are Not Alone* share their struggles of feeling isolated and unnoticed and detail how our awesome God helped them overcome every obstacle to find what truly matters: Him. These stories and devotional teachings shed light on the truth of your significance and value. You are never alone!

Despite all the adversities we face throughout our lives, God is the source of our hope. As you read the pages of this book, you will see firsthand how God brings *Hope Alive* to every person who is yearning for a reason to go on. Like a broken tree in a dark place is primed for new growth, God can use the rich soil of your dark place to prepare a new life to sprout in you.

The authors of *Miracle Mindset: Finding Hope in the Chaos,* have experienced the wonders of God's provision, protection, and guidance. These stories and teachings will ignite a spark within you, propelling you to encounter the marvel of God's miracles, even in the chaos.

Life is full of storms and rough waters. The stories in *Navigating Your Storm: By United Men of Honor* will give you the ability to see the light of God and navigate your storm victoriously.

With *Joy Unspeakable: Regardless of Your Circumstances,* you will learn how joy and sorrow can dance together during adversity. The words in this book will encourage, inspire, motivate, and give you hope, joy, and peace.

*Surrendered: Yielded With Purpose* will help you recognize with awe that surrendering to God is far more effective than striving alone. When we let go of our own attempts to earn God's favor and rely on Jesus Christ, we receive a deeper intimacy with Him and a greater power to serve Him.

*United Men of Honor: Overcoming Adversity Through Faith* will help you armor up, become fit to fight, and move forward with what it takes to be an honorable leader. Over twenty authors in this book share their accounts of God's provision, care, and power as they proclaim His Word.

*Embrace the Journey: Your Path to Spiritual Growth* will strengthen and empower you to step boldly in faith. These stories, along with expertly placed expositional teachings will remind you that no matter what we encounter, we can always look to God, trusting HIS provision, strength, and direction.

*Victories: Claiming Freedom in Christ* presents expository teaching coupled with individual stories that testify to battles conquered victoriously through the power of Jesus Christ. The words in this book will motivate and inspire you and give you hope as God awakens you to your victory!

# WPP's Mission

World Publishing and Productions was birthed in obedience to God's call. Our mission is to empower writers to walk in their God-given purpose as they share their God story with the world. We offer one-on-one coaching and a complete publishing experience. To find out more about how we can help you become a published author or to purchase books written to share God's glory, please visit: **worldpublishingandproductions.com**

This phenomenal story of rescue, restoration, hope, healing, and forgiveness will captivate you. *Who Is Able? The Dana Louise Cryer Story* is an incredible journey of tremendous pain, pierced by tumultuous circumstances and filled with twists and turns. God's incredible love transforms this true-life survival account into a miraculous outcome of total freedom. This book will leave you breathless and in tears at what only God can do.

At seventeen, Audrey Marie experienced a sudden and relentless excruciating firestorm of pain. *Chronically Unstoppable* tells of her true-life journey as she faced pain, developed strength, and battled forward with hope.

The world has become a place where we don't have a millisecond to think for ourselves, often leaving us feeling lost or overwhelmed. That is why Max Gold wrote *Planestorming!*—a straightforward guide to help you evaluate and change your life for the better. It's time to get to work and make the rest of your life the BEST of your life.

THE BULLIED STUDENT
WHO CHANGED ALL THE RULES

A NOVEL BY
ROBERT M. FISHBEIN

Riley Rossey is not your everyday bullied student, but one who discovers how to utilize his talents to assist other shy and picked-on individuals. Journey with Riley as he meets bullying head-on and becomes a God-given blessing to so many in *The Bullied Student Who Changed All the Rules* by Robert M. Fishbein.